ADVANCE PRAIS

The Economics of I

I welcome Mark Anielski's *The Economics of Happiness,* an important contribution to the vital and growing debate on how to re-define and measure wealth and progress.

— HAZEL HENDERSON, author of *Paradigms in Progress:*
Life Beyond Economics and Ethical Markets: Growing the Green Economy

In *The Economics of Happiness,* Mark Anielski has visualized an arresting and, importantly, a possible future, in which affluence will be measured in terms of more happiness and less stuff. That is a world to which all of us can aspire and for which we can work, for the sake of our grandchildren's futures and theirs. Read and lift your expectations; a saner world is possible, and surely most desirable.

— RAY ANDERSON, Founder and Chairman of Interface, Inc.

Mark Anielski does a wonderful job in laying bare the difference between money and genuine wealth and relating them to our economic growth addiction. It sounds easy but we all need a lot of training in the use of economic concepts if we are going to be able to find a cure for the monetary madness in this world.

— OSCAR KJELLBERG, President & CEO, JAK Members Bank, Stockholm

An inspired and readable inquiry into an "oikonomia for the people." Great questions, with a wealth of perspectives and insightful answers.

— RAFFI CAVOUKIAN, C.M., singer, author, ecology advocate,
founder of Child Honouring

It is essential that we transform our societies from ones that worship greed into ones that are sustainable, compassionate, and peaceful. *The Economics of Happiness* provides a rationale for beginning this journey immediately and offers a detailed methodology for measuring our progress along the path.

— JOHN PERKINS, *New York Times* bestselling author of *Confessions of an*
Economic Hit Man and *The Secret History of the American Empire*

The Economics of Happiness will spark an important discussion about one of the major challenges of our time: how to achieve a balanced, sustainable way of life, where notions of progress and genuine wealth are understood as being fundamentally interrelated. To help us on this journey, Mark Anielski points to the promise of transformational work in raising our understanding about a new perspective for how we conduct our present and future.

— HON. ROY ROMANOW, P.C., O.C., Q.C., Former Premier of Saskatchewan, Chair, Canadian Index of Wellbeing Network Board

If those who set the goals of society and measure success in reaching them behaved rationally, they would long since have ceased to use per capita Gross Domestic Product as the major guide. Until now there has been no full-scale study demonstrating this and developing a more appropriate alternative. With *The Economics of Happiness,* the last shred of justification for the exclusive focus on market activity is gone. If this focus is continued, that can only mean that those who profit from our wearing blinders control policy.

— JOHN B. COBB, JR., theologian and co-author of *For the Common Good*

What is the purpose of our economy and our work if not to support happy lives? *The Economics of Happiness* shows how far we have drifted from that goal and details ways to get back on the path to happiness in our personal lives, in our businesses and in economic policy.

— GIFFORD PINCHOT III, Founder and President, Bainbridge Graduate Institute

Reading *The Economics of Happiness* is a real treat; it is not often that one finds ecomonics, philosophy and ethics brought together so closely. "Beggar the next generation" is no longer acceptable in resource policy. In other words, make room for ethics. That is the message throughout this book.

— RT. HON. EDWARD R. SCHREYER, P.C., C.C., C.M.M., O.M., C.D former Premier of Manitoba, former Governor General of Canada

For far too long the economics profession has held sway over our society, and convinced us to worship the god of endless economic growth. In this powerful, insightful book, Mark Anielski exposes how this approach actually stunts our growth and prevents us from achieving a life that is rich in all senses of the word. Breaking ranks with his fellow economists, Anielski shows how we can make the economy serve the interests of society, not the other way around.

— LINDA McQUAIG, author and journalist

Mark Anielski's *The Economics of Happiness* provides an interesting and informative look at money, economics, wealth and what it all means. The lessons in this book provide a timely guide as our society begins the paradigm shift away from crass consumer capitalism toward more sustainable economies and communities where people and the planet matter.

— DEAN KUBANi, Environmental Programs Manager
for the City of Santa Monica

In these times, even the best of us are falling short in courageously charting new maps — and more importantly avoiding heading out without a map at all! Mark Anielski is a great pioneer of our time, and *The Economics of Happiness* is "the emperor has no clothes" rallying cry our world so desperately needs. This book is a critical part of the architecture of a new system. It is a must read for anyone serious about living differently with each other and the planet. Quite simply — LOVE is the only true economics, and when we express love it does not get used up, it multiplies.

— ANITA M. BURKE, Sustainability Elder and former Senior Advisor to the
Committee of Managing Directors at Shell International

The Economics of Happiness helps organizations evolve from satisfying "Show me the money!" demands from shareholders to satisfying "Show me the genuine wealth!" demands from stakeholders. Mark Anielski has provided a timely guidebook for organizations undertaking that challenging journey. This book is a must-read for enlightened business leaders.

— Bob Willard, author of *The Sustainability Advantage* and
The Next Sustainability Wave

The Economics of Happiness joins leading voices critical of the dominant economic paradigm, but it does much more than this. Being a critic is easy enough, and so is dreaming dreams. But designing the practical and modelled path to connect the two in different and meaningful strategic alternatives, is the work of exceptional people, and I rank Mark Anielski as one of these.

— PROFESSOR MARILYN WARING, Institute of Public Policy,
Auckland University of Technology

Mark Anielski is one of those rare Canadians, an economist/civil servant who cut loose from the system and became a true public servant. He did so by following his values. In so doing he changed his own life, and we are all the beneficiaries. *The Economics of Happiness* pushes economics back to its more honorable roots and, in so doing, shows us the way towards what is truly a new common wealth.

— BOB WILLIAMS, Senior Research Fellow,
Vancouver City Savings Credit Union

We live in a world where money, always a means for something else, has become a goal in itself. We need, now more than ever, an economic framework that helps us remember what economy is all about: careful use of life sustaining resources to ensure love and happiness. Why has no one thought to write such a book before?

— KARL-HENRIK ROBÈRT, MD, PhD,
Founder of The Natural Step International,
Adjunct Professor of Sustainable Product Developoment,
Blekinge Institute of Technology

THE ECONOMICS
of HAPPINESS

BUILDING GENUINE WEALTH

MARK ANIELSKI

NEW SOCIETY PUBLISHERS

Cataloging in Publication Data:
A catalog record for this publication is available from the National Library of Canada.

Cover design by Diane McIntosh. Photo: iStock.

Printed in Canada.
Second printing May 2009.

New Society Publishers acknowledges the support of the Government of Canada
through the Book Publishing Industry Development Program (BPIDP) for our
publishing activities.

Paperback ISBN: 978-0-86571-596-7

Inquiries regarding requests to reprint all or part of *The Economics of Happiness*
should be addressed to New Society Publishers at the address below.

To order directly from the publishers, please call toll-free (North America)
1-800-567-6772, or order online at www.newsociety.com

Any other inquiries can be directed by mail to:

New Society Publishers
P.O. Box 189, Gabriola Island, BC V0R 1X0, Canada
1-800-567-6772

New Society Publishers' mission is to publish books that contribute in fundamental
ways to building an ecologically sustainable and just society, and to do so with the least
possible impact on the environment, in a manner that models this vision. We are committed to doing this not just through education, but through action. We are acting on
our commitment to the world's remaining ancient forests by phasing out our paper supply from ancient forests worldwide. This book is one step toward ending global defor-
estation and climate change. It is printed on acid-free paper that is 100% old growth
forest-free (100% post-consumer recycled), processed chlorine free, and printed with
vegetable-based, low-VOC inks. For further information, or to browse our full list of
books and purchase securely, visit our website at: www.newsociety.com

NEW SOCIETY PUBLISHERS   www.newsociety.com

To my grandparents,
who taught me the importance of frugality,
giving and receiving.

To my parents for teaching me about integrity and hard work.

To my wife, Jennifer, who loves me.

To our children,
Renée and Stephanie,
who teach me to love unconditionally.

There is no wealth but life:
life, including all its powers of love,
of joy, and of admiration.

That country is the richest which nourishes the greatest
number of noble and happy human beings.

That man is richest
who, having
perfected the
functions of
his own life
to the utmost,
has also the
widest helpful
influence.

JOHN RUSKIN
1819–1900

Contents

Acknowledgments

This book is dedicated to all those who are pursuing genuine happiness and spiritual well-being.

To my grandparents, on both sides, especially my Opa (Grandfather in German), Peter Mitterer, who died at the grand age of 95 and my Oma, Catherine Mitterer who lives on at the age of 95. Peter, an immigrant to Canada from Austria in the early 1920s, was a gardener all his life. He understood what made life worthwhile: the value of time spent with those he loved and in the many gardens he nurtured.

To my parents, Hans-Ulrich and Mary Ann Anielski, who taught me how to dream and act on my dreams with conviction and leadership. They taught me about how to live a life of faith, love, meaningful relationships and about the virtue of meaningful, life-giving work as vocation.

To my life partner and wife, Jennifer Haslett, who has taught me the joys of love and reciprocal relationship; of reconciliation, laughter and most importantly of open and honest dialogue. And to our two daughters Renée and Stephanie, who teach me every day about unconditional love and real happiness. Like my Opa and our elders, my children are teaching me how to celebrate life in the moment of experience and how to breathe love in each precious second of living. Children have a remarkable gift for asking tough questions; this book is dedicated to answering some of those questions which still linger into adulthood.

Like the book of life, this book is the result of years of many wonderful conversations and enduring relationships with friends and colleagues around the world. I would like to thank David Korten for encouraging me to write this book and my students at Bainbridge Graduate Institute near Seattle, especially Kate Kaemerle who took the first steps with me on this journey by compelling me to "write it down, Mark!" To Chris and Judith Plant and Ingrid Witvoet of New Society Publishers for believing in my message. To Betsy Nuse, my wonderful editor whose loving edits have helped shape this book into a crystal of wisdom. To Sue Custance and Diane McIntosh for the exquisite cover design that adorns this book, including the idea for a

Fibonnaci sequence which is the golden ratio revealed in nature especially flowers. To Jane Haslett, my mother-in-law whose unwavering dedication to the initial edits of this book and her wonderful encouragement continually buoyed my spirit. And to many other friends and colleagues who have inspired and shared in my spiritual and earthly journey including Judi Hoyt, Robert Felty, Aaron Braaten, Anita Burke, Joey Hundert, Michael Haynes, Bill Harder, Ernie Zelinski, Orest Andre, Dominic Misho, Boudewijn Wegerif (deceased), Jeff Wilson, Kelvin Hirsch, Randy Hirsch, Steve Janzen, Derek Rasmussen, Pat Klak, Bernard Lietaer, Libba and Gifford Pinchot III, Pat Carmack, Mel Hurtig, Oscar Kjellberg, Karl-Heinrik Robert, Leslie Christian, Bob Willard, Bob Williams, Herman Daly, John Cobb Jr., Ken Chapman, Marilyn Waring, Hazel Henderson, Janine Benyus, Linda McQuaig, Harold Wynne, Brian and Mary Nattrass, Michael Percy, Colin Soskolne, Bill Rees, Dan Rubenstein, Sandra Zagon, Laszlo Pinter, John Rudolph, Edward Schreyer, Susan Sharpe, John McMurtry, Rob Smith, Sara Wilson, Rob Taylor, Heather Tischbein, Amy Taylor, Rob Macintosh, Peter Haslett, Joy Hecht, John Helliwell, Robert Putnam and Raffi Cavoukian. To all the others whom I treasure as friends — for real wealth is measured in terms of enduring relationships.

This book is intended to inspire both current and future builders of the new economy of well-being in the genuine pursuit of happiness and spiritual well-being. I believe our hearts intuit better ways that are in genuine alignment with our core values to design, measure and manage our personal, community and world economies. We know that life is more than consumption and having more material possessions. We long to build living economies founded on the premise of well-being that are just, sustainable and flourishing; a society which is guided by the virtues of love, respect, shared responsibility, forgiveness, stewardship, cooperation, reciprocity, giving and receiving and restorative justice. This book is offered to those hearts and minds alive with understanding the wisdom of the Dalai Lama, Pope John Paul II, Mother Theresa and St. Thomas Aquinas who teach us that love is the ultimate source of enduring power in the universe.

My final thanks go to God and the Holy Spirit whose loving kindness taught me to get out of the way of my own ego and sense of knowing and to realize that all things come down to a singular breath: LOVE.

Foreword

by HERMAN DALY

SUPPOSE THAT GOD sent an auditor to Earth to review the accounts of individuals, firms, municipalities, and nations, with the purpose of assessing their stewardship of Creation and their success in converting resources into good lives lived abundantly, righteously, and joyfully. What accounts or ledgers would this auditor want to review, and by what criteria would he judge their adequacy? In reading this book I could not help thinking of Mark Anielski as "God's auditor." I do not want to attribute to Mark any divine authority or ability (he certainly does not claim such), nor am I sure that the Almighty would not ask for some parts of the report to be redone. Of course an omniscient God has no need of an auditor's report, and the intended audience and beneficiary of the audit is us human beings.

The main criterion guiding the audit is "genuine well-being" which is derived from "genuine wealth," which in turn consists of five capital accounts that assess both the quantity and quality of each type of capital. These five capitals are: (1) *human capital* — individual minds, bodies, spirits and their capabilities; (2) *social capital* — quality and strength of our relations in community: trust, honesty, common values, including tolerance; (3) *natural capital* —stocks and funds of things in nature that yield flows of natural resources and life-supporting ecosystem services; (4) *built capital* —machines, tools, durable consumer goods; (5) *financial capital* — money and other liquid assets, fungible and acceptable for payment of transactions and debts.

Our current system of national accounts focuses on (5), pays some attention to (4), and ignores (1), (2), and (3). The problem is that it is the first three that are most responsible for genuine well-being. While there is some marginal substitution possible among these different forms of capital (often overemphasized by economists who advise not to worry about depleting, say, natural capital as long as you accumulate an "equal amount" of built capital or human capital), it is important to recognize, as Anielski does, that the different forms of capital are mainly complementary. A shortage of any one limits the productivity of the others. In particular financial capital quickly becomes worthless as natural capital is excessively depleted. And a lack of trust (social capital) limits the value of knowledge (human capital), etc. The fact that financial capital is the most measurable category has biased our attention too much in its direction. But just how measurable is money really? Do we mean M_1, M_2, or M_3, and what kind of measuring rod is it that can be created out of nothing and then destroyed, and while it exists can become longer or shorter? We must not make a fetish out of measurability. What really counts is often not countable. Assets can be recognized and celebrated and maintained and cared for even if we cannot add and subtract them.

Anielski learns from many people: from Luca Pacioli the Italian inventor of double-entry bookkeeping, from Karl-Henrik Robert of the Natural Step, and Mathis Wackernagel of the Ecological Footprint analysis, and from many others, including even me, which makes this old professor feel good. He looks at examples ranging from Ray Anderson's Interface Carpet Co. with its ecological closed loop materials accounting, to China and the idea of *xiaokang*, or the "moderately well off society" as an alternative to the ever-growing economy. He studies the Italian province of Emilia Romagna, the Inuit, Bhutan, and the city of Santa Monica. The style ranges from textbook to personal memoir, to philosophical reflection, but all aimed at elucidating and applying the concept of Genuine Wealth.

So, gentle reader, I will take up no more of your time with further summary and endorsement. After all, you now have the book in your hands, so by all means read it carefully. You will be glad you did.

— HERMAN E. DALY

Herman E. Daly is currently Professor at the University of Maryland, School of Public Affairs, and has previously served as Senior Economist in the Environment Department of the World Bank. He is the author of over a hundred articles in professional journals and anthologies, as well as numerous books, including Beyond Growth *and, with John B. Cobb, Jr.,* For the Common Good. *He has received Sweden's Honorary Right Livelihood Award, and the Heineken Prize for Environmental Science awarded by the Royal Netherlands Academy of Arts and Sciences.*

Introduction

I BELIEVE WE ALL SHARE a common yearning for happiness and ultimately love. Each of us has our own unique journey in discovering these ultimate ends. But what are the determinants of happiness and our conditions of well-being — our genuine wealth? What, as Robert Kennedy challenged, makes life worthwhile? How might we measure our happiness and incorporate these measures into conventional economic measures of progress like the GDP?

Prompted by such nagging questions I began a journey into the origins of economic thought and economic systems. I realized that economics is more like a religion than either art or science. The more I probed its tenets, the more the scales of economic dogma fell from my own eyes and the eyes of those with whom I shared my ideas. In a sense our hearts began to open to truths that have long been stifled.

While some have defined economics as the dismal science, I find it akin to religion precisely because economic principles and tools form the guidance system of our modern states. Economists are the high priests of our capitalist systems. I count myself among the economic priesthood — but I am a priest who longs to understand the very premises and value-origins of our thought. As a professor of business and economics, I have found a hunger among my students to understand more clearly the articles of faith behind business practices. Many students question whether profit and financial wealth maximization should be the primary goals of business; they long for a more meaningful world where corporations are governed by ethics and principles of social and environmental responsibility. I am buoyed by this new generation of business and economic graduates who understand at the heart level that the current "new world order" can and must change.

In economics we have reduced humanity to a collection of individual, independent, utility maximizing creatures. Success is defined by the accumulation of material and financial wealth over a lifetime. We are born into this free market ideology without questioning its morality or ethical foundations. So watermarked is this spirit of economics and capitalism on our lives that even though our hearts cry out for a more meaningful and genuine existence, we are sucked back into the squirrel cage of capitalism, running faster and faster to "keep up with the Jones," lamenting as we imagine a simpler, more meaningful, more genuine life.

I firmly believe we are at an important tipping point in human history. A shared consciousness is emerging which will be supported by enlightened, life-affirming economics. This book presents my future vision: stewardship of what I call Genuine Wealth — those conditions of well-being that align with our heartfelt values about what makes life worth living.

The Economics of Happiness has four primary goals. First, I explore the nature and spirit of the current economic system. I want to better understand why many in the sustainability movement can't seem to move towards a genuine, living and sustainable economic system. I wonder how Adam Smith's seminal economics text, *The Wealth of Nations,* failed to consider the Old English origins of the word "wealth," which literally means "the conditions of well-being." The important work of Amitore Fanfani traced economic and capitalistic thinking back to the European Middle Ages where Fanfani located a pre-capitalist model that the sustainability movement may find desirable.

My second goal is to introduce the concept of Genuine Wealth: a new and compelling model for managing our personal, household, business and community well-being in accordance with the values that define our quality of life. Genuine Wealth is a practical system which measures and manages for sustainability the total capital assets of a community or organization. Synthesizing emerging concepts like natural capital and social capital, Genuine Wealth creates a more comprehensive accounting system where human, social, natural, built and financial capital are all integrated into the balance sheet. This vision of a living, sustainable economy is founded on the mutually reinforcing and integrated principles of efficiency, equity and reciprocity and was inspired by the cooperative economy of Emilia Romagna, a flourishing and vibrant region of Italy.

Thirdly I provide examples of applications of the Genuine Wealth model at the personal/household, corporate/business, community, state/provincial and national scales. I present stories from Nunavut in Canada's Arctic, the City of Santa Monica, California and Leduc, Alberta and explore systems like the US Genuine Progress Indicators (GPI) and the Alberta GPI Sustainable Well-being Accounting System.

Fourthly I examine the nature of money and the current debt-based banking system. Mountains of unsustainable debt and the practice of charging interest on loans actually lead to the destruction of living capital and fundamentally undermine sustainable economies of well-being and happiness. I offer examples of alternatives to the current banking systems like the JAK Members Bank in Sweden, a cooperative member-owned bank that does not charge interest on loans. I present a Genuine Wealth money and banking model that returns the power of money creation to the people in community. Money could be created to serve the genuine needs of an economy of happiness, and private banks, by providing wise financial counsel to households and businesses, could contribute directly to the development of genuine economies of well-being.

While there is a growing library of books about sustainability, I offer here a new paradigm which is also a pragmatic system for the management and stewardship of the common wealth of nations. While other books might despair at the sad state of the world and our environment, *The Economics of Happiness* holds out hope that a genuine renaissance in economics, accounting and business practices is possible and that you and I can build communities of genuine well-being and happiness, a vision that is shared by many. This book is optimistic and predicated on faith that people of all nations understand intuitively what needs to change in order for humanity to move towards a more sustainable future.

— Mark Anielski
Edmonton, Alberta, Canada

CHAPTER 1

My Journey to Genuine Wealth

MANY PEOPLE HAVE ASKED me "how did you get to where you are?" My professional background includes economics, forestry, accounting and religious studies. After three university degrees and years working as a professional economist, I have developed an overview of the ways economic systems operate throughout the world. In my inquiry into economic systems I continue to ask the simple question "why?"

- Why do economists, financial analysts, politicians and media fixate on growth measures (such as the GDP or gross domestic product) as the key indicator of human progress?
- Why do economy and stock market indices have to keep growing if a community has achieved levels of material self-sufficiency and quality of life?
- What is money and where does it come from?
- Why is money always scarce?
- What's wrong with a steady-state, subsistence economy which has achieved sufficiency and homeostasis?
- Why does free-market, capitalist economics look more like a cancer cell than the self-renewing life cycle of an ancient forest?
- What is driving our more-growth, more-consumption obsession?
- Why aren't economists and our leaders asking hard questions: more growth of what? for whom?

These are just some of the questions I began to ask myself as an economist working in the Canadian province of Alberta. As a senior government

economic policy analyst at Alberta Environment my primary task was to de-
rive monetary value for Alberta's natural capital assets or natural resources;
many of them, like wilderness, had no price in a market. I was puzzled that
we had to reduce the value of everything to a monetary figure so it could
count. If something had no monetary value — like the joy of a wilderness experience or the sight of a grizzly bear — did this mean that it was worthless?
I began questioning the meaning of the word value. I was learning that there
might be market and non-market values. Economist and author Marilyn
Waring offered my first plain language lesson in the art of national income accounting and the shortcomings of the gross domestic product (GDP) as a
measure of progress.[1] Marilyn noted that if you want fantastic GDP growth
you would deliberately crash an oil tanker like the Exxon *Valdez* into an
Alaskan reef rather than deliver its cargo of oil safely to a Seattle port. Marilyn was the first economist to point out to me the origins of the word value
(from the Latin *valere* meaning "showing worth"). Her warnings about the
shortcoming of the GNP (the gross national product, the GDP's cousin) as a
measure of progress had been voiced by Robert Kennedy in 1968 just a few
weeks before his untimely assassination. Kennedy lamented that while the
GNP might be great at adding up all the money we spend on goods and services in an economy, it was a lousy measure of what mattered most to Americans: their quality of life. No other politician has given such a poignant critique of the world's key measure of progress.[2] For me, Kennedy's rebuke was
a clarion call to research and develop better systems of measuring human
progress and well-being that make common sense to average citizens and
align with their values.

Learning about natural capital and sustainability

With these insights, I began to examine new models for measuring progress,
sustainability and well-being. I began to explore new methods for accounting
or measuring sustainability, first focused on natural capital and then expanding into other forms of capital accounting including human capital (like
time, knowledge and health) and social capital[3] (like trust and the strength of
relationships). In 1991 I discovered the pioneering work of Robert Repetto at
the World Resources Institute in Washington. Repetto argued that accountants should treat nature's capital in the same way they treat manufactured or
produced capital like buildings, equipment and computers. Accounting
should acknowledge that nature's capital — like forests, oil and agricultural

soils — can either depreciate (that is, be depleted or degraded) or appreciate (that is, grow in volume or quality). Repetto's primary argument made good sense. I began to ask "why don't we keep a balance sheet for nature's capital assets like forests, oil, gas, coal, wildlife, water and soils that are so vital to Alberta's and Canada's economy?" I reasoned that economists ignored the value of nature's capital either because it was too hard to measure or count or because it was politically expedient.

With my curiosity piqued, I began informally examining Alberta's natural assets beginning with forests, oil/natural gas and carbon. Were Alberta's forests being managed sustainably? How many years of oil and natural gas supply did Alberta have left? My preliminary results suggested that Alberta's forests might be approaching an unsustainability threshold: more trees were being harvested and destroyed by fire and insects than the reported annual growth of the total forest. More disconcertingly, I lacked confidence in the annual growth rate of the forest. That was akin to lacking confidence in the revenue line on a conventional income statement or the interest rate on my bank account! When I looked at oil and gas natural capital accounts, I was shocked to discover that the reserve life or years of future production of conventional oil and natural gas left, at current production rates, was shrinking rapidly. By my calculations Alberta would exhaust its precious oil and gas reserves within 12 years without new discoveries. Without information which natural capital accounting provides to guide economic policy decisions, how could Alberta decision makers insure the long-term sustainability of Alberta's natural capital assets? How could there be so little interest shown in natural capital accounting practices by a government committed to accountability and performance measurement?

In constructing these early natural capital accounts I learned an important lesson. While we had mountains of data and information, we seemed to lack the wisdom or capacity to understand what all the information was telling us about sustainability. We had lost sight of the forest, so focused were we on making money on the harvesting and export of trees. I realized that there was an important role for accountants and economists to play in developing new capital accounting tools to assess the long-term sustainability of nature's capital assets as well as human and social capital. Economists could begin developing revised national income accounts and adjusted GDP figures that counted natural, human and social capital depreciation. I knew that such accounts could be constructed from the data we currently collected on the physical state of our forests and other natural capital. Yet I knew that, like all major changes, a move to incorporate natural capital into the balance sheet of the nation would be faced with resistance and reluctance to change. Fortunately almost 15 years later, the term natural capital has been popularized by others (including by the Canada West Foundation in Calgary). Yet even today neither Canada's nor Alberta's income accounts or GDP figures count natural capital assets that are critical to the well-being of Canadians.

Since the early 1990s the idea of natural capitalism — that nature's assets or capital form one of the key foundations of an economy — has gained popularity in many books, countless articles and conferences. *Natural Capitalism* by Paul Hawken, Amory Lovins and Hunter Lovins contributed to this debate. Its authors suggested that the world is on the verge of a new industrial revolution founded on the principles of a system called natural capitalism. They argued that traditional capitalism has always neglected to assign monetary value to its largest stock of capital — namely, the natural resources and ecosystem services that make possible all economic activity and all life. Natural capitalism, they stated, takes a proper and full accounting of these costs and redesigns industry on biological models that result in zero waste, shifts the economy from the episodic acquisition of goods to the continual flow of value and service and prudently invests in sustaining and expanding stores of natural capital. These words were music to my ears.[4]

Encouraged by pioneering reports

Moving to Alberta Treasury in 1995, I entered an exciting area: measuring the overall performance of the government and the quality of life of Albertans. Measuring Up[5] was one of the first triple-bottom-line performance reports in which a government described the conditions (using 24 core indicators) of people, prosperity and preservation (the 3-Ps of progress). Measuring Up rivaled pioneer quality of life indicators in Oregon (Oregon Benchmarks), Minnesota (Minnesota Milestones) and Seattle (Sustainable Seattle). Alberta became one of Canada's (indeed North America's) models for government accountability, business planning and performance outcome measurement by reporting to citizens on the outcomes of economic, health, social and environmental progress. The result expanded conventional economic reporting to include such indicators as life expectancy, crime rates, educational attainment, the sustainability of forests, the stock of oil and gas resources and the quality of air and water. Working with these new performance measurement and policy outcome indicators provided a personal opportunity to see the world in all its complexity and begin to understand the true meaning of the word wealth.

We had begun to diagnose the conditions of well-being — by definition the real wealth of Alberta. I realized that if we could account for nature's capital through resource accounts, we could also expand our accounting into the unchartered waters of human and social capital accounting. I imagined a new way of taking inventory and a new expanded balance sheet for our nation, province, communities and businesses. If we could measure the conditions of well-being of nature's capital assets, then we could measure the human and social conditions of our communities.

In 1997 a most remarkable study landed in my inbox: the US Genuine Progress Indicator (GPI). The GPI was developed by a group of researchers in 1994, led by Cliff Cobb at the San Francisco-based economic policy think tank Redefining Progress. The GPI is an alternative measure of economic progress that starts with the GDP and makes adjustments for the value of unpaid work (e.g. volunteerism and housework) and for various social and environmental depreciation costs. While the GDP measures growth by the amount of money exchanged for goods and services in the economy, the GPI attempts to measure well-being according to what most people might define as progress. For example, while the GDP currently adds things like the financial costs of auto crashes or the social costs of problem gambling, the GPI would deduct these expenditures as regrettable costs. The GPI represented a baby step towards addressing both Robert Kennedy's and Marilyn Waring's challenges that measures of progress should reflect genuine improvements in societal well-being. Economists could use GPI accounting to contrast GDP growth with such regrettable trends as the depletion of nonrenewable oil reserves, the health costs associated with air pollution or the cost of failed personal relationships. Most of us would consider such costs as regrettable and thus deductible as human, social or natural capital depreciation costs against national income. The US GPI results for the period 1950 to 1995 showed a remarkable trend: while the GDP and GPI rose in tandem from 1950 to 1973, the GPI reached its peak in 1973 and then declined steadily even as the GDP continued to rise. The economists' mantra that a rising tide of the GDP lifts all economic boats had been soundly repudiated.

After reading the US GPI work I knew that my life as an economist would never be the same and that a lifetime of new research and development opportunities lay ahead. The US GPI work inspired me to replicate this important well-being measurement in my home province of Alberta and throughout Canada. I dreamed of creating a Redefining Progress Canada and dedicating my professional life to developing more meaningful tools for measuring progress and well-being. Sometimes life sends wonderful surprises. In the spring of 1998 Redefining Progress asked to interview me for the position of Sustainability Measurement director in San Francisco to oversee future US GPI work. It seemed the opportunity of a lifetime. My wife Jennifer and I were flown down to San Francisco during the Easter long weekend of 1998. Wined and dined, I was smitten by the idea of working with such a talented group of creative researchers and living in San Francisco! During my series of interviews with Redefining Progress staff I presented my own vision of a more expansive GPI/well-being measurement system that went beyond full-cost accounting of regrettable social and environmental costs included in the GDP. My vision was to create a system of well-being accounting that would measure what mattered most to people: their actual physical and qualitative conditions of well-being. I reasoned that behind the monetized GPI estimate of progress lay people's real experiences of living which could be measured and used to create both a new index of well-being, but more importantly a new well-being accounting and reporting system.

Yet, as compelling as the idea of working with Redefining Progress in San Francisco was, my own quality of life assessment (comparing the realities of the high cost of living in San Francisco with life in Edmonton close to family) revealed that Edmonton held a clear quality of life advantage. After many long discussions with Jennifer and with my own full-cost accounting figures in hand, we concluded that a move to San Francisco would likely lead to a net loss in our overall family well-being. In the end, our relationship with our family and friends was more important than moving to a dream job and a dream city. Our decision was an important lesson in both my professional and personal life and was a turning point. It brought my professional interest in well-being measurement down to a practical and personal level. We had made our decision about economic well-being based on a review of our values and what we felt mattered most to the well-being of our relationship: our children and our respective families. We had made a decision to stay home, in Edmonton — the community in which I had grown up and which Jennifer now calls home. Our decision was not based on money, income or material quality of life but on intangible, qualitative attributes of life that cannot be easily quantified. Neither money, material gains nor career advancement meant as much as being close to family, growing old with my grandparents and maintaining life-long friendships in Edmonton, North America's most populous Northern city. I realize now in retrospect that we had made a choice based on my first personal Genuine Wealth assessment.

After making this important decision, another door opened. Several months after the trip to San Francisco when I had returned to consulting work, I received a call from the woman who had accepted the position at Redefining Progress. She said that the Ford Foundation (the key funder of the GPI work) would like to see the GPI updated for 1999. "Unfortunately," she said, "I don't have the skills to do the work. Would you be interested in performing the work on contract and as a Senior Fellow?" I was stunned. The opportunity of a lifetime had returned. After contemplating the idea for a few days and discussing the opportunity with Jennifer, I decided to leave my high-paid position as a senior policy analyst with Government Policy Consultants (GPC) International and conduct the US GPI work from my home in Edmonton. Working closely with Cliff Cobb and co-author and journalist Jonathan Rowe, I completed the US GPI study update by January 1999. This work was a dream come true. It was one of the most important turning points in my career, opening up new windows of opportunity to work in this exciting and emerging field of real economics.

Completing the US GPI work turned out to be one of the most challenging and arduous economic exercises I had ever undertaken. In Washington DC, I had the opportunity to meet some of world's most progressive economists at the World Bank, Resources for the Future, World Resources Institute and the University of Maryland to discuss their views of the future of GPI-style accounting. Most were bullish that the GPI was an important measurement effort that should be sustained, but that the model required more rigorous quantitative economic analysis to improve the full cost accounting estimates and care that the measure not become too value-biased. My most memorable experience was sitting down with Dr. Herman Daly in his tiny University of Maryland office. I consider Daly, one of the founding fathers of the transdisciplinary field of ecological economics, to be one of the greatest living economists of our time and deserving of a Nobel Prize for economics. I asked Herman a question that would change the course of my economics career: "Is it possible that our efforts at devising a money-denominated indicator of economic well-being (the GPI) might be futile since we are attempting to monetize quality-of-life issues which have value beyond monetary terms?"

Daly responded to my question with enthusiasm and encouraged me to pursue the answers with all of my life energy. His challenge has shaped my life in ways I could not have imagined that afternoon sitting across from this humble, loving and courageous economist. To understand the importance of the nature of money and how it is created, Daly encouraged me to read Michael Rowbotham's *The Grip of Death* (the title inspired by the French word *mortgage* — meaning "a pledge unto death") which was one of the most important books I read on my long journey to discover the nature of money.[6] Daly explained that over 90% of the world's money supply was actually created in the form of bank debts, not as paper currency created by governments. I then understood that GPI-accounting paled in importance to more fundamental changes required in the nature of money creation and banking. I later came to see that the failure of the sustainability movement to understand and address the nature of our debt-based money system would lead to a dead end street, since genuine sustainability, based on principles of material sufficiency and subsistence, is anathema to the high priests of our debt-money-economic-growth system.[7]

In January of 1999, my co-author Jonathan Rowe (an economic journalist with Redefining Progress) released the 1999 update to the US GPI resulting in almost no US media attention. The first US GPI estimates by Cliff Cobb, Jonathan Rowe and Ted Halstead in 1995 had won the attention of the *Atlantic Monthly* with a lead article and magazine cover proclaiming "If the GDP is Up, Why is America Down?"[8] Other media also inquired into the results at that time. With the 1999 update, it seemed that Americans were more intent on levitating stock market indices than on regrettable news of a sustained slide in the US GPI.

Beginning the work in Canada

If updating the US GPI had been my economic Mt. Everest, my next goal was developing a solid and permanent base camp to advance GPI accounting in Canada. I wanted to develop Redefining Progress Canada and take the original US GPI work to a new level of sophistication and practical application. My friend and former economics thesis advisor, Dr. Michael Percy now Dean of the Faculty of Business at the University of Alberta, gave me the chance to create and run a research think tank at the University of Alberta to explore alternative accounting and measurement systems. What I had hoped to accomplish in San Francisco I would try to do in Canada. I co-founded the Center for

Performance Measurement and Management to conduct applied research on alternative measures of economic well-being and performance. For two years I served as the center's Executive Director and co-taught a course in business and the environment with Dr. Ray Rasmussen. During my time with the center, my vision for expanding the original GPI accounting system took shape. This was the genesis of the Genuine Wealth system. In the winter of 1999 I developed a conceptual grand research agenda for creating a transdisciplinary network (well-being.net) of University of Alberta's top researchers to work on the development of a genuine well-being indicators accounting system. My mission was to design a sustainability accounting system for Alberta to assess the long-term sustainability of Alberta's human, social, natural, produced (built) and financial capital assets. Unfortunately, it soon became apparent from discussions with senior members of the University of Alberta that creating a place for such interdisciplinary research would take years of complex negotiation.

Fortunately my vision of advancing GPI-sustainable well-being accounting caught the attention of Rob Macintosh, the co-founder of the Pembina Institute for Appropriate Development, one of Canada's premier environmental think tanks. In the fall of 1999, Rob encouraged me to join the Pembina team on a part-time basis. I accepted the opportunity and began splitting my time between the University of Alberta and the Pembina Institute. Rob asked me to co-author one of many green budget proposals for the National Round Table on the Environment and Economy (NRTEE) which would be presented to then Canadian Finance Minister Paul Martin for his *Budget 2000*.

I proposed that NRTEE create a research Center for Applied Sustainable Economics. The proposed center, with a $10 million three-year budget, would have two main goals:

1. To apply improved or innovative methods for measuring the total wealth or well-being of Canadians that leads towards economic, ecological and social sustainability
2. To revise existing fiscal policy instruments to help Canada move towards a future where quality of life and competitive efficiency are shared objectives in a world of ecological limits

My proposal also included revising national income accounts and the GDP to incorporate natural, human and social capital accounts to complement existing economic/financial accounts.

The final version of the document proposed developing a set of environment and sustainable development indicators for Canada that would be reported in parallel with other conventional economic indicators of progress. To my surprise, the Chair of the NRTEE Dr. Stuart Smith fully embraced this proposal and brought it forward to Finance Minister Martin, who subsequently announced a three-year, nine million dollar initiative in his spring Budget 2000. Martin's remarks as part of this budget presentation shocked even the most seasoned policy analysts when he stated:

> Finally, as we move to more fully integrate economic and environmental policy, we must come to grips with the fact that the current means of measuring progress are inadequate. Therefore, we are announcing today that the National Round Table on the Environment and the Economy and Environment Canada, in collaboration with Statistics Canada, will be provided funding over the next three years to develop a set of indicators to measure environmental performance in conjunction with economic performance. *In the years ahead, these environmental indicators could well have a greater impact on public policy than any other single measure we might introduce* [my emphasis].[9]

I knew that a new era in economic reporting in Canada had begun. I spent the next three years traveling to Ottawa as Sustainability Measurement Director of the Pembina Institute, developing Canada's first set of environment and sustainable development indicators. Our work was completed and released in May 2003. The final results were somewhat disappointing: only five natural capital indicators (forest cover, freshwater quality, air quality, greenhouse gas (GHG) emissions, extent of wetlands) and one human capital indicator (educational attainment) would augment familiar economic data, including the gross domestic product (GDP) and the consumer price index (CPI). However, the most important outcome was the recommendation that Statistics Canada begin to explore the options for expanding the System of National Accounts (from which the GDP is derived) to include more detailed information on natural, human and social capital. If this recommendation was implemented, Canada would be the first nation in the world to adopt a total capital accounting system that could measure the overall sustainability of the nation. Could my recommendation to Paul Martin for a new balance sheet for the nation to measure the well-being or Genuine Wealth of Canada become a reality? I began to feel that the possibility existed, given the good fortune my journey was enjoying on a provincial level.

While still working part-time at the University of Alberta in January 2000, I had proposed to Jason Brisbois, senior economist of the federal government department of Western Economic Diversification (WED), and Brant Popp, senior policy analyst at WED, a research project to develop the first provincial-scale prototype GPI sustainability accounting and measurement system for the province of Alberta. Both Jason and Brant were enthused by the idea and suggested I submit a formal proposal. At the same time Rob Macintosh encouraged me to do this work through the Pembina Institute. I decided to leave the University of Alberta School of Business and form my own Pembina Institute sustainability measurement research team. My research project proposal to WED was accepted in April of 2000, and a team of five researchers at the Pembina Institute began work on the *Genuine Progress Indicators Pilot Project — Alberta Case Study: Accounting for Sustainable Development.* Our goal was to develop a sustainable well-being accounting and reporting system with Alberta as the case study. I began to assemble my Alberta GPI research team: Amy Taylor (resource economist), Mary Griffiths (PhD medical geography and scientist), Sara Wilson (ecological economist), Jeff Wilson (ecological footprint analyst), with guidance from Barbara Campbell (accountant). We began by developing a blue-print for the Alberta GPI accounts identifying three key domains: economic/financial, social/human health and environmental. Between April of 2000 and March of 2001 our Pembina team developed 51 economic, social, health and environmental well-being indicators (GPIs) accounting for Alberta's progress over four decades from 1961 to 1999. We combed hundreds of statistical databases (mostly from Statistics Canada) to construct our well-being ledgers. We wanted to answer key questions: Has the overall quality of life of Albertan's improved over forty years? Are we on a sustainable course for our children? We built on the original US GPI full-cost accounting framework, estimating the full costs of environmental, social and human capital values and depreciation costs. We also expanded the US GPI model to what I envisioned as a new sustainable well-being accounting system with well-being ledgers that would account for the quantitative (statistical data) and qualitative (opinion data) conditions of well-being. Our 51 indicators, which included the GDP, were based on the Alberta Government's 24 performance indicators for people, prosperity and preservation in *Measuring Up,* plus other indicators that we felt would resonate with quality of life issues important to Albertans. These indicators included time spent with family and friends, volunteer time, leisure time, income inequality, personal debt levels, divorce rates, disease and suicide rates, problem gambling rates and the ecological footprint (a robust measure of the sustainability of our individual lifestyles). Our overall goal was to complete a comprehensive well-being checkup of Alberta, as a doctor would complete an annual health checkup.

After many long nights of research, number crunching and analysis we released the Alberta GPI report on Monday morning, April 23, 2001. Titled *Alberta Sustainability Trends 2000: The Genuine Progress Indicators Report 1961 to 1999,* our report hit a home run in terms of media coverage. It made the front pages of Canada's national newspaper, the *Globe and Mail,* on April 23, 2001 with the title "Fat Cat Albertans Struggle with Happiness" and the front page of the *Edmonton Journal* with the title "Alberta's Natural Capital Slipping." I was stunned by the media attention. The phone rang off the hook that day. I was interviewed for CBC television's nightly newscast *The National* broadcast on both French and English television channels. Radio interviews included Alberta-broadcast CHED 630 radio and CBC radio in Montreal and Whitehorse. After an exhausting media-frenzied day, I knew that we had tapped into a deep current of public consciousness. The average Albertan understood that real progress should be measured by more than an increment in the GDP or stock market indices. We had put a quality-of-life-reality-mirror up to the GDP using a Genuine Progress Index that revealed that while Alberta's GDP had risen an average 4.4 percent per year over the period 1960 to 1999, the more comprehensive Genuine Progress Index had declined at an average rate of 0.5 percent during the same period. Indeed, throughout the 1980s and 1990s the GPI was virtually stagnant as the GDP continued its ascent. The economic credo that a rising tide of the GDP lifts all boats had been repudiated again.

Our results were not unlike the US GPI study. Although Alberta's Genuine Progress Index had remained relatively steady throughout the 1980s and 1990s, the US GPI had been in steady decline since the mid 1970s. The GPI well-being diagnosis also revealed that the average real (deflated for inflation) disposable incomes of average Albertans had stagnated since 1981 even as the GDP continued to rise through to 1999. Most Albertans could relate to this reality. Other regrettable economic and social trends included rising rates of suicide, divorce, problem gambling and personal debt. Many of the environmental indicators also showed negative trends including declining oil and gas reserves, massive fragmentation of forest ecosystem and rising levels of toxic waste production.

Our report sustained media and public attention for several weeks. I was invited to speak at numerous conferences about our findings. We had provided the basis of an important dialogue in Alberta addressing economist Stanley Küznets' challenge: more growth of what and for whom? Interesting, but not surprising, was the lack of any formal response from the Alberta Government and most notably from Alberta Premier Ralph Klein. Klein's response was simply that we were entitled to our own view of progress — a compliment given his penchant for polemic outbursts. The relative silence from the Alberta Government suggested that our longitudinal well-being check-up of Alberta's economic, social and environmental progress was relatively fair and accurate. Our report had its critics, primarily economists who argued that the creation of a composite well-being index was fraught with methodological problems, including indicator selection biases and giving all indicators equal weight. Ironically, few economists take exception to rough estimates of the regrettable social and environmental costs used to adjust Alberta's GDP, despite the creative accounting involved. The criticism about our choice and weighting of indicators were valid, in that our research could not be grounded in the expressed values of Albertans in the absence of longitudinal value surveys. Without the revealed quality of life values of Albertans, it was anyone's guess as to which well-being and sustainability indicators should be more important. I learned from this critique of the indexing process that future well-being indicator work should have a firm foundation in quality of life values expressed by citizens in the community.

The release of the Alberta GPI report suddenly opened up whole new professional development opportunities for me. The positive media and public attention given to our report affirmed my intuition that this kind of honest and transparent well-being measurement and reporting would resonate with people's common sense. During this exercise, I began to envision a new well-being measurement system which would report to Canadians on the well-being of all of our most important assets: human, social, natural, built and financial capital. It was then that I first discovered the origins of the words wealth, economics, ecology and value. While the word genuine had always given me some discomfort — it had a presumptive tone — I soon realized that if genuine referred to being true to one's values (i.e. authentic) then it might be appropriate to marry genuine with my new-found definition of wealth (namely, the conditions of well-being). Thus the concept of Genuine Wealth was born.

My work caught the attention of author David Korten of Bainbridge Island, Washington. David's influential books, *When Corporations Rule the World* and *Post Corporate World,* are two of the most important books that I have read on the nature of corporations and a vision for a sustainable, living economies. Challenged by a graph David presented at a public lecture in Edmonton in 1999, I conducted some preliminary research comparing the long-term trends in the US GDP, stock market indices, US total debt levels, the US GPI and other quality of life indicators. The resulting graph[10] of the trends from 1950 to 1999 clearly showed that while the financial indicators of progress including the GDP were rising exponentially, virtually every quality of life indicator showed a decline since the early 1970s. David encouraged me to write a book about the graph itself. That encouragement led me to write *The Economics of Happiness.*

CHAPTER 2

The Language of Wealth and Economics

Where is the life we have lost in living?
Where is the wisdom we have lost in knowledge?
Where is the knowledge we have lost in information?
— T. S. ELIOT[1]

TO BEGIN THIS STORY of Genuine Wealth, we must critically examine the words which tell our current story of progress: namely, the language or words of economics and business that we hear on the news and read in our newspapers every day. I want to reclaim the true meaning of the language of economics and business: words like wealth, economics, capital and competition. Only by reclaiming their authentic nature can we hope to begin to tell ourselves and our children and grandchildren a new story of development. Only then can we define a new road map for a journey whose ultimate destination is flourishing societies and economies of well-being and happiness.

What is wealth?

One of the most powerful and important words in the English language is wealth. Most of us have come to believe that the word denotes material possessions, financial assets, property and ultimately power. The dictionary defines wealth as: "much money or property; great amount of worldly possessions; riches."[2,3] In economics, wealth is defined as "a stock of all those assets capable of earning an income."[4] Wealth is often associated with power; those with more money, property, material possessions or riches are those with the most financial power in society and most likely to be successful. Every year various publications like *Forbes* list the world's richest or wealthiest people, measured in terms of net worth or income. According to *Forbes* in 2006 Bill Gates of Microsoft was the wealthiest person on the planet with an estimated net worth of US$50 billion.[5] Consider that the net worth of the richest human on earth is comparable to the 2005 GDP of Lithuania ($49.41 billion), a country with a population of 3.586 million people.[6]

Wealth (Old English): the conditions of well-being[7]

While the dominant meaning of wealth is associated with money, riches and worldly possessions, the word means much more. Examining the origins of the word in either the *Oxford* or *Webster's New World Dictionary* you will find that it comes from combining the Old English words *weal* (well-being) and *th* (condition). Therefore, the word wealth literally means "the conditions of well-being" or "the condition of being happy and prosperous." In Greek the word for wealth is *euporeo* which can be broken down into two components: *eu* (well) and *poros* (a passage).[8] In other words, wealth is a means to or way of being well. The Greek interpretation of the word wealth is important since Greek is the original language of the New Testament which has provided spiritual, moral and ethical guidance to Christians for centuries.

As an economist, for me to discover the authentic meaning of the word wealth was both earth shattering and exciting. It meant that wealth could no longer be narrowly defined in terms of the money-value of material possessions but must include the many, often intangible, things that contribute to our quality of life including our spiritual well-being, hope, happiness, the joy of our play and the strengths of our relationships. These were the attributes Robert Kennedy astutely noted were missing in our current measure of economic progress, the GDP. The importance of this revelation cannot be over emphasized. We are called to expand the concept of wealth to include human wealth, social wealth and natural or environmental wealth. Combining these forms of real wealth with financial or monetary wealth and built wealth (e.g. infrastructure, buildings, roads, hospitals, etc.) leads to a more genuine or authentic understanding of all the conditions that contribute to our well-being, both individually and collectively.

How have the Christian and Jewish religions defined the word wealth and economic life, in general? The first use of the term in the Christian Bible comes in the book of Genesis:

They [the sons of Jacob] took their sheep, and their oxen, and their asses, and that which was in the city, and that which was in the field, and all their wealth, and all their little ones, and their wives took they captive, and spoiled even all that was in the house.[9]

Here wealth refers to worldly possessions. In the Old Testament, wealth is defined in terms of the abundance of property. Hebrew words for wealth portray the meaning of *faculty, ability,* and *power* in relation to acquiring goods and influence.[10] In the book of Proverbs:

...wisdom is better than rubies; and all the things that may be desired are not to be compared to it.[11]

The Old Testament has a long-standing tradition of seeing wealth as a positive affirmation of God's blessing as long as it is obtained ethically and wisely.[12] God is not opposed to personal monetary wealth so long as we have the right relationship and perspective on these riches; all true wealth flows from the loving provision of God. We are called to use our stewardship of these gifts of wealth in a sensible manner as faithful stewards. What matters is not how much we possess but how wisely we use this wealth with which we are entrusted.

Jewish and Christian traditions seem to have a common appreciation of the importance of stewardship. According to the Jewish economist Meir Tamari: "The divine origin of wealth is the central principle of Jewish economic philosophy."[13] According to Tamari, all wealth (in which he also means all material possessions) belongs to God, who has given it temporarily to humanity on a stewardship basis, for his or her physical well-being. According to Jewish and Christian tradition, we learn that we are not owners of the earth but at best co-stewards with God, ultimately completely dependent on God for our sustenance. In other words the key issue is not that we are to feel guilty about monetary or worldly possessions, but rather understand that Genuine Wealth (our conditions of well-being) are in essence original blessings or gifts from God to be used wisely. According to Tamari, God taught humanity that our "economic welfare was something provided by God, and therefore to be regulated according to the Divine will."[14] Thus from God's point of view, it seems that wealth is not limited to money or worldly possessions; the real issue is our right relationship with wealth.

A close examination of the New Testament reveals that Jesus never once used the word wealth in his teachings. Jesus operated with a positive viewpoint of wealth as in the Old Testament teachings; wealth is seen as a blessing and to be used wisely for the good of others, especially the poor. He warned us of the dangers and pitfalls of an unhealthy relationship with money and material possessions, imploring us to avoid finding joy in hoarding of worldly things and using our wealth as a source of power to suppress others. Jesus challenged: "What good will it be for a man if he gains the whole world, yet forfeits his soul?"[15] He taught a radical reordering of our priorities challenging us that we can not serve two masters (*mammon* or money and God) at the same time.[16] I believe Jesus' life, by example, teaches us to use wealth frugally (in small amounts) and for the service of humanity, according to the will of God, focusing on the health of our spiritual life of faith, our love for each other and our love for God.

> That which seems to be wealth may in verity be only the gilded index of far reaching ruin.
> — JOHN RUSKIN

Jesus taught that the poor and children were rich in the sense of being free, being less encumbered by concerns over worldly possessions and power. For Jesus, power and financial wealth should in fact be inverted; it is harder for a rich person to enter the kingdom of God than a poor person. Jesus ultimately demanded a reordering of our spiritual, relational and financial priorities.[17]

What about more contemporary treatments of the word wealth? One of the most important books in economics and one which uses the word wealth in its title is *The Wealth of Nations* (1776) by Adam Smith, the eighteenth-century Scottish political economist. When I searched an on-line version of his famous economic treatise for each occurrence of the word wealth I was genuinely surprised to find that Smith had never defined the word according to its Old English origins. In his first reference, he defines "real wealth" as "the annual produce of the land and labour of the society."[18] While Smith's use of the word wealth coincides somewhat with the first Old Testament definition related to livestock and land, it clearly falls short of the more holistic Old English definition that would encompass all conditions of life that contribute to well-being. How unfortunate that such an important theoretical treatise would limit the world of economics to such a narrow treatment of wealth for more than 200 years.

One of the few genuine statements about wealth as a state of being fully conscious to the powers of life was by John Ruskin, the nineteenth-century Victorian philosopher, writer and artist:

> There is no wealth but life. Life, including all its powers of love, of joy, and of admiration. That country is richest which nourishes the greatest number of noble and happy human beings; that man is richest who, having perfected the functions of his own life to the utmost, has also the widest helpful influence, both personal, and by means of his possessions, over the lives of others.[19]

Ruskin was one of the few writers in modern times to understand that the true meaning of the word wealth has more to do with quality of life than the accumulation of worldly possessions. If Ruskin is correct that real wealth is life (the powers of love, of joy, of full life functionality), then I would suggest that real economics should be concerned with real life issues, including the study and measurement of the quality of life conditions of individuals and households that make up a community. For too long, economics has been a mathematical abstraction of the real world substituting a value-less, monetary metric for the real attributes of well-being. Monetary measures of progress (e.g. gross domestic product, inflation and stock market indices) dominate our reportage and consciousness. Economists concerned about real wealth should be assessing or diagnosing the actual conditions of well-being of households and communities. In other words, economists could become "well-being doctors."

If true wealth represents all those conditions of life that contribute to our individual and community well-being, how do we decide what factors matter most? I would argue that our values, principles and beliefs define the conditions of well-being. What we value most about life defines our real wealth. You could probably jot down on a napkin a dozen things you consider most precious and valuable for a good life. Such values will be diverse and varied across cultures, gender, age groups and other demographic strata. But for each of us, these values are genuine — that is, grounded in how we choose to live. And if each of us can define real wealth personally, the term common wealth can then be defined as conditions of well-being of the commons or community, not only as concern for the common good.

Measuring real wealth we should include not only monetary and worldly possessions but qualitative attributes like health (physical and mental), spiritual well-being, healthy relationships, love and respect, the conditions of our physical living environment and the well-being of nature. All factors that contribute to well-being could be called life capital or life assets. We might say, then, that a truly wealthy person enjoys a full and robust life in a manner which is authentic or true to that person's core values. For example, I believe that the most precious and scarce form of life wealth is time. We each have a limited amount of time in the hourglass of our life. How and where I choose to invest every grain of sand of time in my life's hourglass reflects my values.

What is value?

> Our values are those principles and qualities that matter to us, that are really important to our sense of well-being. On one level, values are the ideas and beliefs on which we base our decisions. They are like an invisible DNA, made up of our sense of right and wrong, that structure our choices... So our values are our beliefs.
>
> — JOE DOMINGUEZ and VICKI ROBIN[20]

It is often said that we too often know the cost of everything and the value of nothing. For example, I might know the money-value of my bank account or investment portfolio, but do I know the real value of things that make my life worthwhile? Typically what we measure and count is what we value. Most of us associate the word value with the monetary price of an item or service — like the price of bread, a car or drycleaning. The first definition of the word value in Webster's Dictionary is a fair or proper equivalent in money, commodities, etc. for something sold or exchanged; a fair price or return.[21] Yet, like the word wealth, the origin of the word value has been lost or forgotten.

Value comes from the Latin *valere* which means to be strong, be worth[22] or to be well.[23] The origin of the word *value* is thus closely aligned with the original meanings of wealth and health.

Value (Latin, *valere*): to be strong, to be worth

But in today's English usage, it is only when we consider the plural form that value takes on a different meaning. *Values* is defined as social principles, goals or standards held or accepted by an individual, class or society.[24] These principles of living could include morals or virtues like goodness. Values are attributes of quality of life which are accepted by individuals, households or a community. They often guide decision making. Values may change over time depending on the various pressures and conditions of life. Some — like "love your neighbor as yourself" — may be common across cultures. Some values will be guided by religious teachings and understanding of supernatural authority, while others may be guided by humanism, the system of thought based on the values, characteristics and behavior that are believed to be ideal or the best in human beings. What is clear is that we experience a diversity of values throughout human communities.

The questions are then: what values currently form the foundation of our modern economies? What beliefs and principles of economic life do we consciously or subconsciously live by? Is there discord between the values espoused by our modern democratic, capitalist and free market system and the values that reside in our hearts about what constitutes "a good life?"

What does it mean to be genuine and have Genuine Wealth?

The word genuine means to be authentic, real, natural, true or pure.[25] To be genuine means to live in accordance with one's values, the shared values of a family or household or the shared values of a community of households. To act against our values means to live disingenuous, counterfeit or artificial lives.

By combining the words genuine and wealth we create Genuine Wealth, *the conditions of well-being that are true to our core values of life.* To develop Genuine Wealth means to improve the conditions of well-being in accordance with one's values or the shared values of the community. A genuinely wealthy community is one which has articulated its values and lives life accordingly. Such communities work in a spirit of collective and shared responsibility or stewardship to ensure that the various conditions of well-being that add to quality of life are flourishing, vibrant, life-giving and sustainable for current and future generations.

This concept of Genuine Wealth is consistent with the principles of sustainability. To sustain something means to hold up something, to give support or relief to, to provide for sustenance or nourishment or to support something as true, legal or just.[26] To sustain the life and real wealth of a community means to ensure that the basic needs of all individuals of a community are being met.

Professor John R. Ehrenfeld, an international leader in the field of industrial ecology and instructor at M.I.T. in Boston, has suggested that sustainability be connected to a more compelling word — *flourishing.*

> I think of sustainability as a possibility that human and other life
> will flourish on Earth forever. Flourishing means not only survival,
> but also the realization of whatever we as humans declare makes life
> good and meaningful, including notions like justice, freedom and
> dignity. And as a possibility, sustainability spoken in this way is a
> guide to actions that will or can achieve its central vision of flourish-
> ing for time immemorial.[27]

I share Ehrenfeld's vision. To be genuinely sustainable means that all the conditions of well-being of a community are flourishing. A sustainable community turns to better stewardship — living with intention — in a spirit of
shared responsibility, freedom, dignity, social justice and equity. To live life
sustainably means to be prudent, frugal and better gardeners of the common
wealth, nurturing life assets and weeding out liabilities to limit genuine
well-being for current and future generations. To live frugally and prudently
is associated with living economically. Yet it seems that the modern world
has lost sight of the original meaning of economy.

What is an economy?

It is instructive to discover that etymologically economy comes from the
Greek, *oikonomia*, which means the management (*nomia*) of a household (*oikos*)
or state.[28] Therefore, real or genuine economics should, in principle, study the
conditions of living which households, families, communities and even businesses experience as stewards of well-being and commonwealth, towards
goals of the common good. The French philosopher Vialatoux states: "Economy as its name indicates, studies the order of the human household, arrang-
ing, according to their respective values, persons and things."[29] John Maynard
Keynes was the last great economist to hold that the economy relates to the
good life. Thus it is fitting that Keynes, when asked about his greatest regret
upon his deathbed, is said to have replied: "I should have drunk more cham-
pagne."[30]

Yet modern economics and modern dictionaries define economy as "the
management of the income, expenditures, etc. of a household, private business, community or government and the careful management of wealth."[31]
Economics is defined as "the science that deals with the production, distribution and consumption of wealth."[32] According to these definitions modern
economics studies economic man (*homo oeconomicus*) — a pleasure-seeking and

material wealth maximizing autonomous species seeking the maximum satisfaction at the cost of minimum effort. Notice that this pursuit of material wealth has no moral or ethical compass to guide decisions. Here again, we fail to ground the language of wealth and economics in its original meaning. Most economists today track minute changes in the production, consumption and distribution of material wealth using money-based metrics of performance like the GDP, consumer price indices, stock market indices and currency exchange rates. Few are focused on measuring those conditions of well-being which households experience in their individual and collective pursuit of happiness, the virtuous or good life. It's no surprise to me that economics has been described as the dismal science, so disconnected has economics become from the real life of people and families. John Ruskin lamented the state of economics speaking to civic leaders in a Bradford Town Hall, April 1864: "All our hearts have been betrayed by the plausible impiety of the modern economist, telling us that, 'To do the best for ourselves is finally to do the best for others.'"[33] John Maynard Keynes' vision of the future of economics gives me some hope:

> The day is not far off when the economic problem will take the back
> seat where it belongs, and the arena of the heart and the head will be
> occupied or reoccupied, by our real problems — the problems of life
> and of human relations, of creation and behavior and religion.[34]

Chrematistics (money) or *oikonomia* (life)

Since modern economics seems to be focused on financial and material wealth management it is instructive to learn that Aristotle, the third-century-BC Greek philosopher, made an important distinction between *oikonomia*/economics and chrematistics.[35] Chrematistics is a word rarely heard in today's economic or business discourse yet it should be because it comes from the Greek meaning the art of money-making, with the root *chrema* meaning money, riches or something useful.

Ecological economist Herman Daly and theologian John Cobb Jr. define chrematistics as "the branch of political economy relating to the manipulation of property and wealth so as to maximize short-term monetary exchange value to the owner."[36] In stark contrast Daly and Cobb define *oikonomia* as "the management of the household so as to increase its use value to all members of the household over the long run."[37] Daly and Cobb draw these distinctions:

Oikonomia differs from chrematistics in three ways. First, it takes the long-run rather than the short-run view. Second, it considers costs and benefits to the whole community, not just to the parties to the transaction. Third, it focuses on concrete use value and the limited accumulation thereof, rather on abstract exchange value and its impetus toward unlimited accumulation. Use value is concrete: it has a physical dimension and a need that can be objectively satisfied. Together, these features limit both the desirability and the possibility of accumulation use values beyond limit. By contrast, exchange value is totally abstract: it has no physical dimension or any naturally satiable need to limit its accumulation. Unlimited accumulation is the goal of the chremastist and is evidence for Aristole of the unnaturalness of the activity. True wealth is limited by the satisfaction of the concrete need for which it was designed. For oikonomia, there is such a thing as enough. For chrematistics, more is always better.[38]

> Chrematistics (Greek): The art of money-making, the science of wealth; the science, or a branch of the science, of political economy.[35]

Daly and Cobb agree that pursuing true wealth satisfies basic and concrete life needs. By contrast, chrematistics is really modern capitalism: the hedonistic accumulation of riches or material wealth without any moral or ethical limiters on sufficiency or a sense of what constitutes a virtuous life. I have made the point to my students at the University of Alberta in the School of Business that chrematistics — not *oikonomia* — is the dominant language and theology of business and economic schools today.

In a world dominated by chrematistics there is no moral or ethical limit to the acquisition and accumulation of more worldly riches and monetary wealth, even if others may be suffering for lack of basic life needs. Moreover, there is no moral or ethical compass that tells us individually or collectively when sufficiency has been reached or when inequality of material wealth has reached such unacceptable levels that social cohesion is at risk in communities. In a chrematistic world, sustainability, sufficiency or even flourishing are unacceptable destinations for progress. Without understanding the very nature of the chrematistic system we live in and the nature of money and its creation in this system, the pursuit of sustainability as an objective will remain an impossible dream. In the mind of a chrematist there are no limits to economic growth, and the market economy as a system behaves more like a cancer cell than a virtuous human being with a conscience. The chrematistic spirit and the spirit of market capitalism are so dominant and powerful on a global scale that they easily crowd out those few who attempt to live a virtuous life. Unfortunately as a teacher and practitioner of economics and business, I see chrematistics continuing to masquerade as real economics. By providing students with the chrematistic tools of commerce and winning in the world of markets, business schools fail to grasp the true meaning of the very basis of commerce: competition.

> Competition (from Latin, *competere* to strive together)[39]

What does it mean to be competitive?

In dictionaries, the word competition is usually defined as the activity of doing something with the goal of outperforming others or winning something; a form of rivalry or contest such as in sports (playing to win a medal or a prize) or in business (for market share, customers, or financial profits). But the word competition actually comes from the Latin *competere* which means "to strive together or to seek (*petere*) together (*com*) some common interest."[40] Based on its word origin, true competition implies working or striving together in cooperation towards a common goal. Genuine competition is therefore supportive of and entirely consistent with building a world of Genuine Wealth, a world based on a foundation of common values striving towards well-being.

Regrettably, we say we "compete" to win a game or war rather than to work together towards a mutually beneficially outcome. Competition has become a euphemism for commercial and trade warfare. Terms like "competitive advantage" suggest an eternal battle over market share where there are only winners and losers in business relationships. Progress and success are defined in terms of profitability and market dominance, not as outcomes of relationships that operate in a spirit of cooperation, mutuality and reciprocity that lead to a win-win world. In the world of Genuine Wealth I envision, where genuine competition is taking place with cooperation and reciprocity, there is no room for the regrettable consequences of such warfare models. We thus have the opportunity — indeed responsibility to future generations —

to rediscover the true meaning of competition and envision a world that is defined by life-giving and reciprocal relationships committed to building Genuine Wealth.

What is capital?

The word capital is undoubtedly one of the most common words used in business and economics. When I searched the usage of the word "capital" using Google, the web search engine, there were 57.8 million hits compared with 21.1 million hits for the word "wealth." The etymological roots of capital are more difficult to source than the word wealth. *Webster's New World Dictionary* defines capital, amongst several options, as: wealth (money or property) owned or used in business by a person, corporation, etc.; an accumulated stock of such wealth or its value and wealth, in whatever form, used or capable of being used to produce more wealth.[41]

It is intriguing that wealth and capital are so closely associated. Perhaps the word capital can also be defined more comprehensively? There may be many types of capital — human, social, natural and built — which contribute to overall well-being. I will expand on this concept later in this book. For the moment, let's just say that the words capital and wealth are effectively synonymous and can be used interchangeably.

Life capital

If wealth and capital are synonymous we might provide a more precise definition of capital that contributes to quality of life or well-being. Professor John McMurtry calls this "life capital." Life capital includes human (people), social (relationships) and natural (environmental) capital. McMurtry, a professor of Philosophy at Guelph University in Ontario, has made important contributions to the Genuine Wealth model through numerous conversations.

McMurtry identifies the importance of "life needs", a need being that without which life capabilities are reduced or destroyed (e.g., the need for nourishing food).[42] When a person's life needs are satisfied then you have the conditions for a good life. A person who is rich in "life capabilities" has the ability needed or the potential for development. That person is endowed with real wealth and the potential to improve well-being for themselves and the community.

CHAPTER 3

What's Wrong with the
Picture of Progress?

Too much and too long, we seemed to have surrendered personal excellence and community values in the mere accumulation of material things. Our Gross National Product [GNP]... — if we should
judge America by that — ...counts air pollution and cigarette advertising, and ambulances to clear our highways of carnage. It
counts special locks for our doors and the jails for the people who
break them. It counts the destruction of the redwood and the loss of
our natural wonder in chaotic sprawl. It counts napalm and counts
nuclear warheads and armored cars for the police to fight the riots in
our cities.... Yet the gross national product does not allow for the
health of our children, the quality of their education or the joy of
their play. It does not include the beauty of our poetry or the
strength of our marriages, the intelligence of our public debate or
the integrity of our public officials. It measures neither our wit nor
our courage, neither our wisdom nor our learning, neither our compassion nor our devotion to our country, it measures everything in
short, except that which makes life worthwhile.

— ROBERT KENNEDY, March 18, 1968[1]

WHAT WE MEASURE reflects what we value and what matters most; what
we use to measure and report progress gets our attention. Robert

Kennedy reminded us just how limited our measures of economic progress can be. Virtually every nation tells its story of economic progress using gross domestic product (GDP): the monetary value of all the goods and services bought and sold in an economy. We are led to believe by economists and politicians that the more the GDP grows the better off we are. But who really cares if the GDP rose another few percentage points, representing billions more dollars in production of many things we don't actually need more of, while ignoring deficits of love, relationships and the health of the environment? The GDP is simply a poor measure of well-being and genuine progress, as Kennedy pointed out.

New research into well-being and happiness is showing that increasing economic growth does not necessarily improve well-being.[2] Well-being is more than making more money and even more than just happiness. Well-being means developing as a person, being fulfilled, and making a meaningful contribution to the community.[3] If economic measures of progress fail to measure that which makes life worthwhile — that is, well-being — where did we go wrong? What can we do to change the ways we measure and manage progress so that they align with our values?

Many of us intuitively know there is something wrong with the current picture of progress where indicators like the GDP measure economic well-being solely in terms of what is bought and sold. We are continually told by economists and even presidents that improving our economic well-being requires stimulating the economy through more economic growth. "Stimulating the economy" means producing more stuff, spending more, and consuming more even if our basic corporeal needs have been satisfied. One of the most poignant moments for me was when President George W. Bush, following the horrific events on September 11, 2001, urged Americans to go shopping. Why? To ensure the economy kept going and growing even if many Americans and Canadians experienced the joys of slowing down, listening to nature as the skies grew quiet from the noise of airplanes, and renewing friendships with neighbors and strengthening our relationships with those we love.

Behind President Bush's invocation for more consumption and more growth is the fundamental economic belief that a rising tide of the GDP ultimately raises the well-being of all households in an economy. Economic growth has been the central objective of most governments over these last 50 years, and the GDP has been the key measure of progress. But has the rising tide of the GDP led to improved conditions of well-being for the average American or Canadian? Are we any happier today with more income and more material possessions than 40 years ago? Lynne Twist author of *The Soul of Money* notes that society is caught up in a myth that more growth, more production and more consumption are good for our lives.[4]

If we examine leading economic indicators like the GDP, stock market indices and consumer spending it is true that after 50 years of progress our capitalist western societies have enjoyed unparallel economic success. We have more GDP per capita, more income, more material possessions, larger homes, more cars and more kitchen gadgets than at any time in history. The average American now spends almost 250 percent more (in inflation-adjusted dollars) in 2005 than she or he did in 1950. Consumer spending is the key driver of the GDP. The following graph shows trends in economic growth in the US. Between 1950 and 2004 the US GDP rose 3,887% in current dollars while total stock market capitalization value rose a fantastic 8,160% (even after the major correction in stock-market values following 9-11-2001). According to economic logic these upward-sloping graphs should mean that overall well-being in the US has improved.

As an economist, I was used to seeing GDP curves like this for the US and Canada. But as a member of my community I felt these indicators were

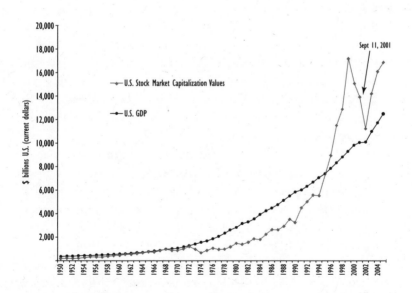

FIGURE 3.1. US GDP and Stock Market Valuations, 1950–2005.

Credit: US Bureau of Economic Analysis & New York Stock Exchange (nyse.com)

masking what was really going on at the household level. While economists and politicians bragged about rising GDP, my neighbors in Edmonton would lament that their personal economic well-being showed little improvement.

The Genuine Progress Indicator (GPI)

The Genuine Progress Indicator or GPI was developed in 1995 by Cliff Cobb, an economist with the San Francisco economic-think tank Redefining Progress as an alternative measure of economic well-being and progress to the GDP.[5] If the GDP was designed to account for the total monetary value of consumption and production in an economy, the GPI was designed to indicate genuine progress in people's quality of life and overall economic, social and environmental well-being.

The GDP's ideal economic hero is a chain-smoking, terminal cancer patient going through an expensive divorce whose car is totaled in a 20-car pile-up, as a result of being distracted by his cell phone while munching on a fast-food hamburger — all activities which would contribute to the GDP. GPI, on the other hand, suggests that many of these "heroic" activities are regrettable and indeed should not be counted as genuine progress.

The GPI addresses seven major fallacies embodied in the GDP and similar national income accounts:

1. The GDP regards every expenditure as an addition to well-being, regardless what that expenditure is for and its effects. By this reasoning a healthy person in a solid marriage that cooks at home, walks to work and doesn't smoke or gamble is an economic villain. The hero borrows and spends; the villain pays cash and saves for the kids' education. What economists call "growth," in other words, is not always the same as what most people would consider good.

2. The GDP ignores the crucial economic functions that lie outside the realm of monetary exchange. The GDP excludes the value of unpaid housework, child care, volunteer work and leisure. Parents do real work. So do neighbors, communities, open spaces, rivers and oceans, the atmosphere and trees. Anyone who doubts this might try getting along without them. Such things contribute more to well-being than does much that we buy from the market. Yet the GDP regards these life-sustaining functions as worthless — until the economy destroys them and we have to buy substitutes from the market or from government. Then the GDP says that the economy has "grown." When parents default and kids need

counseling or foster care, the GDP goes up because money has changed hands. When a parent cares for kids at home the GDP stagnates; when that same parent takes care of other peoples' kids and calls it "daycare" the GDP goes up. When the city cuts down shade trees to widen a street and homeowners have to buy air conditioners for cooling, the GDP goes up again. It looks like economic growth, but no real increases have occurred. Instead, something that used to be free now costs money; social and environmental decay has been transmogrified into "growth" through the myopic lens of the GDP.

3. The GDP does not account for natural resources that are required to sustain current and future economic development — implying that the future has no value. The GDP excludes natural resource capital, environmental resources services, human resources, research and development. All that matters is the present. The implications of current economic activity for our kids and grandkids do not enter the calculation. For example, the GDP counts the depletion of natural resources as current income rather than as the liquidation of an asset. This violates both basic accounting principles and common sense. Similarly, saving doesn't add much to the GDP; economists actually chide Japan for its high savings rate. But maxing out on credit cards makes the GDP soar.

4. The GDP ignores totally the distribution of income, the social costs of inequality and poverty. Changes in the GDP are insensitive to income inequality, poverty and the distribution of personal consumption and wealth. Even assuming that the GDP represents a rising tide of beneficence, it can't have that effect unless all share. If the economy is getting bigger but the benefits are going mainly to those who need it least, the result are material accretion not economic advance. This is true even in conventional economic terms. For a family struggling on the minimum wage, a tenth that amount can mean the difference between macaroni and chicken for many nights.

5. The GDP contains intermediate and regrettable expenditures that do not contribute to economic welfare. It includes government spending for weapons. It also includes personal costs related to commuting, crime, environmental protection and automobile accidents.

6. The GDP minimizes the value of expenditures on education, health care, social services and environmental protection because it does not reflect the outcomes or returns on investment from such expenditures. Such

outcomes might include physical well-being (e.g. life expectancy), intellectual and labor market skills, educational attainment and improved quality of the environment.

7. The GDP does not directly measure investment in social capital. Social capital includes investments in the health and wellness of communities, social institutions and democratic processes.[6]

When you add up all of these fallacies, is it any wonder that economists and leaders may see current economic reality and the future as rosy and while many Americans and Canadians intuit there is something wrong with the picture of progress they are given?

The GPI attempted to address these shortcomings of the GDP by measuring the social and environmental costs and benefits which the GDP either ignores or counts as economic progress. The GPI made intuitive sense to me and seemed to address the fundamental challenges posed by one of the creators of national income accounting, Simon Küznets. Küznets had deep reservations about the limits of the new national income accounting and in 1934 cautioned the US Congress that "the welfare of a nation can scarcely be inferred from a measurement of national income [as defined by the GNP]." Almost 30 years later Küznets had come to the conclusion that national income accounting should be completely rethought. Writing in the *New Republic* in 1962 he noted "Distinctions must be kept in mind between quantity and quality of growth, between costs and return, and between short and long run." He noted further that "Goals for more growth should specify more growth of what and for what." Küznets foreshadowed the need for an alternative measure of economic well-being stating that eventually "national income concepts will have to be either modified or partly abandoned, in favor of more inclusive measures, less dependent on the appraisals of the market system. The eventual solution would obviously lie in devising a single yardstick."[7] John Kenneth Galbraith, one of the 20th century's greatest economists, echoed Küznets' concern: "There is a major flaw in measuring the quality and achievement of life by the total of economic production — (GNP/GDP) — the total of everything we produce and everything we do for money." Galbraith noted that measures such as the GDP override and obscure deeper and more important aspects of economic life, failing to take sufficient account of the value and enjoyment of what is produced.[8]

To calculate the GPI, we begin with the personal consumption expenditures. We include capital investment, government spending and net exports. But the GPI adjusts personal consumption expenditures by:

- Adjusting GDP for income inequality — the gap between rich and poor
- Adding the values of unpaid housework, parenting and volunteer work
- Adding the value of the service from household infrastructure
- Adding the value of the service from streets and highways
- Subtracting the value of time including costs of lost leisure time, family breakdown, commuting time, unemployment and underemployment
- Subtracting the costs of crime, auto accidents and cost of consumer durables
- Subtracting the costs of long-term environmental degradation, air pollution, water pollution, ozone depletion, noise pollution, loss of farmland, loss of forests, loss of wetlands and
- Adjusting for net capital formation and net foreign borrowing

In other words, the GPI reveals hidden environmental costs as well as several measures of both social progress (value of unpaid work) and decline which the GDP obfuscates. I realized that the GPI, while itself incomplete and methodologically challenging, nevertheless represented one of the most heroic attempts in economics to present decision makers with a more meaningful and accurate picture of human progress. In my mind, the GPI represented a gold mine of economic research opportunities.

In 1999 I helped to update the US GPI to the year 1998 as a Senior Fellow with Redefining Progress. The results in Figure 3.2 showed erosion of natural, human and social capital in the US while the GDP continued to rise. The loss of economic well-being since the mid-1970s went on through the 1990s even when US stock markets were red hot. While the GDP per capita rose by 1.4 percent per annum throughout the 1990s the GPI was declining at an average annual rate of 2.7 percent.

The key negative drivers or costs causing the sharp decline in the US GPI through the 90s included soaring income inequality (the gap between the rich and everyone else), the cost of the depletion of nonrenewable resources ($1.3 trillion), long-term environmental damage ($1.0 trillion), the cost of commuting and loss of leisure time ($638 billion combined) and increasing foreign indebtedness.

The strength of the GPI is that the results are expressed in the same dollar or monetary terms as the GDP. For example, the US GPI account update I completed in 1999 revealed that personal consumption expenditures (which makes up 65% of US GDP) were $4.9 trillion (in 1992 dollars) in 1997. But when the benefits of unpaid work (+$2.6 trillion) are added and the costs of the loss of nature, family breakdown and other social costs are deducted (-$5.7 trillion) from economic progress, the result is a net GPI for 1997 of only $1.7 trillion. Some of the positive social benefits included in GPI, but otherwise unaccounted for in GDP, include the value of unpaid housework, parenting and volunteerism — a benefit of $1.97 trillion — that amounts to an equivalent of 27% of the value of the 1997 US GDP. On the negative side, the costs of pollution and environmental degradation — $1.44 trillion — represented 20% of the 1997 US GDP. The cost of resource depletion (including loss of forests, farmland, wetlands) totaled $1.84 trillion or 25% of the US GDP.

Making money, growing poorer

In the fall of 1999, David Korten, author of *When Corporations Rule the World,* gave a public lecture at the University of Alberta. He presented a graph which he believed reflected the current state of US economic as well as quali-

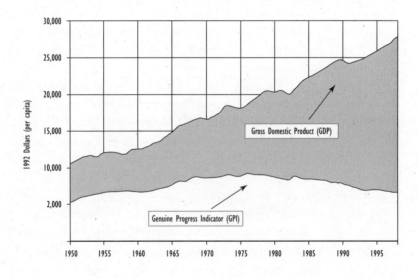

FIGURE 3.2. US GDP versus the Genuine Progress Indicator (GPI), 1950–1997

Credit: Jonathan Rowe and Mark Anielski. *The Genuine Progress Indicator 1998 Update — Executive Summary.* Redefining Progress, 1999.

ty of life indicators. The lines on that graph were constructed with fictitious numbers, so I decided to reconstruct Korten's graph with actual data including 50 years of US statistics on GDP, stock market indices, the US GPI and other quality of life indicators. Being a student of the nature of money in our economy, I identified a key indicator missing in Korten's graph: the total amount of outstanding household, business, government and foreign debt in the US. The following graph emerged.

This graph shows an incredibly robust set of economic indicators: a rising GDP as well as a rising stock market, with the noted collapse of stock market values following 9-11-2001. The current market capitalization value of all domestic stocks traded in the US have risen over 12,254% (over 12 times its value) since 1950 reaching a value of $16.9 trillion. Over the same period the US GDP (in current dollars) has risen 4,143% reaching $12.5 trillion in 2005. The US GPI line is hardly noticeable while the estimated costs of environmental degradation and natural capital depletion in the US is evident in the line which declines steadily. The most remarkable line in this graph is the total amount of outstanding US debt. This includes all forms of

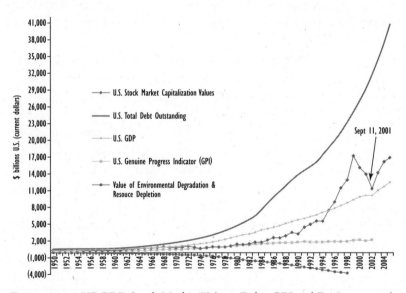

FIGURE 3.3. US GDP, Stock Market Values, Debt, GPI and Environmental Degradation Costs.

Credit: 1: US GDP: US Bureau of Economic Analysis; 2. Stock Market Values: New York Stock Exchange (nyse.com); 3. US Total Credit Debt Outstanding: US Federal Reserve; 4. GPI: Redefining Progress; 5. Environmental Degradation Costs: Redefining Progress.

debt including government (public), household, business and foreign debt. Between 1950 and 2005, the total debt outstanding (as reported by US Federal Reserve statistics) has risen 7,935% reaching a staggering $38.3 trillion by the second quarter of 2005. The increase in total debt is so dramatic that it has reached parabolic heights which appear unsustainable in the long-run.

This graph clearly illustrated that while the US was making money it was also growing poorer in genuine economic and environmental terms. This graph also affirmed something I have come to appreciate: that there is a direct relationship between debt and the GDP. The graph shows that debt places a permanent claim on life's capital, like an insatiable cancer cell sucking life from its hosts. The graph implies that eventually the host/economy will die because outstanding debt can never be repaid out of current production. We can see how the unrepayable debt load of the US exerts insatiable pressure on that economy to keep growing *ad infinitum.* Perhaps this is why President George W. Bush urged Americans to go shopping after the tragedy of 9-11; without continued spending the outstanding mountain of debt could not be serviced and the economy would face a heart attack. Moreover, the graph warns that even if we want to pursue an economy of moderation based on ethics of sufficiency this would be impossible with the debt overhang that exists in the US as in most nations.

The epiphanies of this analysis led me to examine other social quality of life and environmental health indicators in contrast to the GDP. Graphing the GDP in relationship with the GPI, the Index for Social Health, the World Wildlife Fund's Living Planet Index and an estimate of the ecological deficit for the US (measured using Ecological Footprint analysis) showed that every key life indicator has been in decline in the US since the mid-1970s.

For example, the Index for Social Health (ISH), a 17-indicator composite measure of societal well-being developed by Marc Miringoff at Fordham University, includes indicators such as suicide rates, teen pregnancy, income inequality, life expectancy and other intuitive social and human health indicators. It declined 45% between 1970 and 1993. Over the same period the GPI declined 29% since its peak in the mid-1970s. The Ecological Footprint deficit[9] of the US continued to rise (revealed by a declining trend line). As a proxy for world ecosystem health, the Living Planet Index — a measure of the health of the world's forests, freshwater and oceans — declined 32% globally over the same study period. There are indicators that show positive improvements in quality of life including increasing life expectancies and improved air quality. But here again is strong evidence that the "progress" represented in conventional economic and financial market indicators masks the cancerous state of many our life support systems.

Our affluent society has been fueled largely by non-renewable fossil fuels. Our GDP, our food and much of our lifestyle is literally soaked in oil. For example, agricultural production is now roughly 90% dependent on oil inputs; our food is literally petroleum based.[10] It takes about three-quarters of a gallon of oil to produce a pound of beef.[11] If all of the world ate the way the United States eats, humanity would exhaust all known global fossil-fuel reserves in just seven years.[12] Every second the world consumes 37,000 gallons of oil, 480 tons of coal and 3 trillion cubic feet of natural gas.[13] The US now consumes more than one-quarter of the world's total fossil fuel production (more than 20 million barrels of day). According to some petroleum geologists the world is facing a stark reality: peak world oil production. Peak oil describes reaching the midpoint between discovery and depletion of finite re-

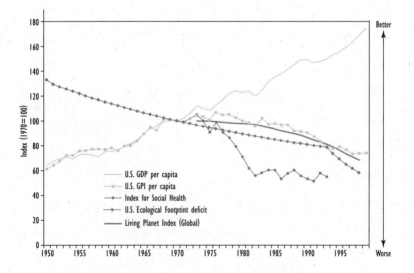

FIGURE 3.4. Genuine Well-being (Quality-of-Life) Indicators versus GDP (1970–100)

Credit: 1. US GDP: US Bureau of Economic Analysis; 2. US GPI: Redefining Progress (rprogress.org); 3. Index for Social Health: Marc Miringoff. 4. UN HDI: UN Human Development Report 1999; 5. US Ecological Footprint: derived from Wackernagel & Rees, *Our Ecological Footprint*, New Society, 1995 and rprogress.org; 6. Living Planet Index: World Wildlife Fund.

serves of oil, gas and other non-renewable energy. At the point of peak world oil production, prices become more volatile as nations scramble to secure the remaining and diminishing supplies of oil. According to the Association for the Study of Peak Oil and Gas (ASPO) the world reached a peak oil situation in 2005; the US and Canada reached peak of conventional oil and gas reserves in the early 1970s.[14]

Figure 3.5 pictures trends in US dependency on non-renewable fossil fuels relative to the GDP (current dollars) between 1950 and 2005. The graph clearly shows how US economic progress has been fueled by the use of non-renewable oil, gas and coal resources. However, the good news is that the US economy is in fact much more energy efficient today than it was 50 years ago — requiring only 6.8% as much total energy input in 2005 per dollar GDP than in 1950; in 1950 a dollar of GDP required roughly 20,314 barrels of oil equivalent (117, 822 Btus) of total energy (fossil fuels, electricity and renewable energy) compared to only 1,383 barrels of oil equivalent (8,020 Btus) in 2005.[15] This suggests that the US economy is in fact more frugal with respect to energy inputs while maintaining high economic well-being.

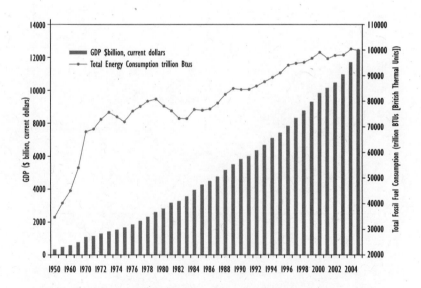

FIGURE 3.5. US GDP versus total fossil fuel consumption, 1950–2005

Credit: 1. US GDP: US Bureau of Economic Analysis; 2. US fuel consumption: US Department of Energy, Annual Energy Review 2005, Section 2: Energy Consumption by Sector.

Yet the US faces a significant challenge from the pressures of peak oil and its continued dependency on fossil fuels. In 2005, of the 99,894 trillion Btus in total energy consumption, fossil fuels still made up 86% of energy consumption followed by nuclear energy (8.1%) and renewable energy (6.1% of which 45% is from hydroelectric power generation). The contribution of renewable energy as a percentage of total energy consumption has actually declined from the high of 10.5% in 1971.

To examine whether the US as a whole was better off today than it was in 1950, I constructed a large database. I wanted to compare trends in economic indicators with quality of life indicators like average real incomes, income inequality, water quality, air quality, the extent of natural environments like wetlands and old growth forests, crime rates, car crashes and a number of health indicators. I asked the simple question: "are today's citizens happier and enjoy a higher quality of life than they enjoyed 50 years ago?" I organized the available indicators according to what I felt people might intuitively say they would want more of and what they would want less of to improve their quality of life. The results of my analysis for the US are sobering. Here I have compared several well-being indicators in the year 2000 with the benchmark year 1950.

These indicators demonstrate again that many life conditions for the average US citizen have grown worse despite increasing levels of GDP and booming financial markets.

The Alberta GPI

As the US GPI update project was nearing completion in January of 2000 I began to construct a similar but more detailed GPI analysis for my home province of Alberta in Canada. I was motivated by a simple question: were Albertans in general better off today in terms of economic, social, health and environmental well-being than they were in 1960 when I was born?

The Alberta GPI sustainable well-being accounts track 51 indicators of economic, social and environmental conditions from 1961 to 1999. The accounts include variables shown in the graph below. These indicators can compare individually with GDP growth or with each other. We also designed a unique data indexing system which allowed us to aggregate indicators into composite indices such as an economic well-being index, a social-health well-being index and environmental well-being index. An overall Genuine Well-being Index was also created, combining all 51 indicators.

Figure 3.6. Is the US citizen better off or worse off today compared to 1950?

What we want more of….	Progress Indicator	Better or Worse (compared with 1950)	Description of Change in Quality of Life since 1950
Happiness	Self-rated happiness	☹ Worse	The number of Americans who say they are "very happy" has declined from 35% in 1957 to 30% in 2002.[16] The US ranked only 16th in the world in 2003 in terms of self-rated happiness.[17]
Longer lives	Life Expectancy	☺ Better	The average life expectancy has increased 6.0 years for American men and women between 1970 and 1997.[18] However, the US ranks only 24th among world nations in terms of life expectancy with Iceland and Japan topping the list.
Overall societal well-being	Index for Social Health	☹ Worse	The Index of Social Health (ISH) has declined 45% between 1970 and 1993.[19]
Healthy youth	Youth suicide rate	☹ Worse	The teen suicide rate has more than tripled since the 1950s.[20]
Prosperous economy	Gross Domestic Product	☺ Better	The US GDP has grown 164% (in real 1992 inflation-adjusted dollars) or 4,183% in current dollars.
Healthy markets	Stock market values	☺ Better	Total stock market capitalization value of all US (domestic) stocks stands at $16.9 trillion and has increased 12,254% in current dollar value from 1950 to 2005.[21]
More money	Personal income Real wages	☺ Better ☹ Worse	Average real (adjusted for inflation) incomes have risen by 229% from $8389 in 1950 to $27,608 by 2005,[22] however, average hourly real wages (in 2005 inflation-adjusted dollars) have remained virtually unchanged since the early 1960s ($16.11/hr. in 2005 compared to $15.94/hr. in 1964).
Genuine Progress	Genuine Progress Indicator (GPI)	☹ Worse	While the GPI per capita increased 22% from 1950 to 1978 it declined 29% since 1978.
More material possessions	Consumption expenditures	☺ Better	Real (inflation adjusted) personal consumption spending on material possessions has increased by 249% from 1950 to 2005.[23]
More leisure time and time with family and friends	Leisure time	☹ Worse	The average US worker enjoys 19% less leisure time today than in the 1950s. TV viewing per household has increased 58%.
Strong and healthy relationships	Divorce rate	☹ Worse	The divorce rate has increased by 195%; the number of kids impacted by divorce has increased 238%.
Healthy farm land	Productive farm land	☹ Worse	The area of productive farmland has decreased by 248% since 1950.
More time to give to others	Volunteer time	☺ Better	169% increase in average hours volunteered per capita.
Reduced dependency of fossil fuels	Fossil fuel use versus renewable energy consumption	☹ Worse	Fossil fuel consumption has increased by 172% since 1950, however, in 2005 it now takes one fourteenth as much energy to produce $1 of GDP. More than 86% of energy consumed in 2005 still comes from fossil fuels (compared with 91.4% in 1950). The percentage of energy from renewable energy sources is only 6.1% of total energy consumed, down from a high of 10.5% in 1971.

Credit: Updated by Mark Anielski. Originally published in Mark Anielski and Colin Soskolne. "Genuine Progress Indicator (GPI) Accounting: Relating Ecological Integrity to Human Health and Well-Being." Chapter 9 in *Just Ecological Integrity: The Ethics of Maintaining Planetary Life*, eds. Peter Miller and Laura Westra. Rowman and Littlefield, 2001, pp. 83-97.

Figure 3.6. (continued)

What we want less of....	Progress Indicator	Better or Worse (compared with 1950)	Description of Change in Quality of Life since 1950
Debt	US total outstanding debt	☹ Worse	Total outstanding US debt (domestic financial, domestic non-financial and foreign) stands at $40.7 trillion an increase of 9,471% between 1950 and 2005. Average household personal debt was $84,454 in 2004.
Violence	Violent crime rate	☹ Worse	While the violent crime rate in 2004 (465 per 100,000 inhabitants) is now 38% lower than the peak reached in 1991 (758 per 100,000), it is still 2.9 times higher than in 1960 (161 per 100,000).
Inequality in terms of both income and wealth	Gini coefficient	☹ Worse	The Gini coefficient, a measure of income inequality, has risen by 18% since 1968 low. 70% of the rise in average family income between 1977 to 1989 went to the top 1 % of the richest families.[24] By 1995 the richest 0.5% of families claimed 28% of net worth, almost as much as the bottom 90% of the population (32%).[25]
Poverty	Poverty rates	☺ ?	According to 2004 UN Human Development Report, 19% of US citizens still live in poverty (50% of median income).
Work	Hours of work	☹ Worse	The average US worker worked 7% more hours per annum in 2000 than in 1950. On average, Americans work nearly nine full weeks (350 hours) longer per year than their peers in Western Europe do.[26] The average American worked 1815 hours in 2002 or more than 473 hours (almost 12 weeks) more than the average Norwegian (1342 hours), the lowest rate in Europe.[27]
Work-related commuting time	Commuting time	☹ Worse	The average commuting time to work and back has increased by 89%; Americans, on average, spend more than 100 hours a year commuting to work (more than the average two weeks of vacation time).[28]
Under-employment	Underemployment rate	☹ Worse	The percentage of Americans who are under-employed has increased by 375%
Automobile crashes, deaths and injuries	Auto crashes	☹ Worse	The number of auto crashes has increased by 200%.
Long-term environmental damage	Cost of environmental damage	☹ Worse	The estimated cost of environmental damage has increased 142%.
Loss of wetlands	Area of wetlands	☹ Worse	6% decrease in the area of total wetlands in Alaska and lower 48 states since 1950; 53% loss of total US wetlands since 1900 (World Watch).
Loss of old growth forests	Area of old growth forest	☹ Worse	69% less old growth forest.
Air pollution	Air quality indices	☺ Better	Ambient air quality has improved by 42%. However, emissions of carbon monoxide are down 13%, nitrogen dioxide up 132%, VOC (volatile organic compounds) down 9%, sulphur dioxide down 15% and particulate matter up 83%.
Reliance on foreign borrowing and debt	Foreign debt outstanding	☹ Worse	Foreign debt outstanding was $1.4 trillion in 2005, an increase of more than 100 times the amount owing in 1950 ($14 billion).[29]

The Alberta GPI project went beyond the original US GPI work by developing well-being "ledgers" or accounts from which any number of indicators of well-being could be derived and reported. I found the accounting metaphors of ledgers, balance sheets and income statements useful to speak not only to the business community but also to average Albertans. A well-being balance sheet shows the conditions of Alberta's human, social, natural, built and financial or economic capital just like a company's balance sheet reveals some of its key financial and capital assets. It reveals both the assets (strengths), liabilities (weaknesses) and distribution of wealth and income in Alberta. I reasoned that such a balance sheet could lead to more informed and wiser stewardship of our common wealth.

Figure 3.7. The Alberta Genuine Progress Indicators

Economic Well-Being Indicators	Social Well-Being Indicators	Environmental Well-Being Indicators
Economic growth	Poverty	Oil and gas reserve life
Economic diversity	Income distribution	Oilsands reserve life
Trade	Unemployment	Energy use intensity
Disposable income	Underemployment	Agriculture sustainability
Weekly wage rate	Paid work time	Timber sustainability
Personal expenditures	Household work	Forest fragmentation (ecological integrity)
Transportation expenditures	Parenting and eldercare	Fish and wildlife
Taxes	Free time	Parks and wilderness
Savings rate	Volunteerism	Wetland
Household debt	Commuting time	Peatland
Public infrastructure	Life expectancy	Water quality
Household infrastructure	Premature mortality	Air quality related emissions
	Infant mortality	Greenhouse gas emissions
	Obesity	Carbon budget deficit
	Suicide	Hazardous waste
	Drug use	Landfill waste
	Auto crashes	Ecological footprint
	Divorce	
	Crime	
	Problem gambling	
	Voter participation	
	Educational attainment	

Credit: Mark Anielski, Mary Griffiths, David Pollock, Amy Taylor, Jeffrey Wilson, and Sara Wilson. *Alberta Sustainability Trends 2000: Genuine Progress Indicators Report 1961 to 1999.* Pembina Institute for Appropriate Development, April 2001, p. 4. pembina.org/pdf/publications/gpi-ab2000-trends.pd.

A new income statement could adjust the GDP for a number of unaccounted benefits (e.g. the value of unpaid work such as volunteerism), net out regrettable expenditures (e.g. cleaning up auto crashes) and adjust for the depreciation costs to human, social and natural capital as a result of their loss or consumption. Such an income statement would provide a rough full cost-benefit accounting of Alberta's economic progress. Moreover, it would help to assess the true benefits (or costs) of various economic development policies — such as forestry or oil and gas development policies or the introduction of legalized gambling (e.g. casinos and video-lottery terminals) in the province in the early 1990s — over time.

While the business section of newspapers and general government economic reporting heralded Alberta's booming oil-based economy, the Alberta GPI accounts told a different if not more honest story. By combining all 51 Genuine Progress Indicators, we derived a composite index—the GPI Well-being Index — which we compared with the GDP over time. Figure 3.8 illustrates this comparison. From 1961 to 1999, Alberta's GDP (in constant

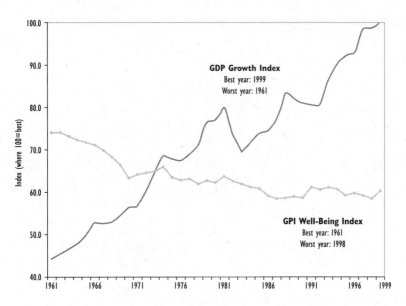

FIGURE 3.8. The Alberta GPI Well-being Index versus Alberta GDP Index, 1961 to 1999.

Credit: Mark Anielski, Mary Griffiths, David Pollock, Amy Taylor, Jeffrey Wilson, and Sara Wilson. *Alberta Sustainability Trends 2000: Genuine Progress Indicators Report 1961 to 1999.* Pembina Institute for Appropriate Development, April 2001, p. 6. pembina.org/pdf/publications/gpi-ab2000-trends.pd.

1998 dollars) increased by over 400%, or 4.4% per annum, while the Alberta GPI Well-being Index declined at an annual rate of 0.5% per year. The GPI Index was highest in the 1960s then declined to reach a plateau in the 1990s despite continued economic growth. Our study indicates that the best GPI Index was recorded in 1961 and the lowest in 1998. In the 1990s, the GDP per capita grew at an annual rate of 2.4% while the GPI per capita was virtually stagnant, growing a mere 0.43% per year, on average.

We also presented all 51 indicators of well-being in a unique spider graph: the Sustainable Well-being Circle Index. Using this graph, you can compare relative conditions of well-being across all indicators regardless of their unit of measurement. This provides a full-length mirror of Alberta's well-being in any given year.

The unique Genuine Well-being Circle Index clearly shows the strengths and weaknesses of various conditions of well-being in Alberta in 1999. This

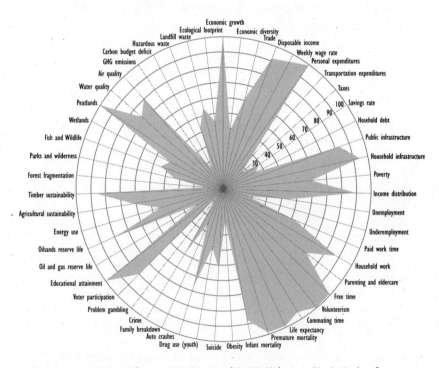

FIGURE 3.9. The Alberta GPI Sustainable Well-being Circle Index for 1999.

Credit: Mark Anielski, Mary Griffiths, David Pollock, Amy Taylor, Jeffrey Wilson, and Sara Wilson. *Alberta Sustainability Trends 2000: Genuine Progress Indicators Report 1961 to 1999*. Pembina Institute for Appropriate Development, April 2001, p. 7. pembina.org/pdf/publications/gpi-ab2000-trends.pd.

Index is like a company balance sheet on which each type of living and produced capital is reported as an index score relative to historical conditions.
This index shows the condition of all capital in Alberta in 1999, each indicator with its own score.[30]

The GPI Circle Index provides a powerful visual image of the overall
condition of economy, society and environment that could be applied at the
local, state or provincial or national level. It provides an alternative to trend
lines and shows clearly the contrast between the condition of the factors that
contribute to quality of life. For example, health indicators such as life expectancy, premature mortality and infant mortality are in good condition—
that is, their scores are close to 100 points. Many social and environmental indicators, on the other hand, were in an unhealthy condition in 1999 compared
with the previous 40 years. While we may not value each indicator equally
(for example, timber sustainability cannot be compared with agricultural
sustainability), the presentation of all indicators together does show relative
conditions for any point in time. Moreover, each of the 51 indicators can be
portrayed as an individual trend line allowing policy makers to visually
contrast, for example, the trend in GDP compared to suicide rate or life expectancy.

The story of 40 years of economic progress in Alberta can be told by comparing GDP growth with changes in other living capital accounts. While real
GDP per Albertan rose 126% between 1961 and 1999 to $109.7 billion or
$37,005 per capita (1998 dollars) the following changes occurred in terms of
economic, social, human and environmental capital between 1961 and 1999:

- While GDP is up, disposable income levels remain stagnant throughout
  the 1990s suggesting that not all Albertans are sharing equally in the
  economic good times
- Taxes (per capita) have increased 494% to $5,172 per capita (1998$)
- Total debt (federal, provincial, household, farm) per capita increased
  262% to $48,182 per capita
- Poverty (% living below the Low-Income-Cutoff) has increased 37%
- Income inequality (after-tax income) has actually decreased thanks to the
  positive impacts of a progressive income tax system and government
  transfers
- The gap between rich and poor is still significant with the eight wealthiest Albertans having an estimated hourly income of $33,307 per hour
  versus $5.90 per hour for a minimum wage earner

- Paid work hours fell 17% while underemployment is the highest in history
- Unpaid work hours (per person) increased 4% and is valued at $32.6 billion or 31% of the GDP
- Time with the kids and parents has fallen 33%
- Family breakdown (divorce and separations) increased 312%
- Life expectancy increased 10% to an average 79.3 years
- Asthma amongst children is up dramatically
- While Albertans have one of the lowest cancer rates in Canada, both the incidence and mortality from all forms of cancer (particularly lung, breast, thyroid, prostate and colorectal cancers) are higher than in 1970
- Obesity has more than doubled since 1985
- Suicide increased 30% to 14.4 suicides per 100,000 population at a societal cost of $365 million in 1999 (0.3% of GDP)
- Auto crashes have increased 37% for a total societal cost of $3.97 billion or 3.6% of GDP
- Crime rates per capita increased 59% with total costs of crime amounting to 2% of GDP
- Intellectual capital has increased with over 54% of Alberta's adult population with some post-secondary education
- Democracy is weaker with fewer Albertans voting in federal, provincial and municipal elections than 30 years ago
- Alberta's ecological footprint increased 63% and is the fourth highest in the world, while the Canadian average ranks 10th in the world
- Forests are younger, more fragmented, and timber supply has become unsustainable with less than 14% of Alberta's boreal forests and less than 1% of Alberta's foothill forests remaining in a wilderness condition
- Oil and gas reserves are dwindling (except for oilsands) with less than nine years of natural gas and seven years of conventional crude oil reserves remaining. More than 300 years of oilsands reserves remain. If valued correctly as depreciation of natural capital, the depreciation cost of oil and gas depletion in 1999 would be $9.9 billion and reduce Alberta's 1999 GDP by 9.4%
- Wetlands and peatlands have declined. Wetlands declining 58% in area since pre-1880 settlement times reduces ecological services such as carbon sequestration
- Alberta's carbon budget deficit continues to increase with forests and

peatlands sequestering no more than 25% of total anthropogenic carbon emissions
- Slightly higher levels of fecal coliform, nitrogen and *E.coli* appear in some Alberta rivers along with reduced dissolved oxygen levels and lower phosphorous levels
- Glacial melt in the Rocky Mountains is increasing and will impact river water flow rates
- Very little is known about the condition of groundwater aquifers either in terms of volume or quality or the potential risk to water from feedlot developments
- Ecosystem health has declined dramatically if measured in terms of ecosystem fragmentation with over 88% of Alberta's forest ecosystem fragmented by roads, seismic lines, well-sites and pipelines[31]

One of our key findings was that while Alberta's GDP continued to increase after the recession of 1982, the economic well-being of Albertans (measured

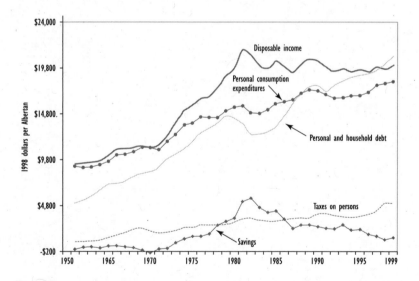

FIGURE 3.10. Real Disposable Income, Personal Consumption Expenditures, Personal and Household Debt, Savings, and Taxes Paid per Albertan (1998$), 1961 to 1999

Credit: Mark Anielski, Mary Griffiths, David Pollock, Amy Taylor, Jeffrey Wilson, and Sara Wilson. *Alberta Sustainability Trends 2000: Genuine Progress Indicators Report 1961 to 1999*. Pembina Institute for Appropriate Development, April 2001, p. 11. pembina.org/pdf/publications/gpi-ab2000-trends.pd.

in terms of income, taxes, debt and savings) had remained virtually un-changed for almost 20 years.

While the real GDP per capita rose 36% between 1982 and 1999, our analysis showed that disposable income (adjusted for inflation) and real week-ly wages per average Albertan have still not recovered to the highs reached in 1982. Personal consumption expenditures per Albertan continued to rise al-though more slowly than GDP growth, but these expenditures are increas-ingly financed through debt rather than through income.

Personal and household debt has increased significantly since 1982. In 1997 for the first time in history, this debt surpassed real disposable income reaching an unprecedented rate of 109% of disposable income in 1999. At the same time, savings have fallen from their peak in 1982. The total of all government taxes and fees paid by each Albertan exceeds the amount she or he is saving.

The big story is that while more money changed hands between 1982 and 1999 (i.e. the GDP was increasing), not all Albertans benefited equally from this increased cash flow. The flow was caused by more economic output

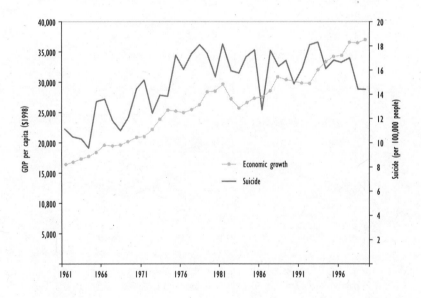

FIGURE 3.11 Alberta's GDP per capital versus Alberta's suicide rate, 1961–1999.

Credit: Mark Anielski. Alberta GPI Accounts: Suicide. Report #10. Pembina Institute, November 2001, p.4.

and more exports. The GPI accounts suggest that in 1999, average Albertans struggled to keep their households afloat against growing debt and higher levels of total taxes (paid by persons), while their disposable income remained in the doldrums, thus eroding their capacity to save for things like retirement and their children's needs. Most Albertans I have talked to in person and on radio talk-shows in Edmonton relate to this evidence.

Figure 3.11 compares Alberta's GDP with its suicide rate. While there is no statistically significant correlation between suicide and the GDP, the suicide rate has increased since the 1960s as did the GDP. Such a striking image provokes one to ask: if the GDP is up, how are other aspects of life?

In 2005, Amy Taylor, an economist with the Pembina Institute and one of the key economic researchers on the original project , released an update to Alberta GPI on the centennial of Alberta as a province. The results showed that most of the trends continued from the 2001 results: incomes, consumer spending and household debt were up but savings rates were down. While life expectancy increased, the gap between rich and poor continued to increase along with poverty, suicide, problem gambling and commuting times. Voter participation in elections also continued its decline. On the environmental side, the Ecological Footprint continued to increase while oil and gas reserves continued to decline along with the area and ecological conditions of wetlands.[32]

The Alberta GPI project accounts for well-being in a manner that intuitively aligns with most people's values. The GPI accounting approach helps us better understand the potential relationship between economic growth and social, health and environmental conditions of well-being, thus enlightening our debate about progress. GPI accounts can be used to develop annual reports to citizens about the changing conditions that affect their lives. Understanding these conditions is critical to charting a sustainable future and ultimately to working towards an economy of well-being. With better information, people are empowered to participate more fully in the democratic process of shaping their future.

A Renaissance in Economics
and Capitalism

U NDERSTANDING THE ORIGINS of economics, accounting and capitalism is essential to thinking about where we are today. A study of the
economics of ancient civilizations like Sumeria, Babylon, Greece, China and
ancient Israel helps us understand how we might construct economies of
well-being based on an economics of happiness. Many of these societies had
economic ethics and principles of right livelihood that would make sense to
most of us, yet they seem to have been forgotten in our era of capitalism. It
has been said that those who do not learn from history are doomed to repeat
it. I hope that rediscovering the wisdom and experience of past civilizations
and eras will inspire a renaissance in economics and accounting creating an
economy of well-being including authentic conditions of quality of life.
What does history teach about moderation, about economic ethics and the
good life?

Economic ethics of ancient Israel

Prior to their first exile from Israel into Babylon in 586 B.C.E., the Jewish people lived by wise ethics, principles and rules for economic life. Meir Tamari, a
former chief economist of the Office of the Governor of the Bank of Israel and
rabbinical scholar, notes that ancient Jewish economic philosophy was based
on the principle that all wealth belongs to God. It was God who gifted
humanity temporarily with wealth, on a basis of stewardship, for physical

well-being. Tamari points out that the seventh-year *Shabbat* (sabbatical year) in which the land was allowed to rest reminded the Jewish people to trust and depend completely on God to provide sustenance or basic needs.

Tamari writes that the Jews had a highly developed social welfare system that provided for the needs of the poor and weak. Their fundamental attitude towards welfare was that any person's property does not belong to that person alone but is held in partnership with God and with the community. Thus, education and religious facilities were financed through tithing and free-will offerings. Taxation was an accepted part of life, reflecting the obligation of the individual to share in all the costs of public policy.

Some of the most important standards applied to the production of goods, money and debt. Tamari states that it was forbidden to produce or sell goods or services that were harmful to their consumers, either physically or morally. Moreover, each individual was responsible for damages caused by one's body or property. Theft or economic dishonesty in any form was forbidden. Each person was required to limit one's appetite for material goods. One's disposable income was automatically reduced by interest-free loans, demands of taxation to finance welfare, education and the physical well-being of the community. Most importantly, it was forbidden to take interest either as a direct payment for loans or in the course of business activities. Interest-free loans were regarded as acts of righteousness and the highest form of charity. These loans allowed the poor to break out of the poverty cycle and prevented the rich from entering it. Loans were repaid according to their nominal value without interest charges. Finally, according to Tamari, the role of money flowed from two concepts: the authority of the state as the issuer of the currency and its acceptance in the marketplace.[1]

According to Rabbi Arthur Waskow, the *Shabbat* (which means pausing or ceasing in Hebrew) was a time to recall the creation story and to free all of society from slavery and financial debts. There was not only the seventh-day *Shabbat* (a day of rest) but also the seventh-year *Shabbat* when the land was allowed to catch its breath and rest. This was also a time to study the Torah and to give thanks to God for the good life. In this year-long *Shabbat* even financial debts were forgiven. And the 50th year Jubilee was honored by redistributing the original land allocated under Moses to each individual tribe, family or individual. The object of the Jubilee was to prevent the accumulation of land (through sales) by a small, monopolistic group of people. It was also a time of personally relinquishing one's attachments, habits, addictions and idolatries.[2]

In other words, this was a time of ensuring the fair and equitable distribution of genuine wealth.

China's *xiaokang* philosophy of moderation

My recent work in China, helping Chinese colleagues design a new national accounting system to take nature into greater account in China's GDP estimates and economic policies, has led me to appreciate an ancient philosophy called *xiaokang* (moderation) first put forward by the Chinese philosopher Confucius. Confucius believed that a society seeking to achieve true harmony should strive for moderation and material sufficiency for all households of the nation. The term *xiaokang* literally means moderately well-off, describing a society that is well-to-do or fairly well-off in which the average person has a living status less than affluent, but better than in need. *Xiaokang* is based on the notion that genuine well-being is achieved when the households have their material needs met (sufficiency), people are living lives of moderation and material needs are equitably available and distributed to all (equity). This philosophy is a very practical one that promises peace and harmony in society.

This ancient Confucian philosophy is complemented by Taoist teachings about the importance of governing the affairs of the household, communities and the nation by seeking a delicate balance or harmony between heaven and earth. Inscriptions on many of the buildings in Beijing's Forbidden City indicate that wise emperors continually walked a delicate line balancing heaven and earth in the ongoing pursuit of the Taoist Way or harmony. In the Hall of Central Harmony (Zhong He Dian) in Beijing's Forbidden City above the throne of the 18[3]-century Qing Dynasty Emperor Qianlong[3] hangs a sign that reads "The Way of Heaven is profound and mysterious and the way of mankind is difficult. Only if we make a precise and unified plan and follow the doctrine of the mean, can we rule the country well." This is in accord with China's ancient Book of Rites which states "When we handle matters properly and harmoniously without leaning to either side, all things on earth will flourish." To follow the Taoist Way means to be in harmony with nature, governing by principles of balance and harmony, returning to naturalness and reality.

Modern economists in China have rediscovered these important concepts and are proposing the idea that China, in order to become truly sustainable, must pursue the ideals of a *xiaokang* society and harmonious development (i.e. economic development that is in harmony with nature). Chinese President Hu Jinatao and Premier Wen Jiabao recently committed China to the all-round building of a *xiaokang* (or moderately well-off) society. Today, according to the average Chinese citizen, *xiaokang* means owning enough property to be self-sufficient or economically comfortable and being free from hunger and cold or simply being comfortably well-off.

The European Middle Ages: An age of moderation

In Europe during the Middle Ages (from the 5th to 16th centuries) the good life was a life of frugality and subsistence, similar to our modern concept called sustainability. Living well during this era meant meeting one's basic needs with a shared responsibility for the common wealth of the community. As among ancient Jewish peoples, in medieval Christian Europe there was underlying trust in God's providence. A person who hoarded financial wealth or material possessions was frowned upon because sharing maintained a good society. Religious celebration took precedence over productivity, and there was generally no work on the more than 150 holy days. In the US today most working people only get about one week off beyond weekends plus vacations (typically another 10–15 days) for those eligible — for a total of 111 days of rest per year. So peasants in the Middle Ages had more time off work than we do today.

If we had lived in the European Middle Ages we would have heard from our church leaders that we must orient our lives to the supernatural, that is to God. Wealth was seen as a gift from God, to be used frugally and wisely. Wealth should not distract us so that we forget to "store up treasure in heaven." People in the Middle Ages lived conscious of these teachings. There was a sense of the common good: that wealth was something available to all citizens not to be hoarded as private property. During this era work and the acquisitive efforts were encouraged, but miserliness was frowned upon. Although the acquisition of goods was considered legitimate up to the point of satisfying the necessities of life, if a man continued to work to gain ever more wealth (to reach a higher social position or to make his sons richer and more powerful, for example) this was seen as a sign of avarice, sensuality or pride and therefore condemned. In medieval Europe, traders and captains of commerce were thought unproductive parasites, corrosive to the harmony and well-being of otherwise vibrant and sustainable living, community-based economies.

The Catholic theologian St. Thomas Aquinas (1225–1274 a.d.), like Aristotle, taught that genuine economics was concerned with the well-being of the household (*oikos*) and was the science of the family and household

stewardship. Aquinas pointed out that sufficiency of material goods is necessary for a virtuous life. He felt that the relationship between individual well-
being and the well-being of the community was in accordance to a divine
plan or the supernatural order.

Aquinas said that genuine happiness required only two things: virtuous
action and sufficiency of material goods, the use of which was necessary for
virtuous action. He wisely noted that external goods and the accumulation of
material wealth was insufficient for genuine happiness. Service and attaining
eternal happiness were the primary goals of each soul. Aquinas taught that
the desire for wealth was unlawful in the eyes of God if one sought wealth as
an ultimate end, with too great solicitude or for fear of lacking necessities. He
declared, "prudence regards things which are directed to the end as a whole"
was admirable whereas "prudence of the flesh" for which the ultimate end lies
in worldly things was a "sin."[4] Wealth becomes an evil when, instead of a
means, it becomes an end and absorbs human activity and consciousness at
the expense of eternal joy in heaven.

The birth of accounting: Luca Pacioli

It's instructive to review the history of modern accounting since accounting
was grounded in stewardship principles. The father of modern accounting
was Luca Pacioli (1445–1514 A.D.), an Italian mathematician and Franciscan
friar who was a friend of and collaborated with Leonardo da Vinci. Luca actually taught Leonardo mathematics. Pacioli's seminal works included *De divina
proportione* (written in Milan in 1496–98) which described the mathematics
of the golden ratio and *Summa de arithmetica, geometrica, proportioni et proportion-
alita* (published in Venice in 1494), his treatise on accounting. Summa syn-
thesized the mathematical knowledge of Pacioli's time, providing methods
for keeping accounts that Venetian merchants used during the Italian Renaissance. Pacioli's system is known today as the double-entry accounting system. Pacioli showed Venetian merchants they could be better stewards of
their businesses using journals and ledgers, balance sheets and income statements. He encouraged merchants to keep account of their assets, particularly
by keeping good inventories and accounting for receivables as well as liabilities, capital and income. Maintaining an inventory was seen as critical to
successful management of not just business but also the household which was
generally connected to the business. The importance that debits should equal
credits was impressed upon merchants; this was consistent with the notion of

divine proportion and harmony. Pacioli's teachings, almost 500 years old, have survived to this day and are little changed.

According to my colleague Dan Rubenstein, an accountant and auditor with the Canadian Auditor General's Office, Pacioli never provided a definition of wealth or profit in an accounting context. For Luca Pacioli, the world of commerce and the material world was an apparition, an illusion. So, his notion of wealth was consistent with the teachings of Aquinas: that wealth was a gift from God and that true wealth was in the afterlife, salvation and heaven. Taking inventory and accounting for the assets and liabilities of a business on the material plane was principally virtuous as it helped one be accountable of one's stewardship to God and to one's neighbor.

Dan Rubenstein also notes that during Luca's era much of European society was organized by guilds, cooperative associations of business people. In a guild society there was no such thing as profit. Indeed, there could be no just, moral residual—only a return on factors of production, primarily labor. Moreover, in Luca's time a business enterprise was closely linked to the household; the well-being of the business related to the well-being of the household and in turn to the well-being of the community. With regards to debt financing, Luca upheld the teachings of the Catholic church at that time: that interest charged on debts was usury, considered a sin against the idea that wealth came freely from God.[5] These teachings were also consistent with the economic ethics of ancient Sumeria and Bablyon.

Because Pacioli and the accounting system he established have never provided a definition of wealth, I suggest we are free to rediscover wealth's true meaning and to develop new accounting systems which measure Genuine Wealth. We are also free to re-examine the nature of profit and imagine a more genuine purpose for businesses and commerce: being the best we can be as innovators and entrepreneurs ultimately in service to the common good. I imagine that Luca Pacioli might approve of our efforts at developing a new Genuine Wealth accounting system, a new total wealth balance sheet that measures wealth more comprehensively (i.e. human, social and natural capital to compliment current accounts of financial and manufactured or built capital) and a new income statement that accounts for the full social, environmental and economic costs of our actions. A Genuine Wealth accounting system can be constructed at any scale of accountancy from enterprise, to community, to the nation. We are capable, with millions of pieces of information already available to us, to construct well-being accounts at any scale we desire. It is only a matter of the will to do so.

It's time for new accounting and economics. It's time for accountants to revisit our generally accepted accounting principles (GAAP) that were founded on Pacioli's works. Some noble efforts are already underway including the development of internationally accepted corporate sustainability reporting guidelines through the Global Reporting Initiative (GRI). These guidelines provide business enterprise and municipal governments tools for reporting a triple-bottom line: financial, social and environmental performance. While the GRI guidelines are still voluntarily used by corporations, I envision a day when they will become generally acceptable for all accountancy from the enterprise to the nation. Then we would have realized the fruits of Pacioli's work and the wisdom of genuine wealth that informed its foundation.

Awakening the true soul of capitalism?

One of the central and least discussed issues in economics today is the very nature and role of capitalism. Supported by neoclassical economic principles and free-market orthodoxy, capitalism has defined our financial, economic, social and environmental policies and economic life in general. If there is to be a renaissance or rediscovery of the wisdom of the economic ethics of past ages, we must examine the very soul and nature of capitalism.

William Greider's book *The Soul of Capitalism: Opening Paths to a Moral Economy* attempts to address these issues: how and why does our current economic system collide with so many of society's broader aspirations and regularly frustrates them? How did these paradoxes develop and how can they be redressed?

Greider points out that most North Americans live materially comfortable lives; we have more than enough and live well beyond self-sufficiency. We have overcome the anxieties and dread of scarcity; indeed many of us realize that the story of scarcity that economics has taught is an illusion, a lie. Greider reminds citizens that we have the luxury and responsibility now to repair this paradox of progress and plenty, to transform the essential purpose of our economic system from the relentless pursuit of "more" to the fulfillment of human needs.[6]

Greider writes:

If capitalism were someday found to have a soul, it would probably be located in the mystic qualities of capital itself. The substance begins simply enough as personal savings and business profits, then flows like oxygen through labyrinthine channels into the heart and muscle of economic life. Once set in motion, the surplus wealth (Marx provocatively called it "stored labor") becomes one of capitalism's three classic factors of production, alongside human labor and nature (the land and resources consumed to make things). Capital puts up the money to build the factory, buys the machines and pays the company's bills until its goods are produced and sold, thus yielding the new returns that pay back the lenders and investors with an expected increase. It is not simple, but that is the essence.

Given the vast wealth of the country, the financial system forms a rather narrow funnel through which tens of trillions of dollars are continuously poured. Yes, the transactions are dizzyingly diverse and complex, involving thousands of large and small financial firms, but the work itself is actually done by a fairly small number of people. On Wall Street (an emblem of the system now dispersed nationwide) fewer than 1 million Americans manage the money. And only a relative handful of those people make the big decisions.

Collectively, they are very, very powerful. Nobody elected them, but their exalted position in American life is reflected in their incomes. My central complaint is with the narrowness of their value system rather than the financial mechanisms. With a few important exceptions, the agents of capital operate with dedicated blindness to capital's collateral consequences, an indifference to the future of society even as they search for the future's returns. The capital system does not authorize financial agents to think about such things and may well penalize them if they do. Yet finance capital shapes and polices the "social contract" in America far more effectively than the government, which has largely retreated from that role.[7]

Greider analyzes dysfunctional ways that capitalism impacts workers, consumers, investors and citizens. He also explores the inequities of wealth distribution providing many examples of lapses or failures in the ethics of business as well as discriminatory government practices. He suggests ways to use the strengths of capitalism to improve it from within. Greider argues that the "house of economics is due for major renovations, if not a complete tear down, because the economic order has lost one of its main emotional suppositions: the motivating fear of scarcity and deprivation."[8] Yet even as a few become alive to the truth of abundance there is momentum in the motivating fear of scarcity that still pervades most of the public consciousness, the news, politics and civic ambitions. To counter this fear, Greider suggests we develop "authentic democracy" in corporations and nation states. He recommends governing by the following seven principles:

1. Produce real new wealth, profit but also genuine value added to the material basis for sustaining a civilized society.
2. Achieve harmony with nature instead of borrowing assets from the future. Disturbing nature is inescapable, but destroying it is neither required nor free.
3. Set up systems of internal governance, which reflects a democratic understanding that one way or another, all of a company's insiders "own" it and together accept the risks and responsibilities. Participatory decision making and equitable adjudication of differences.
4. Concrete covenants with communities in addition to obligations to investors or creditors.
5. Mission includes promoting unbounded horizons for every individual within it.
6. Commitment to the bedrock institutions of society, from viability of family life to integrity of representative democracy.
7. Culture that encourages altruism: selfless acts on behalf of the whole.[9]

Greider concludes that the future fate of fixing capitalism and rediscovering its very soul belongs to those whose hearts are alive to the truth of abundance (versus scarcity), to genuine competition (not economic warfare): our youth. "One of this book's implicit objectives is to encourage a little impudence, especially among younger people. I do not expect my prose to blow away their caution and skepticism. But, I do hope they keep their minds open to the possibility that some of what I have observed may be right and that it speaks to their own experiences and thinking. If so, they need to ask some questions, to entertain more doubts about the system, less doubt about themselves. Curiosity and doubt are the first steps toward action, especially when accompanied by well-earned anger at the way things are."[10]

Many Americans, Canadians and others in the capitalist world are seeing the flaws that Greider has observed. Many no longer believe the premise and promises of capitalism and the ideologies of free-market economic orthodoxy. We have begun to seriously question the gospel of more. We are questioning the theology of efficiency, productivity and growth which are at the heart of the economic system, of accounting systems and of capitalism itself. Like Simon Küznets we are asking ourselves "more of what?," "for whom?" and "why more?" If we have more than enough, if we are truly self-sufficient with respect to life's basic needs, why must we produce more and consume more? Why is there still poverty amidst plenty and growing inequality between the haves and have-nots, between the rich and the poor? If there is more than enough or plenty to go around why does the economic order still require impoverishment, the loss of nature and dependency on debt-based money? Why does the capitalist process and system of economics, accounting and politics continue to defend or ignore its many forms of social injury and ecological destruction?

The good news is that many of us are beginning to come alive to the truth of genuine abundance as is reflected in nature itself; in nature there is no scarcity, only abundance, harmony and equilibrium. This is occurring at all levels in society from within our families, in conversations across the fence with our neighbors, in conversations in cafes and in the board rooms and offices of the world's largest corporations. We are beginning to see that generating more economic output and consuming more stuff does not necessarily generate what society wants and needs. We are beginning to renew our faith in the infinite capacities of ourselves and each other to give and receive. Many of us are awake to the truth of abundance and the real purpose of life, which is to pursue life, liberty and happiness.

Many are hard at work in redesigning and rethinking capitalism; tinkering at the margins. Some of us are experimenting with small changes in our own lifestyles. We are beginning to walk a new path as we become alive to the truths of abundance. These are not simply utopian in nature but practical changes that collectively are moving the system as a whole to a more enlightened economic system. Young filmmakers, entrepreneurs and business people like Adam Cormier are exploring such a future. Cormier is producing a documentary called "Fixing Capitalism" that is exploring how enlightened captains of commerce are beginning to rethink their roles and responsibilities as stewards of the common wealth. The new champions of this renaissance in economics, commerce and accounting include Ray Anderson (Interface Inc.), Paul Hawkens, Amory Lovins, Hazel Henderson, Leslie Christian (Progressive Investment), William McDonough, Dan Rubenstein, David Korten, Anita Burke, William Greider, Raffi Cavoukian, Gifford Pinchot III, Libba Pinchot and Jennifer Haslett and many more.

Greider believes the system will be changed not by activist government or activist protests but by a variety of small-scale incremental reforms led by those enlightened souls working within corporations and the existing economic system. Greider proposes that government expenditures and tax policies be redirected from the current system of corporate subsidies and corporate welfare to long-term social investments for building and sustaining social and human capital. He wisely recommends that the changes necessary will have to come through experiments at the local level rather than at the grand, global scale. I have long believed that sustainability must begin in our own lives, our households and extend outward, one-person-at-a-time to our neighbors, our communities and nations.

So what are we afraid of? I believe we are the ones we have been waiting for. For me, truth is revealed when I look at the consequences of our actions through the eyes and hearts of my children. To listen genuinely to the voices and questions of my daughters, Renee and Stephanie, is to act in a way that takes into consideration their well-being. I believe Raffi Cavoukian, the children's troubadour, is right in his eloquent book *Child Honoring:* that to turn this world around we must return to the wisdom and joy of the inner child and that our children are here to remind us of what we must do.

Capitalism as a religion and spirit?

Some might say that William Greider and I are foolish to believe that any remnant of heart and soul resides in capitalism. Greider trusts enlightened self-interest, believing that a few enlightened and well-meaning individuals can change the world. While I do not disagree that it takes one person who is awake to truth to affect any change (the "Mother Teresa approach" to change) Greider may be naïve to the deeper possibility that capitalism itself is a form of religion or spirituality. Indeed many have identified faith in free-market economics as a kind of orthodoxy.

What if capitalism is not simply a system but is fundamentally a religion imbued with spirit? This is the subject of a little known book *Catholicism, Protestantism and Capitalism* published in 1935 by Amintore Fanfani, an economic historian, Prime Minister of Italy and President of the United Nations General Assembly. Amintore Fanfani philosophized, theorized and analyzed the historic relationships between capitalism and Christianity.

According to Fanfani, capitalism is unbounded by morals, ethics, virtues or the laws of nature. The capitalist rebels against the notion of self-sufficiency and taking full responsibility for his or her actions when it comes to the impacts those actions have on the well-being of community and nature. Indeed, the capitalist acts as if without conscience in acquiring and accumulating material and financial wealth. The capitalist worships money and material wealth accumulation as an end itself rather than a means to happiness. Fanfani points out the inconsistency of this capitalist dogma to the teachings of Thomas Aquinas, the Catholic and Protestant Christian churches.

Fanfani argues that the triumph of capitalism is that it effectively ignores these teachings and the very laws of nature, of spirit and the supernatural order, which are common to most world religions. He argues that capitalism acts as if it has no morals, dogmas or theology when in fact it does. Fanfani writes that capitalism is a system of methods, means, institutions and economic forms for the production, circulation and distribution of wealth without considering its ends.[11] It is thus hedonistic in spirit. He argued that when capitalism is operating without a strong juridical framework which places it at the service of human freedom in its totality the core of which is ethical and religious, then capitalism becomes pathological.[12] To the extent that capitalism is a complete social system, Fanfani argued that capitalism is a religion. He stated unequivocally that capitalism itself is imbued with a spirit which acts in direct opposition to the supernatural order of creation or against God as love!

Fanfani notes that capitalism's theological codex is characterized by a set of beliefs. Today one could call these "the DNA of capitalism:"
- Capital (financial) predominates
- Labour is "free"
- Competition is unbridled
- Credit expands
- Banks prosper
- Big industry can assume gigantic dimensions (transnational)
- World markets become one
- The accumulation of wealth has no moral or ethical limits[13]

Fanfani wrote that capitalism rationalizes that people are by nature capitalistic when they live by these principles:
- Wealth accumulation (hoarding) is the best means for an ever more complete satisfaction of every conceivable need
- A capitalist lifestyle is the best means for improving one's own position
- Goods are instruments to be used without limit by their possessor

- The possessor of wealth does not recognize the rights of third parties to claims to personal wealth possessions, and
- The possessor sees no problem with obtaining, increasing or reproducing their possessions at diminishing costs[14]

The importance of Fanfani's vision today cannot be overstated. What may be surprising to many is that Fanfani points to the importance of the teachings of Christianity, insisting that Catholic and Protestant churches begin to speak the truths about the supernatural order which is God's laws as they pertain to right livelihood. This truth can also be found in Judaism, Islam, Buddhism, Taoism and the traditional teachings of indigenous cultures.

Fanfani compels Christians in particular to remember that churches historically taught us to care for the whole community. This cannot be reconciled with individual, hedonistic, capitalist concerns.[15] He argues that the Christianity in general, and the Catholic Church particularly, will always diametrically oppose the capitalist spirit because "the true and deep seated reason for conflict between Catholic and capitalistic ethics, lies in the diverse manner of correlating human action in general and economic actions in particular to God. The Catholic Church appraises the legality of every action by the criterion of Revelation.... The capitalist does not doubt the lawfulness of any act that corresponds to what he considers the exigencies of human reason. The Catholic order is a super-natural order, the capitalistic order is a rational order in the sense of the Enlightenment."[16] This conflict represents an unbridgeable gap between the Catholic ideals and capitalism.

Fanfani argues that faith-based religion, unlike capitalism, is voluntary while capitalism becomes binding in so far as social and justice institutions are ordered to protect the capitalist's interests. Catholicism he notes favors state intervention while capitalism seeks free trade markets. Catholicism accepts the existence of the capitalist "gene" within humanity but has always acted to hold this tendency of humanity in check to avoid a regrettable state of sinfulness. Catholicism does not disagree with private instruments of capitalism but does reject the ends to which capitalism is directed and the manner in which they are organized. Capitalism seeks liberalism of political and social systems, as well as freedom from ethics and morality, with a focus on efficiency and utility; Catholicism fundamentally rejects economic rationalization but holds that such rationalization should be bounded by the other principles that order life.

A way forward

It has been said that which is true is true for all ages. Ancient societies and cultures remind us of basic truths about economics, wealth and money. Many of us today are alive to these truths; through the material benefits of the capitalist system we have realized the truth of abundance. But can we celebrate genuine abundance and true sustainability together? Can we shift our societies, our economic systems and our politics of "more" to a society of "sufficiency, moderation and enough?"

Fanfani's bold challenge and vision penned over 70 years ago reminds us that the choice we must ultimately make, individually and collectively, is between an economy of love, happiness, well-being and right livelihood (that is oriented towards the Divine or God) or wealth and riches (one oriented towards *mammon*), between the pursuit of the supernatural or divine and earthly treasures. Great spiritual leaders including Jesus Christ, Buddha, Krishna and Lao Tsu have continuously reminded us that this is the challenge of being human.

This is a daunting challenge, yet I believe many of us are ready for it. A renaissance in economics, accounting and a conversion of capitalism to an economics of well-being and happiness requires each of us to examine ourselves in the mirror Amintore Fanfani presented. If capitalism is a religion then it is time to be honest about its theology, to celebrate the gifts of what modern capitalism has provided and to then to redesign an economy based on the principles of right livelihood, stewardship, giving and receiving (reciprocity), genuine competition (striving together), abundance, moderation, sufficiency and harmony with nature.

CHaPTeR 5

The Genuine Wealth Model

ECONOMICS, AS WELL AS BUSINESS, must be reoriented towards the genuine development of human well-being, in balance with the well-being of nature, not simply the pursuit of efficient economic growth for growth's sake. I am not alone in this proposal for a new and more compelling vision of human development. Amartya Sen, winner of the 1998 Nobel Prize in Economic Science, argues in his book *Development as Freedom* that freedom is the ultimate goal of economic life and the most efficient means of realizing general welfare. Sen attempts to redefine economic development not in terms of GDP but in terms of the real freedoms that people enjoy. Sen's view of well-being is formulated as follows: "We all want the capability to live long (without being cut off in our prime) have a good life (rather than a life of misery and unfreedom)" and "We would all like to lead a kind of life that we have reason to value."[1] He addresses an even larger question: What is the relation between our economic wealth and our ability to live as we would like?[2]

My proposal for the new paradigm of Genuine Wealth for current and future generations considers these ultimate goals. Genuine Wealth is grounded in what I believe we value most about life: love, meaningful relationships, happiness, joy, freedom, sufficiency, justice and peace. The ultimate goal is an economy and society dedicated to well-being. Well-being constitutes a more compelling vision than simply more economic growth and more material possessions; well-being is about quality of life.

Philosophical foundations

Like the foundation of a house or the roots of an oak tree, Genuine Wealth is based on the belief that if we measure our progress in accordance with what makes life worthwhile, then we will live authentic and flourishing lives: the "good life." By measuring what matters most to our quality of life and ultimate happiness, we are more conscious of those conditions of living we should celebrate and those we could work to improve. Only then can we say that we are genuinely pursuing happiness and the good life for the common good of all.

At the philosophical heart of Genuine Wealth are some fundamental tenets. First: true wealth represents all the things that make life worthwhile, not simply monetary or material possessions. Second: true wealth is abundant, not scarce. Third: true wealth is more abundant when freely given and freely received through the spirit of reciprocity. Fourth: true wealth ultimately comes as a gift from God; each one of us has a responsibility to be co-stewards with God for this wealth. This is particularly true of natural capital or the gifts of nature which are abundant yet priceless. Fifth: the management of our genuine wealth is grounded in sustaining the integrity and vitality of the assets which contribute most to our pursuit of love and happiness; that is, the pursuit of flourishing individuals, households, communities and ecosystems.

We can add to this model tenets from many religions, from the sustainability and environmental movements. Genuine Wealth is intended to celebrate each individual's, each household's and each community's unique values and principles. There is no single set of "right" principles.

Figure 5.1. Old Economy of Scarcity vs. New Economy of Well-being

Old Economy of Scarcity	New Economy of Well-being
Resources and money are scarce	All wealth, including money, is abundant since it is a gift from God for all to receive and share
Progress is driven by consumption and productivity	Progress is driven by the pursuit of happiness and genuine well-being
Consumer	Citizen
Politician	Statesman
Hoarding and profit maximization	Sharing, gifting, reciprocity
Fear of not enough	Joy in sufficiency
More growth is good and necessary	Sustainability and flourishing communities are good

Credit: Mark Anielski, Anielski Management Inc.

In the Genuine Wealth model, each individual first realizes his or her genuine wealth. This realization then extends to the household or family. From the family the awareness of Genuine Wealth extends to the neighborhood and communities at large.

A practical tool for measuring well-being

The Genuine Wealth model is not only a philosophy but also a process and practical tool to account for conditions of life that both contribute or detract from our genuine well-being and state of happiness. Built on the principles and tools of the 500-year-old accounting model developed by Luca Pacioli, Genuine Wealth takes inventory of all of the conditions of life that contribute to our individual and collective well-being. The model recognizes that these assets of well-being are in various conditions from excellent to poor. In this sense we establish a true wealth balance sheet showing us both our assets and liabilities with respect to quality of life.

Conducting a Genuine Wealth Assessment is akin to the full medical checkup we get from our doctor every year, except that it provides a full-length mirror of our physical, mental, emotional and spiritual well-being, as well as our financial well-being and the well-being of the environment in which we live and work. Through this assessment we become more aware of our key strengths but also identify areas for improvement.

Examining our values, principles and virtues

As a process, Genuine Wealth Assessment begins by examining our values. Our values define us. What really makes life worthwhile? What defines our state of happiness? What are the ends that our hearts desire? We require honest answers to these key questions:

a. How's life?
b. What's going well in life?
c. What areas would we like to improve?

Answers to these questions lead us to attributes and indicators we can use to assess our well-being. This is true at the individual, household and community scale.

Genuine Wealth Assessment also requires articulating the *principles* which guide our lives, our families, our workplace and our communities. Principles are important underlying assumptions or laws. Principles are akin

to the words contained in the US Declaration of Independence. They are statements of things we believe, we aspire to and which guide the ways we act.

GWA may also require examining what we call *virtues*. Virtues are particular qualities that are morally good or admirable. E.F. Schumacher noted that
the mother of all virtues is prudence, meaning seeing reality with clear-eyed
objectivity. Prudence can only be perfected when one silently contemplates
reality, temporarily silencing humanity's egocentric interests. Schumacher
concluded that "Prudence implies a transformation of the knowledge of truth
into decisions corresponding to reality."[3] Virtues such as these are central to
genuine wealth.

Raising awareness of the wisdom of virtues is critical to building economies of well-being. Whether we begin by examining our values, principles
or religious virtues, the process requires a deep heart-felt connection to what
defines us and the good life. This is both an individual and collective exercise.

What is the good life?

Genuine Wealth Assessment (GWA) examines the good life and distinguishes between ends and means. In his book *Small is Beautiful* published in 1973,
economist E. F. Schumacher examined economics through Buddhist eyes.
Schumacher had lived in a Burmese Buddhist monastery. He observed that a
Buddhist economist would define the good life according to Buddha's teaching of Right Livelihood — the path and means to enlightenment, the ultimate end of life. Schumacher noted that in Burma, there was no conflict between religious values and economic progress. There, spiritual health and
material well-being were not enemies but indeed natural allies; Burmese people felt they had a sacred duty to link both their dreams and their actions to
their faith. Schumacher criticized western neoclassical economists, noting
that they suffer from "metaphysical blindness, assuming theirs is a science of
absolute and invariable truths, without any presuppositions. Some go as far as
to claim that economic laws are as free from 'metaphysics' or 'values' as the
law of gravitation."[4]

In Buddhist philosophy the fundamental source of wealth is human
labor; work and leisure are complementary parts of living, and one can enjoy
work without compromising the bliss of leisure. For a Buddhist economist
the essence of human civilization is not in the multiplication of wants and
material possessions but in the purification of the human character and ultimately the enlightenment of one's soul.

George McRobie, reflecting on Schumacher's book twenty five years after it was published, notes that Buddhist economics would distinguish between misery, sufficiency and excess; that economic growth would be good only to the point of sufficiency. In a Buddhist view limitless growth is disastrous; an economy founded on renewable resources and hence an economics of permanence would be the norm. Modern economics views consumption and hence economic growth as the sole end and purpose of all economic activity. In our current era few remind us of this ancient wisdom which articulates the principles of good life. Without strong philosophical foundations our modern economies steam along that path of unlimited growth even as the crisis of ecological Armageddon looms large.

Consider this vision of the good life:
- Meaningful and flourishing life defined by a productive work day (but no more than three or four hours)
- Time for personal re-creation, quality time with friends and family celebrating the genuine wealth of nature and each other
- A life of genuine giving and receiving, of reciprocity
- Forgiveness of financial debts and ultimately the elimination of interest on debts
- Equitable redistribution of financial wealth
- Regular Sabbaths: periods of resting or pausing to thank God for the gifts of the good life

Could anyone deny that such a vision is more compelling than the current culture sick with affluenza and consumption yet hungry for meaning? We have the capacity to achieve a good life defined by moderation and sufficiency.

A taxonomy of needs, wants, wealth and poverty

In order to identify the genuine wealth of an individual, household or community it is critical to distinguish between human needs and wants, between what constitutes true wealth and poverty (the absence of genuine well-being). What are the basic needs for well-being? Well-being research is a complex, new and emerging field of study. Historically, it began with psychologist Abraham Maslow's hierarchy of needs. Maslow defines basic needs — physiological, safety, love, esteem and self-actualization — in hierarchical order moving from bottom (physiological) to top (self-actualization). Each plateau of need must be satisfied before a person can act unselfishly. According to

Maslow, so long as we satisfy needs, we are moving towards growth and self-actualization.[5]

Chilean economist Manfred Max-Neef and his colleagues have provided an important taxonomy of human needs and a process by which communities can identify their wealths and poverties according to how these needs are satisfied.[6] Max-Neef says human development is "focused and based on the satisfaction of fundamental human needs, on the generation of growing levels of self-reliance, and on the construction of organic articulations of people with nature and technology, of global processes with local activity, of the personal with the social, of planning with autonomy, and of civil society with the state."[7]

Max-Neef's work goes beyond Abraham Maslow's by clearly distinguishing basic human needs from what provides a good life. Human needs are few, finite and classifiable — clearly distinct from the conventional economic notion that wants are infinite and insatiable. Max-Neef notes that "human needs are constant over all cultures and unchanging; what is different and what changes over time is how these needs are satisfied or met."[8] Satisfiers can have different characteristics. Some satisfiers while meeting a specific human need may in turn destroy the possibility of satisfying other needs. There are also some synergic satisfiers that lead to satisfaction in more than one area of life.

Max-Neef classified fundamental human needs under nine headings: subsistence, protection, affection, understanding, participation, recreation (that is, the sense of leisure, time to reflect, or idleness), creation, identity and freedom. He defined needs according to four existential categories (being, having, doing and interacting), and from these dimensions he developed a 36-cell matrix filled with examples of satisfiers for those needs.

Unlike Maslow's hierarchy, Max-Neef's framework recognizes that human needs, like a forest ecosystem, are interrelated and interactive. In other words none is more important than the other; each is a necessary complement to the other though trade-offs are made constantly in the process of satisfying needs. But as in an ancient Redwood forest, there is continuous movement toward harmony.

The Max-Neef taxonomy of human needs and satisfiers provides a useful framework for Genuine Wealth Assessment. Using this taxonomy we can identify impediments to meeting fundamental human needs but also highlight synergies which help achieve higher states of well-being and happiness.

Distinguishing between means and ends

In addition to understanding basic human needs that lead to happiness, we must distinguish between basic life needs and wants and between the means of well-being and ultimate ends.

Building on the earlier work on Max-Neef and Maslow, ecological economists Herman Daly and Josh Farley have proposed a framework for understanding a spectrum from the ultimate means to the good life (basic human needs) to the ultimate ends (highest aspirations). At the base of this

Figure 5.2. Max-Neef Matrix of Human Needs

Fundamental Human Needs	Being (qualities)	Having (things)	Doing (actions)	Interacting (settings)
subsistence	physical and mental health	food, shelter, work	feed, clothe, rest, work	living environment, social setting
protection	care, adaptability, autonomy	social security, health systems, work	co-operate, plan, take care of, help	social environment, dwelling
affection	respect, sense of humor, generosity, sensuality	friendships, family, relationships with nature	share, take care of, make love, express	privacy, intimate spaces of togetherness
understanding	critical capacity, curiosity, intuition	literature, teachers, educational policies	analyze, study, meditate, investigate	schools, families, universities, communities
participation	receptiveness, dedication, sense of humor	responsibilities, duties, work, rights	cooperate, dissent, express opinions	associations, parties, churches, neighborhoods
leisure	imagination, tranquility, spontaneity	games, parties, peace of mind	day-dream, remember, relax, have fun	landscapes, intimate spaces, places to be alone
creation	imagination, boldness, inventiveness, curiosity	abilities, skills, work, techniques	invent, build, design, work, compose, interpret	spaces for expressions, workshops, audiences
identity	sense of belonging, self-esteem, consistency	language, religions, work, customs, values, norms	get to know oneself, grow, commit oneself	places one belongs to, everyday settings
freedom	autonomy, passion, self-esteem, open-mindedness	equal rights	dissent, choose, run risks, develop awareness	anywhere

Credit: Manfred Max-Neef. "Human Scale Development: An Option for the Future." 1987

continuum are the ultimate building blocks or means of life including natural resources, matter and energy (natural capital). This is the realm of physics, biology and science. This is followed by intermediate means including human labor, tools, factories and the processing of raw materials into things that bring material comforts such as good food and shelter. This is the realm of technology and engineering. After one's ultimate means and intermediate means are satisfied comes another realm of intermediate means including our health, personal safety and living comforts. This is the realm of economics and politics. Finally, there are ultimate means which include happiness, well-being, enlightenment, love and union with God. This spectrum of means and ends could help us construct an inventory of life conditions at the individual, household or the community scale. Such an inventory would identify areas of strength and weakness, offering an objective mirror of reality.

Of course there are other ways of distinguishing between the basic needs and ultimate ends of life; each culture must define its own. It is thus important to distinguish between needs and wants. A want is a wish, craving or desire for luxuries that extend beyond our basic life needs or sufficiency. In their book *Your Money or Your Life,* Joe Dominguez and Vicki Robin describe the relationships between the money we spend on meeting our basic life needs and our level of fulfillment. They argue that people fall somewhere on a spectrum of economic well-being from survival mode (subsistence) through a comfort zone (sufficiency of basic needs) to the zone of wants, luxuries and a

Ultimate Ends (well-being)
  • happiness, harmony, fulfillment, self-respect, self-realization, community, enlightenment, love, God

Intermediate Ends (human capital and social capital)
  • health, wealth, leisure, mobility, knowledge, communication, consumer goods

Intermediate Means (built capital and human capital)
  • labor, tools, factories, processed raw materials

Ultimate Means (natural capital)
  • solar energy, the biosphere, earth materials, the biogeochemical cycles

FIGURE 5.3. The Means and Ends of the Good Life

Credit: Adapted from Herman E. Daly. *Toward a Steady-State Economy.* W.H. Freeman, 1973, p. 8.

threshold they call "enough" — that point of maximum fulfillment of everything we need for a good life. Spending beyond "enough" gets you more luxuries with possible diminishing happiness or fulfillment. At some point more stuff does not bring added happiness.[9]

Another word for "enough" might be self-sufficiency or sustainability: the place genuine wealth might be realized. This might be a zone of genuine happiness. Each individual has the freedom to choose a level of sufficiency without value judgment, knowing that spending additional effort and money in accumulating more luxuries (which requires more life energy) does not necessarily translate into higher returns to happiness.

In today's most affluent economies, most people's basic needs have been fulfilled. I would expect to find that the vast majority are living well beyond "enough," beyond material sufficiency. Many have enough and more. Yet, I also expect that a Genuine Wealth Assessment would reveal deficits of meaningful work, meaningful relationships, spiritual hunger and a collective deficit of love. This is the kind of inventory would provide a practical tool for building an economy of genuine well-being.

Another way of constructing a Genuine Wealth inventory, especially at the individual level, is to use a framework which defines the well-being of individuals. The New Economics Foundation's *Well-being Manifesto* identifies key determinants of well-being from a growing body of research into happiness economics and well-being analysis. They identify three key factors that contribute most to the well-being of the individual:

1. About 50% of your well-being can be attributed to your genetics, including your upbringing, childhood, parents and your environment
2. About 40% can be attributed to your social and recreational activities including socializing, exercising, engagement in meaningful work, appreciating and savoring life and "looking at the bright side"
3. The final 10% of well-being is attributed to your life circumstances, including your income, material possessions, marital status, the weather and where you live (your neighborhood)[10]

What is remarkable about these findings is the relative insignificance of money or income and the importance of having loving and meaningful relationships both early and throughout life.

According to this new well-being research, life satisfaction can be defined as:

- Being engaged in life
- Being curious
- Feeling life as a flow (where time seems to stand still)
- Personal development and growth
- Autonomy
- Fulfilling your potential
- Having a purpose
- Feeling that life has meaning

People who are happy and report a high satisfaction with life tend to be more sociable, creative, altruistic, generous, tolerant, productive, creative, healthy and long-living.[11]

The work by the NEF and well-being research in general is critical to managing an economy of well-being. Genuine Wealth must be firmly grounded in research into the key determinants of well-being. We need this research in order to measure Genuine Wealth at the individual and community scale.

The five capitals of Genuine Wealth

Genuine Wealth integrates and harmonizes five categories of wealth or capital which collectively contribute to the good life and form the basis of an economy of well-being.

The image I use to portray the harmony and integration of the five forms of capital is a flower with five petals surrounded by a circle. This is very similar to the medicine wheel of many indigenous cultures in North America. The five petals of this Genuine Wealth flower should be viewed as complementary, integrated, in harmony and genuinely competitive (that is, striving together) because all forms of capital are necessary to optimum well-being and ultimately happiness. This image is consistent with Max-Neef's concept of the integration and complementarity of human needs, recognizing that trade-offs are necessary. It also reflects Luca Pacioli's vision of divine proportion.

What are the five capitals?

Human capital

Human capital means people: the sum of our individual minds, bodies, spirit, souls, dreams, visions, knowledge, skills, competencies, capabilities and other human attributes. Human capital also includes our mental, physical, emotional and spiritual health. A flourishing individual, household or community is one in which the human community is diverse, enjoys meaningful work balanced with meaningful leisure time, and time to pursue the aspirations of the heart and soul.

Social capital
Social capital refers to the strength of our relationships with each other. It refers to intangible qualities like trust, the ability to work together towards common goals, shared responsibility, reciprocity, neighborliness and a sense of belonging in community.

Natural capital
Natural capital includes the free gifts from nature: natural resources (forests, agricultural soils, oil, natural gas, coal and mineral resources), land, and ecosystem services like clean air, water and climate regulation from forests,

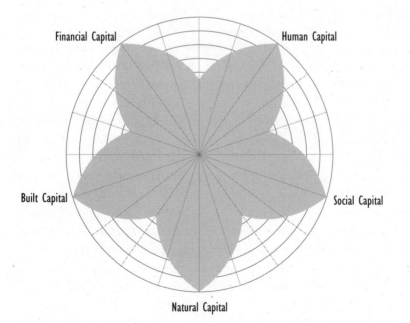

FIGURE 5.4. Five Capitals of Genuine Wealth

Credit: Mark Anielski, Anielski Management Inc.

watersheds and wetlands. While natural capital may be freely given by nature, it is perhaps the most important form of wealth. We cannot survive without it.

Built capital

Built capital includes all things that have been made or manufactured with both human and natural capital including equipment, factories, tools, buildings and other physical infrastructure. Manufactured capital contributes to our overall economic well-being by providing the intermediate means to a good life. Manufactured capital includes private and public infrastructure: homes, household appliances, cars, factories, hospitals, schools and roads. It also includes new technology, designs, patents, processes and ideas.

Financial capital

Financial capital is essentially money or anything denominated in monetary terms including cash, savings, investments. This includes debt, mortgages and other loans. Most money in our modern economies is in the form of debt or financial liabilities to which interest charges are attached.

Another way to visualize the Genuine Wealth model is by thinking of an oak tree or mighty redwood whose roots secure and nourish the tree, drawing water and nutrients from the soil. An oak tree has a strong, thick trunk and branches and an expansive root system. The tree roots represent our values, principles and virtues: they are the foundation of our life's journey. A tree with weak roots can be blown down by the many stormy challenges of life. An individual or community which is not in touch with its core values is subject to blow-down. A redwood tree has a huge girth from years of growth; many mature redwoods reach 500 years of age. Walk through forest of old redwood trees, and you will appreciate the harmony, balance and reciprocity of that ecosystem.

A tree's trunk increases in circumference with each year and growth season; each ring of growth is like a diary of the conditions of life that the tree experienced in one season of existence. Some tree rings are thick, representing periods when living conditions were ideal; thinner rings may reflect a poorer season. In our lives too, some periods are productive and flourishing while others offer challenges that test our well-being. Trees also have strong and diverse branches whose leaves draw free sunlight. Through the magic of photosynthesis sunlight is converted into pure energy that nourishes the tree and helps the branches, trunk and roots to grow. In our own lives, there are many branches that affect our overall well-being — physically, mentally and spiritually.

Each tree in a forest is like an individual human being in a family, household, neighborhood or community. Like trees, we live in community or in an ecosystem. Each individual brings a unique set of skills, capacities and spirit that together contribute to a healthy, vibrant and flourishing human ecosystem of reciprocal relationships. While each of us is unique, together we constitute a true economy or a household.

Accounting for the five capitals of Genuine Wealth

How do we measure Genuine Wealth? To measure something we must observe it; we can observe exterior appearance or what is revealed of interior spirit. We usually measure exterior appearance with the different tools and units of measure of objective measurement. Yet, no matter how carefully we measure "objectively," something is still something missing: softer, intangible attributes of a thing or experience or what we feel in our hearts. Measuring subjectively requires getting in touch with how we feel about a thing or experience.

Take crime or violations of our sense of safety as examples. We can measure the crime rate in a community; that's an objective proxy measure of a community's collective safety. But, a rate lacks an important subjective attribute: how we feel personally about safety in our community? Do we, for example, feel safe walking alone in our neighborhood at night? Do we let our nine-year-old daughter walk to the grocery store for a popsicle without worrying about her safety? Measuring genuine well-being requires both objective and subjective indicators. Even then measuring the conditions of any attribute of well-being will be incomplete. It's as impossible as describing completely how a tree functions, how photosynthesis works or how a forest can remain in apparent harmonious development for centuries.

Measuring Genuine Wealth attributes can be done whether we are looking at an individual person, a family or household, a neighborhood or community, a city, state, province or nation. Each may have different well-being characteristics for which different objective and subjective indicators are necessary.

Measuring Genuine Wealth at the individual level is about measuring our personal physical, emotional, mental and spiritual conditions. At the household level, it's about measuring the five capital conditions that contribute to the quality of the household or family. At the neighborhood or community level it assesses the overall quality of life conditions (social, environmental, economic). At the workplace level it considers whether your work is meaningful and your work environment is stimulating and flourishing. At the level of cities, provinces, states or nations Genuine Wealth Assessment includes economic, social and environmental conditions at the broadest possible scale. Measuring Genuine Wealth requires multiple approaches to the physical and qualitative conditions of the five forms of capital. It may also involve conducting a full monetary accounting of the costs and benefits associated with each of the five forms of capital.

This overall inventory of well-being conditions can use the Max-Neef human needs and satisfier framework or Herman Daly and Josh Farley's means-to-ends framework to establish a series of well-being ledgers or accounts. In some applications (for example my work with the community of Leduc, Alberta[12]), soliciting the values from citizens in a community helps to establish well-being themes and to create associated well-being indicators as proxies for these themes.

Well-being ledgers reveal the strengths (assets) and weaknesses (liabilities) of a household's or community's genuine wealth (their five capital assets or well-being themes). Indicators are used as proxies for the real conditions of each of the five capitals. Indicators can be objective or subjective. Objective measures are things like statistical data (e.g. crime rates); subjective measures include indicators of how we feel or our perceptions of a certain issue or condition (e.g. how we feel about our personal safety). The results can be presented in a new Genuine Wealth balance sheet which shows the assets, liabilities and the distribution of genuine wealth within a community.

The Genuine Wealth Assessment life cycle

Like a medical checkup, Genuine Wealth Assessment (GWA) is a comprehensive well-being checkup for a household, business, community, city, state, province or nation. It allows an individual, household or community to examine itself in a mirror and to celebrate its strengths or assets while acknowledging its weaknesses or liabilities. The GWA is a particularly useful tool which allows organizations or communities to plan for sustaining their assets, to mitigate any well-being deficits and to achieve genuine sustainability, a flourishing legacy.

The GWA process follows a series of steps in the life-cycle shown here:

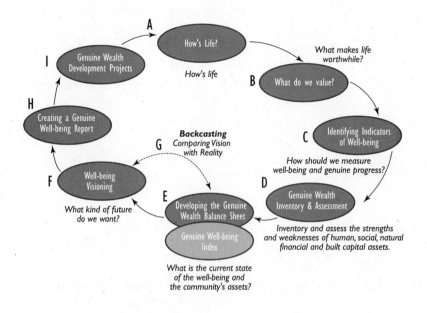

FIGURE 5.5. The Genuine Wealth Model for Communities
Credit: Mark Anielski, Anielski Management Inc.

How's life?

The first step in the GWA involves a self-examination of our own quality of life. Take a long look in the mirror, examining your strengths and weaknesses. It's a mirror of light and dark. Ask yourself and your community questions in these five fundamental areas:

1. How's life? How happy are you about life today (your personal life, your physical health, your spiritual life, your family life, your work life, your sex life, your community life)? Do you feel you have strong and loving relationships with loved ones? Do you feel the work you do is meaningful?
2. What do like most about your quality of life, your family's and your community's? What are your strengths, your skills and your capacities?

This is your light mirror. It can be as simple as asking a child: what makes you happy?

3. What do you feel are your weaknesses or areas you could improved (in your own life, your family and your community)?
What do you like least about your community? What do you feel
are the liabilities for realizing the good life? What areas do you
feel are currently hindering or interfering with your pursuit of
genuine happiness? When asking a child: what makes you sad?

This is your dark mirror.

4. What is currently going well for you personally in your family
and your community?

From answers to these questions we can celebrate our assets.

5. If you had the power to change anything about the your personal
quality of life, your family's or your community's, what areas
would you change or like to see improved? When asking children
I ask: if you could wish for anything for your family, what would
it be? This provides the basis of envisioning a new and improved
tomorrow.

Considering these questions is exciting and meaningful for people. We love
to examine these quality of life issues and talk about them openly with our
families and our neighbors.

There are many tools for gathering information including using telephone surveys, on-line, web-based surveys or using dialogue with citizen
groups. In my experience, surveys are less meaningful than engaging people
in dialogue. I like to talk with high school students, with senior citizens in
retirement homes or with club members. My favorite process is called conversation or world café: small groups of people (usually no more than eight in a
cluster) come together, explore questions and share their responses. We are
after all social creatures, and we love to talk and share stories. Stories are powerful; each of us has our own story to share and tell.

I have witnessed many magic times when people came together to share,
to listen and to participate in respectful dialogue. While dialogue processes
take time, I believe they are most important because they allow people to feel
they are having meaningful input into the processes of civil society and in the

stewardship of our shared economy of well-being. Through dialogue we come to appreciate that each of us has unique gifts and dreams for happiness and the good life. We come to appreciate each other's strengths and can see the benefit of sharing — of giving and receiving each other's gifts. We begin to realize genuine wealth as the diversity of human being. Such dialogue creates democracy in which everyone is invited to contribute.

What do we value?

The second step is values assessment: a personal and collective examination of our values and principles of living. We address the fundamental question: what makes life worthwhile? Remember that the word value refers to that which is worthy or good. What do you feel contributes most to a happy and good life — for yourself, your family and your community? What values form the foundation for a healthy and vibrant workplace or a vibrant, flourishing and sustainable community? What principles form the foundation of our decision making? Does your family, organization or community have a set of principles? Imagine writing your own declaration in the way Thomas Jefferson wrote the US Declaration of Independence. What would such a declaration hold up as the highest goals and virtues of a good society, a happy and good life? Without a sense of what we value we are like ships without rudders.

We might turn to existing statements of principles and values for right livelihood. This could include principles and virtues that come from our religious practices and spiritual convictions. We may find inspiration from statements like the Declaration of Independence — statements we feel have meaning across generations and cultures. These principles may be new, like the four system conditions of The Natural Step which speak to the need to live in harmony with nature and right stewardship of renewable natural resources while avoiding the use of chemicals and other things that are not otherwise food for nature (that is, toxic).[13]

For most people identifying values is difficult since we rarely examine our core values — what we find to be worthy and true in our hearts. We must put aside what we have been conditioned or taught to believe about the way the economy and world works. We may discover that what we actually value in our hearts is disconnected from what the world teaches us. What an opportunity to go deeper in a genuine reflection of what we value most and to enter a genuine dialogue with our family members, our neighbors and co-workers!

This, in my experience working with organizations and communities, can be exhilarating and meaningful.

Answering larger questions create a values inventory: a set of statements of what makes life worth living; what we hope and dream for; our vision for the future well-being of our children and grandchildren. The values form a blueprint for the construction of our good-life household or community. Because we are individually unique, with unique skills, capacities and dreams, each household and community may have a different well-being blueprint. That's OK because humanity is diverse; we all have something important and unique to offer in the economy of well-being.

Identifying indicators of well-being

The next step in the GWA is to identify indicators of well-being, quality of life and sustainability. We are trying to identify measures that matter — that align with our values. The indicators we create are meaningful proxies. They can be objective or subjective. Some will be measured statistically while others will be measured in terms of our perceptions (how we feel about a particular issue). Engage citizens by asking them to identify measures of progress that they would want to hear about on the morning news. Would they be curious to know how each neighborhood in a city rated their happiness? Indicators must resonate with people's sense of what matters.

Complementing citizen consultation, it's critical to include the input of experts and professionals. In our communities there are many who gather statistics and information ranging from crime statistics (police), real estate values (real estate agents), financial statistics (bankers), health statistics (hospitals, doctors, health authorities) to environmental statistics (municipal officials, provincial/state government experts or environmental groups). I liken these experts to doctors: they know how to diagnose conditions in their particular area of interest or sector and can provide an expert and informed opinion about the conditions of various attributes of the human, social, natural, built and financial capital assets of a community.

The next step is to compare notes from the citizen-based input and the expert input to find areas of overlap and convergence. Very often, citizens will provide input that is based on their intuition or simply common sense. This is critical. Experts, on the other hand, often will provide counsel based on the parameters of their field. However, experts may not be in tune with citizen perceptions of what is meaningful. At the same time, citizens may be unaware of various conditions of well-being that experts understand. Both citizens and experts can learn from their respective input.

Next, attempt to align the expressed values of citizens and the indicators that both citizens and experts have identified. This task often reveals gaps; what may be a value (e.g. healthy democracies) may lack meaningful indicators for measuring a condition. These gaps suggest where we must explore for new indicators and gather new data.

Genuine wealth inventory and assessment

As Luca Pacioli reminded Venetian business people, keeping a good inventory of one's assets is important to running a flourishing business. Taking a Genuine Wealth inventory is more comprehensive; it involves assessing the physical, qualitative and monetary conditions of five forms of capital assets. Working with statistical agencies (e.g. Statistics Canada), information experts along with various key groups in a community, the new economics conducts a comprehensive inventory of the current and historical conditions of human, social, natural and built and financial assets. These conditions can be measured in physical (or quantitative) terms and qualitative terms, as well as in monetary terms (that is, in terms of the full cost or benefit attributes of a capital asset). Such an inventory can be conducted on any scale from household to nation. What gets inventoried should be aligned with the values and well-being indicators which were identified. The inventory is the database that populates the indicators with information.

A community Genuine Wealth inventory creates a map of community assets. Assets might include items like skills, capacities, personal free time, parks, bike trails, infrastructure, financial assets or natural resources (trees, water, green space). In addition, community deficits or weaknesses should also be identified and recorded. The intention is to celebrate one's assets while identifying weaknesses that become tomorrow's to-do list of actions.

Prof. John McKnight, author of *The Careless Society,* makes a clear case for mapping a community's assets (resources) and liabilities (needs). He argues:

> Each community boasts a unique combination of assets upon which to build its future. A thorough map of those assets would begin with an inventory of the gifts, skills and capacities of the community's residents. Household by household, building by building, block by block, the capacity mapmakers will discover a vast and often

surprising array of individual talents and productive skills, few of
which are being mobilized for community-building purposes... In
a community whose assets are being fully recognized and mobilized, these people too will be part of the action, not as clients or re-
cipients of aid, but as full contributors to the community-building
process.[14]

Developing the Genuine Wealth Balance Sheet

Once the inventory of community assets and liabilities is complete we prepare a Genuine Wealth Balance Sheet which reveals the physical, qualitative
and monetary conditions of a community or organization's five capitals. This
balance sheet, unlike traditional financial balance sheets, is a comprehensive
and integrated assessment of human, social and natural capital combined
with an accounting of the built and financial capital assets that are all necessary for sustainability and flourishing communities. If any one asset is weak
then one knows that the community as a system is also less robust than it
might be.

How can so many indicators be compared with each other given that different units of measurement are used? We are accustomed to using money as
the only common measure of comparison. However, it is possible to compare
indicators that use different measurement units through a process of indexing
normalizing data: converting the original data into a common unit of measure that can be compared to any other indicator. In essence this involves converting original raw statistical data (e.g. crime rates) to an index score using a
scale of 0 to 100 basis points where a score of 0 would reflect the poorest possible condition (the worst crime rate in 50 years) while a score of 100 would
represent the best possible condition (the lowest crime rate in 50 years).

This process of indexing requires the selection of a benchmark. A benchmark may be a starting point in a statistical series, like a base-year (e.g.
1970). A benchmark can also be a target or predefined objective. It can also be
a specific condition of well-being that is the optimum state over a period of
time. For example, using life expectancy as an indicator of a population's
overall health, the longest life expectancy achieved over the time series would
be used to establish the benchmark. Regardless of how a benchmark is chosen, all other data points are compared against it, allowing users to determine
whether conditions have improved or declined over time. Understanding
trends is important to decision makers.

The Alberta GPI shows the conditions of 51 economic, social, health and environmental indicators for 1999 using the scale of 0 to 100. All indicators are placed on a single graph in the shape of a wheel or circle which constitutes a Genuine Wealth Balance Sheet showing both strengths and weaknesses in Alberta's well-being. What is immediately apparent are the strengths (e.g. economic growth, personal expenditures and life expectancy) in contrast to the weaknesses (e.g. savings rates, obesity, suicide and several environmental conditions) of Alberta's overall state of well-being.

While the capacity to compare otherwise incomparable data may avoid using money as the common metric, the process of benchmarking can involve value judgments. For example, if we were to use an indicator like the divorce

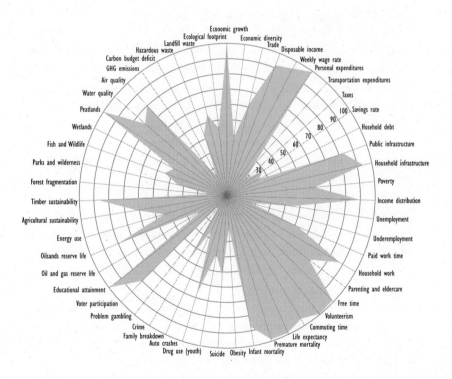

FIGURE 5.6. Alberta Genuine Progress Index, 1999

Credit: Mark Anielski, Mary Griffiths, David Pollock, Amy Taylor, Jeffrey Wilson, Sara Wilson. *Alberta Sustainability Trends 2000: Genuine Progress Indicators Report 1961 to 1999.* Pembina Institute for Appropriate Development. 2001.

rate what should the benchmark be? If we choose the lowest divorce rate as the benchmark we might be accused of moral bias against divorce. Another example is taxes: is a higher rate of taxation desirable or undesirable? The answers depends on how society views taxation or divorce. This is why a values audit is so important.

A key strength of setting benchmarks is that a number of indicators can be added together to create composite indices. For example, we could add environmental well-being indicators together to create a environmental well-being index. We could also add up indicators of all the five capital conditions and create a Genuine Well-being Index.

Aggregation assumes that all indicators in an index have equal weight and thus equal value. Equal weighting of indicators is controversial. Critics argue that composite indices are misleading since they assume that all indicators have the same value. This is a fair criticism. A good values audit can help determine the relative importance or weighting of indicators. However in practice, coming to consensus on whether, for example, the suicide rate is more important than the GDP, is ethically or morally difficult. I prefer to simply report and contrast the various indicators in their current condition, presenting a composite picture of well-being in the form of the Genuine Wealth flower index or circle/spider graph. The controversies of weighting can be avoided while retaining the benefit of a common unit of measurement for comparison of indicators.

Well-being visioning

Looking at our community, households or organizations through Genuine Wealth Assessment, it is now possible to ask ourselves "given this reality, what kind of future do we want for ourselves, our children and their children?" Visioning defines a desirable future state of well-being based on reflections in the mirror of current reality.

To vision the future of a community we celebrate our assets but genuinely acknowledge the challenges towards achieving genuine well-being and sustainability. What can each one of us do tomorrow to be a better steward of the resources, assets and genuine wealth that we are blessed with? With the Genuine Wealth Assessment as a baseline, a community is better equipped to answer this question. This process must involve the entire community across the spectrum of age, sex, culture, race and socio-economic conditions. Every voice is important in visioning a well-being economy.

Backcasting

Backcasting means comparing current conditions of well-being with our vision for the future. In that examination we look at the gaps between the desired future and the actual conditions of reality. How big are those gaps? How can we narrow them? What investments of time, resources and other factors will be necessary to get us from our current state to the desired future state? Backcasting can be a powerful process that leads us to change behaviors, business plans and policies. We must ensure that all wealth is conserved and that the integrity of all forms of capital is maintained — even improved — so that services may flow to future generations. This is at the heart of sustainability.

Creating a Genuine Well-being Report

Drawing all the information together from the previous steps, we can prepare a Genuine Well-being Report to citizens just like the annual reports of publicly traded corporations to their shareholders. A Genuine Well-being Report reveals the economic, social and environmental conditions of well-being using indicators that actually matter to people. Such a report articulates the values and principles of the community. It reveals the results of a quality of life audit and information on changes in people's self-rated happiness. The report also talks about the distribution of wealth in the community addressing the all-to-often-ignored issue of the inequitable distribution of financial and material wealth. Such a report is intended for the coffee tables of every household, for every boardroom and the office of every business. It could provoke discussion and debate at town or city council meetings and in social agencies, informing policy and planning decisions about where to invest taxpayers' monies to improve or sustain the community's genuine wealth. A Genuine Well-being Report helps everyone vision what kind of community we want tomorrow and where and how we can invest the resources and assets that are available to realize that vision.

Genuine wealth development projects

Reflecting on the results of a Genuine Wealth Assessment, households, businesses and decision makers can then plan to invest their time, money and other resources in actions and projects that will sustain or improve the genuine wealth of the community. Projects should improve the conditions of well-being of the community as a whole; they will improve the state of the community's balance sheet and build real assets. A direct budget link needs to be made between any proposed project and the Genuine Wealth Balance Sheet so that real returns to improved well-being can be accurately accounted for and reported. We might call this genuine well-being budgeting.

All of these strategies imply commitment to full cost and benefit accounting. Full cost accounting refers to a process of collecting and presenting information, costs as well as advantages or benefits, for various alternative decisions. Costs and advantages can be measured in terms of environmental, economical and social impacts; these can be both tangible and intangible. The US and Alberta GPI projects used full cost accounting at an economy-wide scale. Other examples of full cost accounting at the policy level are examining the full social, economic and environmental costs of auto crashes to a community or analyzing the full value of recycling programs. Full cost accounting provides critical information for more informed decision making.

The Genuine Wealth process is a life-cycle of designing-building-operating communities focused on improving their overall well-being. One can repeat the process on a regular (e.g. annual or biennial) basis tied to existing planning processes like strategic business planning or long-range municipal development planning. The process could also become key in the political process by providing newly elected governments with a baseline well-being profile against which they could monitor their progress from one election to the next. A Genuine Wealth Assessment provides a unique, comprehensive and high-level perspective on a community's overall well-being which other planning processes tend to lack. I call this taking a 30,000 foot aerial perspective on a community. The process becomes one of sustainable Genuine Wealth management.

Personal Genuine Wealth

G ENUINE WEALTH LIES within you. Each of us is unique in our skills, capacities, aspirations and dreams. Each one of us has a unique life's journey towards our own inner genuine wealth. Your own story could fill this chapter if not an entire book.

Too often we look for meaning and fulfillment outside of ourselves. We may hope to find happiness in money, material possessions or expectations that other people will bring us genuine happiness or an authentic life. I have learned that true peace, joy and love come from my inner teacher, my soul and spirit. Doing a Genuine Wealth Assessment means looking deep within your heart for the real you.

A personal Genuine Wealth Assessment means looking in the mirrors of light and dark. In the light mirror we examine what we love about ourselves and what others love about us. In the dark mirror, we look at the things we don't like about ourselves or what others dislike about us. We may agree or disagree with what we see, but these mirror images help to create a complete and honest profile of our physical, mental, emotional and spiritual well-being.

Conducting a personal Genuine Wealth Assessment

A personal Genuine Wealth Assessment takes a 360-degree perspective on our personal, professional, environmental, social and financial well-being. We identify strengths and areas needing improvement in our personal lives (love, spirituality, physical fitness, diet) as well as the strengths and weaknesses of our professional and work life, our physical environment (e.g. our

89

household and our work place) and our financial and material wealth. We need to ask ourselves: what makes life worthwhile? what makes us happy, inside? what do we value most about life?

We might define our five Genuine Wealth assets according to skills, capabilities, dreams and relationships. For example, our Genuine Wealth account might include:

- Our happiness with life
- Our physical, mental and spiritual health
- Meaningful and satisfying work
- Healthy eating and lifestyle
- Friendships
- Loving relationships with our spouse, children, and family
- Belonging to organizations, clubs and associations with others
- Quality time for personal reflection, prayer and "smelling the roses"

FIGURE 6.1. Personal Genuine Wealth Circle

Credit: Mark Anielski, Anielski Management Inc.

- Financial security
- Enjoying the wonders of nature

Each of us will define "the good life" from our own unique perspective and experience.

The purpose is to be fully in touch with our gifts and our values. What do you love about life? What would you change? What agreements have you made with yourself in the past that hinder you from celebrating your real wealth, the real you? Have fun with these questions; sit down and write out all the things you would like to improve as well as areas of your life you would like to heal. A Genuine Wealth Assessment is about connecting with your inner teacher, going deeper and peeling back the onion of your life so far. Moreover, it's about both giving and receiving; some may have difficulties giving of our gifts while others struggle with receiving the gifts of others. Living genuinely we celebrate our own and each others' gifts.

Taking the Personal Genuine Wealth Survey

In Chapter 5, we learned from the emerging science of happiness that there are three key determinants of well-being:

1. Our parents, our upbringing, and our childhood experience
2. Our social relationships and recreational activities in community
3. Our current economic situation, including our income, material possessions and education.

Find a quiet place where you can be reflective and get in touch with your inner self, your heart and soul. Let's consider some detailed questions based on these key contributors to well-being and happiness.

Your overall quality of life

Q1. What are the most important values in your life? What makes life worthwhile for you?

Q2. Overall, how would you rate your quality of life, from poor to excellent?

Q3. What is going well in your life right now?

Q4. What is not going well in your life right now?

Q5. What areas of your life would you like to improve today?

Q6. Overall, how would you rate your level of happiness?

Q7. Are you happy with your spiritual life?

Q8. Do you ever feel depressed?

Q9. If you've felt depressed sometimes, very often or all the time, have you ever considered suicide?

Q10. If you said you felt depressed sometimes, very often or all the time, have you ever taken medication?

Your upbringing

Q11. Thinking of your childhood (age 0–12), how would you rate the quality of your life, from terrible to excellent?

Q12. How would you rate your teenage years (ages 13–19)?; your young adult years (ages 20–29)?; your adult years (ages 30–39); your mature adult years (ages 40–49)?; your seasoned adult years (ages 50–64); your golden years (65 + years)?

Q13. Do you come from a home where your parents separated or divorced?

Q14. Have you ever physically, mentally or emotionally abused another person?

Social activities and relationships

Q15. Do you spend enough time with your family?

Q16. Do you have enough quality time for yourself (e.g. recreation, reading, praying, thinking/dreaming)?

Q17. How often do you take an overnight vacation?

Q18. Do you get enough sleep, i.e. do you feel rested and rejuvenated when you awake?

Socializing

Q19. How often do you socialize with people outside your immediate family?

Q20. Do you belong to a social group, church/religious group or other social organizations?

Exercising

Q21. How often do you do physical exercise in a week?

Meaningful work

Q22. Do you find your work rewarding and meaningful?

Q23. Do you like your job?

Q24. On average how many hours per week do you work?

Love of life

Q25. Do you feel you are living life to the fullest?

Q26. What do you love most about your life currently?

Current life circumstances

Q27. What is your current marital status (single, married, cohabiting with a partner, divorce, remarried)?

Relationships

Q28. How would you describe your relationship with your spouse or partner?

Q29. How would you describe your relationship with your immediate family?

Q30. How many close friends do you have?

Income and material possessions

Q31. Do you feel you are earning a sufficient and living wage?

Q32. Do you feel you have enough material possessions for the quality of life your desire?

Your physical environment

Q33. Do you live within walking distance of green space (e.g. parks, open spaces, walking trails)?

Q34. How often do your walk or ride your bike to work, to the store and to meetings?

Q35. What is your ecological footprint (Take an Ecological Footprint survey and find out how much of the earth you consume every year to meet your needs.) What can you and your household do to reduce your footprint?

Q36. Do you like the neighborhood where you live?

Q37. Do you trust your neighbors?

Q38. How long have you lived in your current neighborhood?

Q39. How many times have you moved homes in your lifetime?

This survey is just the beginning of celebrating your genuine wealth. Have fun with it. Share your findings with your partner, your kids and your friends. Consider the questions as the basis of writing your own story.

What the Inuit taught me about genuine wealth

I have had the good fortune of working with many wise indigenous peoples over the past few years. I have helped them assess their own genuine wealth, celebrating their gifts and the gifts of nature, which are so abundant. My most important teachers have been the Inuit, of Nunavut in Canada's Eastern Arctic.

Many indigenous cultures of North America see a person holistically in the shape of a wheel or circle. Within that circle, the human is composed of four attributes: mental, spiritual, emotional and physical. An Inuit elder taught me how important it is for each of us to have the right balance of these four attributes so that we go through life with genuine integrity. A healthy person is one who finds the right harmony and balance on the journey through life. However, each person is free to choose how to use her or his respective gifts. No person is the same, since each will have a unique set of attributes, volition and path to walk. Any imbalance in one's wheel suggests that one's walk may be wobbly or that one element in life is not as complete or full as it could be. To walk the path in harmony and integrity is to live according to all the gifts you were given and all the being that you are.

The Inuit (their name, in their own language, which means "the people") taught me that in order for their culture to survive and flourish in the harsh climate of the north a set of core skills, competencies or assets are required. These skills are held individually but shared collectively; the illustration shows the range of everything critical for the good life, depicted again as a wheel, emphasizing balance, harmony and complementarity. No one competency is more important than another. In Inuit culture an individual and society is fully formed when they are endowed with a full set of core competencies or skills. The health or integrity of an individual or community can be assessed in terms of the capacity (wealth) of individuals and families in a community to have knowledge or skills to practice these core competencies with fluency. What is remarkable about this inventory of genuine wealth is the range of attributes and aptitudes. A fully endowed individual has some knowledge or skill capacity in each of the 10 core competencies that would then contribute to the collective well-being of a community or society. How many of us in affluent southern communities would or even could count these skills as assets?

What was immediately apparent to me is that these are the basic skills for living sustainably. The Inuit have long understood that the strength of their communities depends on the capacities of one or more individuals to be a good hunter, a good singer, a good healer, a good storyteller and a good builder of igloos, dog sleds or utensils. All skills are needed to flourish and to be self-sufficient. Yet relationship with the land, nature and wildlife is also important. The Inuit had no history of counting (numeracy) or literacy (writing or reading). Their traditions, knowledge and wisdom came from direct relationship and experience with nature and with each other in social environments, and were passed down from one generation to the next through an oral tradition of storytelling.

The family is the central economic unit of Inuit culture. It is from the family that knowledge, skills and wisdom (*isuma*) is developed and sustained through generations. According to the study of Inuit values by Jaypeetee

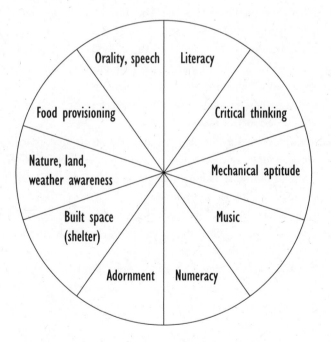

FIGURE 6.2. Inuit Core Life Competencies

Credit: Mark Anielsk and David Pollock. *The State of Inuit Well-being in Nunavut, 2001.* Report prepared for the Nunavut Social Development Council, p. 13.

Arnakak of Iqualuit, the traditional Inuit family plays the following economic roles:

- The family is the primary life support system for all its members
- The family is a node in a larger dynamic social network — part of a varied web of contacts and commitments
- The family is the primary means of transferring ever-evolving knowledge, skills and values that are essential for producing contributing members to families and society
- The family is the fundamental unit of economic activity in traditional Inuit society[1]

Like other human families, Inuit families are formed by sharing knowledge, skills, wisdom and culture. It is the network and interrelationships of families in community which form Inuit society. This cooperative reliance, unlike the individualistic approach of western economies, has allowed the Inuit to flourish and sustain their quality of life. The Inuit also have a close relationship with nature, the land and animals.

In addition to the core competencies of an individual, there are also social skills that are critical for ensuring a healthy community and cohesive society:

- Interpersonal/socialization skills: teaching; childrearing; cheerfulness; empathy; sense of responsibility to others; sensitivity to body language and social cues; social cohesiveness.
- Leadership/decision making skills: judgment; arbitration; proficiency at inspiring and mentoring others; sensitivity to others' perspectives; ability to find compromise and reconcile conflicts; ability to maintain peaceful relations within the community.
- Healing/life transition skills: midwifery; herbal knowledge; ability to perceive and guide people through passages of life (birth, marriage, family, illness, old age, death)
- Transpersonal/transcendent skills: intuition; deeply nuanced insights; sensitivity to past/future events; comprehension of overall life patterns; psychic/metaphysical connection to people/animals/nature.[2]

Measuring actual knowledge or skill capacity with respect to these core social competencies presents an important measurement challenge to economists. Many indicators would elude objective measurement like surveys or statistics and would require qualitative descriptions like storytelling. But I believe there would be great value in conducting a Genuine Wealth Assessment using the Inuit or other indigenous models of the nature of human being.

Why not ask the children?

My children are perhaps my greatest teachers on how to understand genuine wealth. Kids are naturally curious, and they ask the most penetrating and arresting questions about why things are as they are.

In recent years I've come to know Raffi Cavoukian, the troubadour who entertained children throughout the 1980s and 1990s with songs like "Baby Beluga" and "Bananaphone" which captured children's hearts and imaginations. Raffi and I have become friends since first meeting at a Canadian Society for Ecological Economics (CANSEE) conference. At the time I was Vice-President of CANSEE and hosting a conference which brings together ecological economists from across Canada and around the world. Our subject was measuring sustainability and measuring what matters. Raffi accepted my invitation to open the conference with two of his new inspirational songs for adults.

The room full of economists loved Raffi's songs and his passionate call for a "child-honouring society." A parent then asked if I would consider involving the children of attendees in any sessions, particularly with Raffi. I jumped at the idea and Raffi joined me in a dialogue with the kids-of-the-conference about what mattered most to them and their happiness. Their responses were, as you can imagine, spontaneous and wonderful.

When asked "what makes you happy inside?" the kids (who ranged from 3 to 15 years in age) responded: the sun, kindness, good food, dogs, spending time with my family, dancing, singing, bugs and chocolate. When we asked them "what is the strongest thing in the world?" they told us: God, a tree, love and honesty. When we asked "what kind of world do you want to live in?" they told us: "I wish our world was safe," "I wish there were no more wars," and "I wish no animals got killed." The kids told us, from their hearts, what mattered most to them. When we presented the kids' session results to the larger conference audience they were struck by their honesty. Our kids were challenging us to value things that make life worthwhile.

Recent research into what children feel they need most from their parents is most revealing. Researcher and mother Ellen Galinsky asked over 1,000 children from a diversity of backgrounds to grade their parents in terms of parenting skills. The most common theme that emerged from this research was that what matters most to children is their parents "being there for me." In other words, a strong and loving relationship with their parents is what matters most to kids. When asked if they could have one wish, the majority of children didn't necessarily want more time with their parents but wished that their parents were less tired and stressed.[3]

Kate Kaemerle's story

We each have our own story about realizing our own genuine wealth. The following is the story of Kate Kaemerle. Kate lives in Seattle with her partner and a few fuzzy friends in a 1910 bungalow. She's a vibrant and innovative 40-something entrepreneur and businesswoman with a passion for doing good by doing right in business and in her community. She owns EnTech Public Relations and specializes in clients with environmentally sound and socially responsible products and services. She also invests locally in real estate to create affordable housing. Kate and I met at the Bainbridge Graduate Institute (BGI), where I taught the economics of sustainability. BGI is a new MBA program located near Seattle on Bainbridge Island. There, a new generation of business people are learning how to create sustainable, socially and environmentally responsible business enterprises. Kate was a student in the very first BGI class or cohort. She had formerly worked at a worldwide public relations agency, consulting for technology firms like Microsoft, but something was calling her to a simpler life less concerned with material possessions and making money. Here, in her own words, is Kate's story about her genuine wealth.

Mark and I met at Bainbridge Graduate Institute (BGI), a new and improved kind of graduate school for MBA students in the fall of 2002. Their mission: to teach business in a socially and environmentally responsible way. Instead of teaching that only the bottom-line counts, BGI's philosophy is to infuse environmental and social responsibility into each course along with financial responsibility, comprising what is called the triple bottom-line. Mark was recruited to teach economics the first quarter the school opened its doors.

It's not an understatement to say that Mark's economics course blew our minds. Yes, we studied traditional economics. Then we learned the rest of the story. Things about economics that really don't make sense when you hear them, but you figure "hey, I'm not an economist, what do I know?" Learning that everything that costs a buck gets added to the gross domestic product, but nothing is ever subtracted. How clever — I wish I could do that with my checkbook. Chemotherapy for Aunt Ellie from all those Marlboros? Ka-ching! Toxic waste clean-up? Ka-ching! Clear-cutting old growth forests? Ka-ching! Everything adds to the GDP even though most people would consider the above examples negatives for society. It's as if you were doing your finances with only the addition key on the calculator functioning — nothing is ever subtracted. How can this be? Nothing is a cost; everything goes in the plus column? How did this evolve? What were they smoking? And more importantly, how do we get off this crazy thing?

The concept of genuine wealth is something so basic that we knew what it was as children. It was about having time with the people we love, petting a puppy, eating fresh peas out of the garden, having time to pursue our passions. Now too many of us have to schedule our time three weeks out with our Palm Pilots to jam a get-together with friends into our busy schedule.

Genuine wealth is about what's really important to us. If you didn't need money, what would you want to do with your time? For me it's time to read, paint, write, garden, enjoy the outdoors, hang out with my family and friends, be involved in my community and just have time to lie around and think or do nothing at all. Genuine wealth goes beyond money. What is genuine wealth to you?

In the beginning

I came to the simple living movement down a side alley and through the back door. Raised in an affluent suburb of Los Angeles with valley girls and surfer dudes, I became a good little consumer with the idea that more — and more expensive — was always better. In college I was on a budget for the first time and it was painful! Somehow I survived on my part-time income, a little help from my friends, much pizza and beer and regular trips home for re-supply runs.

After college, I made a trek to Alaska for the summer and ended up staying for more than a decade. Got married, got the career path going, bought new cars, city and country homes, shopped at Nordstroms and took frequent vacations to warm and tropical destinations. The credit card companies loved me! At the same time, I deepened my love of nature in this beautiful, wild place. I also absorbed the do-it-yourself independence of the Alaskan spirit, even while I carefully spiked my high heels into the ice as I strode across the slippery parking lot to my advertising agency job. Who needs crampons?

I lived in a log house on seven acres and could walk through the woods to several lakes or a river and go fishing or canoeing. I had a huge garden that I had to protect with a tall fence from the moose, plus a greenhouse. For a time, I raised chickens and ducks and was blessed with fresh eggs all year and cute fuzzy babies in the spring. I picked berries and rosehips with my friends every fall. With my friends we canned salmon and made jam. My homestead had many of the makings of permaculture — the creation of a self-sustaining landscape — although I'd never heard that word at the time. And all the while I was driving off to work five days a week to my advertising agency job where I encouraged everyone to part with their hard-earned money for that touted new car or living room set in the slick commercials. Or telling them the oil companies were really good corporate citizens and part of the community. I did not yet see or feel the disconnect between my work and my heart.

It's only money, honey

Then a tumult of change in my life — divorce, catastrophic illness of a family member, moving 1500 miles to a new city, underemployment where I made half as much money and my expenses were higher. Watching my bank account hemorrhage, I made major changes. I quit using the credit cards, got a roommate to share expenses, shopped less, did more things myself, sold the car to get rid of the car payments and bought a used one for cash. And although it wasn't easy, it worked. I was living comfortably on half as much money. Half as much! That was shocking news. I thought I needed the new car, the fashionable clothes, the perfectly furnished home and the expensive haircut. In reality, I didn't need any of those things at all; I merely wanted them. Desired them. It was the fantasy of happiness through more stuff, spurred by the advertising industry that I knew only too well. It was a freeing revelation to let go of my artificial desires for the material and focus on what was really important. Life was important, not things.

I'm not going to say any of these changes were easy. Most of them were not. But the debt relief was a huge monkey off my back. And I learned to live a rich life in ways that were simpler and more meaningful. Expensive evenings out socializing at restaurants and nightspots became parties at home with an intimate group of friends and just as much fun was had by all, if not more. And without the bar tab and the cigarette smoke. Shopping excursions were replaced by the Saturday morning sport of garage sale-ing with friends where we could still fulfill our hunter/gatherer needs for a couple bucks and no credit card bills. Plus I could get an antique wingback chair for the price of a new blender! Instead of exotic vacations to Hawaii or Mexico, we went camping. I even ended up doing marketing for an import company and spent several months in Thailand and Nepal — and got paid for it.

From here to simplicity

I lived in the same neighborhood in Seattle where the Simple Living movement officially started,[4] so one day I saw a flyer at the local cafe and went to see what it was all about. I joined a Simplicity Circle and discussed with others why it seemed like a good idea to simplify our lives and how we were doing it. The conversations were enlightening. The reasons we wanted to purposely simplify our lives were many. To have more time for the things that mattered to us — family, friends and community, activities and interests long ignored. And the single biggest reason and the one that was often the first to go out the window was time for ourselves. That seemed to be the first casualty when our lives were hectic.

Since those days of Simplicity Circles and lean economic times, I've gone up the corporate ladder and reaped the rewards. But fortunately, I didn't forget that less is more. The less I have, the less I have to work to maintain what I have. And the more time I have for my passions such as pursuing an MBA degree, writing and painting. When I left my last position with a global PR firm to strike out on my own, I knew initially I'd have much less money. But I'd have more freedom and less stress. That seemed like a good trade-off to me. And I could look for the kind of clients I wanted to work for: people that are making the world a better place, not companies that are extracting the natural capital from the earth and driving up consumer debt through slick advertising and focus groups.

I recently was house-hunting. Instead of looking for the biggest house I could afford, I looked for the smallest house that could fit my needs. Less home to maintain and clean means more time for my passions. And the last time I moved, I sold most of my possessions and only kept the basics and what was important to me. What I have now will fit in a parking space. So even though the real estate agent was recently stumped by my insistence on a small house, I know that I don't even have enough things to fill a two-bedroom bungalow. More garage sale-ing will definitely be in order.

Living in a sustainable world

The latest piece of my desire for simplicity is the recognition that our American lifestyle is not sustainable. Even though I have opted out of the much of the consumer rat race (where even if you win, you're still a rat!), I find I have a ways to go.

Economics, which is from the Greek word *oikonomia* meaning household management, should increase value to all members of a household over the long run. Economics is more about quality of life than money. To me, managing a household for the good of all members involves two households: 1) the actual household I live in and 2) in the larger sense the planet we all share.

From a planetary perspective, my ecological footprint (EF) seemed a good measure of how I am living. According to Redefining Progress in Oakland, California (rprogress.org), your ecological footprint is the biologically productive area required to produce the natural resources you consume expressed in acres. They have a thirteen question quiz to determine your ecological footprint. Being an organic food eating, simple living, compact car (OK, it's a sports car) driving citizen, I thought I'd do pretty well. Not really. My footprint is only 71.9% of the average American's, which in my mind is an SUV driving, Big Mac eating, TV watching schmuck. I took the test again. This time I projected some attainable alterations in my lifestyle with major changes like better transportation habits (primarily less air travel) and eating fewer animal products. In this projected case I would score an ecological footprint as low as 41.6% of the average American. Before I celebrate too much about this potential improvement, while it may be a pretty good score in the US the average person worldwide has an EF of 5.4 acres. My best-case scenario, without moving to Montana and living like the Unabomber, is an EF of 11.1 acres. It would be a start, but no cause for celebration.

Learning about the state of the US economy today, with the rising mountain of debt and money constantly being loaned into existence and not backed up with other funds, reminds me of the opening scene of the movie "Jackass." A bunch of young men pile into a giant shopping cart at the top of a hill, and as they careen down the middle of a city street with the inevitable crash at the bottom with bodies flying akimbo through the air, I know that at least they have medical assistance standing by for their stunts. Our economy has no such medics in the wings. Our economy is one big global casino, and Vegas always wins, baby.

Think globally, act locally

So what is a new personal economic plan that works? One where I don't have to live on sticks and nuts foraging in the outback, a life where I still have DSL and a good cup of coffee in the morning? Where I don't have to bet my retirement account on the global casino that already sucked much of my 401K away with the dotcom crash? Think globally, buy locally may be a catchy bumper sticker, but it works in practice as well. How do I help keep my economy local and contribute to the kind of world I want to live in? How do I walk the path of sustainability in every part of my life — including work, investing and buying the necessities in life? Here are five ways I'm exploring to contribute to a sustainable local and world community.

Investments

I recently moved most of my money out of the global casino (stock market) and into community banks that loan money in the neighborhoods they're in, such as ShoreBank Pacific and Self Help Credit Union. When my money is in a regular bank it could go to fund a Wal-Mart or oil exploration. Do I want to loan money to them? I don't think so!

Work

Recently starting my own PR firm, I'm working with and pursuing clients that are contributing to their stakeholders and the environment in positive ways. And I work from my home office so I can commute in my bunny slippers. I'm working less than 40 hours a week right now so I have time to pursue my passions.

Volunteering

This is an area that previously brought much richness to my life; I was involved in community activities such as participating in my local community council. The last few years I have not had time for this passion of mine and am anxious to make a contribution of my time and energy once again.

Purchases

When you buy new products, you are voting with your dollars. I try to buy local whenever possible. The local pharmacy instead of the big chain, the farmers market rather than a nationwide supermarket. I examine each purchase and think of the ramifications. I no longer buy clothes that need to be dry cleaned because of the nasty chemicals used in the process. A long distance phone company such as Working Assets or Earth Tones supports organizations I believe in. I'd rather give my money to them than to Sprint, MCI (WorldCom) or AT&T. Buying in the local economy with dollars that stay in the community with the locally owned businesses that employ my neighbors makes a difference. Imagine if more people bought locally? That is happening in many communities whose dead and boarded-up downtowns are now coming back to life with new stores, restaurants and businesses. What if everyone bought locally in their community? Maybe a few of those box stores will get boarded up for a change.

Philanthropy

To reduce my ecological footprint, I donate to organizations that supply clean power or plant trees to offset my impact on the earth. To assist the poor, I donate to help the homeless in my community, and I've donated funds to Bangladesh's Grameen Bank for their micro-credit program. Grameen Bank's founder, Mohammad Yunus, was awarded the Nobel Peace Prize. Their micro-credit program gives small, collateral-free loans to the poor which enables them to build small businesses. Millions of poor around the world improve their lives through micro-credit programs.

Conclusions

Americans are under the misguided notion that more stuff brings more happiness. We have more stuff and we're not happier. We have bigger houses and more cars and guess what? We're not happier.

The US Quality of Life index has been going down since the 1970s, and prescriptions for anti-depressants have skyrocketed. We're working more hours than ever. The rich are getting richer and the rest of us, well, we're not. We believe the advertising that if we drive the right car, we'll get the beautiful girl or guy. Instead we have an over 50% divorce rate, and consumer debt is at an all-time high and climbing an unsustainable upward curve. Many think if they work hard and stoke their corporate 401Ks, they can retire and then have time for their passions. Is this any way to live? I think not.

Being into more instant gratification than the thought of retirement can give me, I want to live a fulfilling life now. And I'm able to do that by simplifying my needs and living with less. Less house, less stuff and less work means more time to enjoy life, create community and just be. In the bigger picture,

I can help contribute to my community and the world by consciously making decisions about my purchases and actions. I can encourage others to be conscious of the economic decisions in their lives through education and example.

What do we really want? I think we really want more quality of life based on life values instead of purely financial values. More real wealth instead of virtual wealth. I will not pretend to understand all the nuances of the science of economics (chrematistics as practiced in America seems to be an easily manipulated house of cards built on often faulty assumptions — wait a minute, maybe I grasp it after all!) What I do understand is the concept of *oikonomia* as it relates to my household and my world. And in my case, less is more.

My own story of Genuine Wealth

In my own life and family, I have come to a new realization that things that make life worthwhile don't take a lot of money or require us to compromise our values. Indeed, to live in accordance with our heart's inner desires and to be true to our inner talents and teacher is to live authentically.

In my experience this has meant connecting with my own relationship with the Divine, with God, as Love. It has meant balancing my spiritual path with my worldly path. It has meant freeing myself of my previous anxiety about money and debts and living each moment with joy. Each situation is pregnant with opportunity. I strive to be a genuine steward of not only my own personal wealth but the collective wealth of my household (my spouse and my daughters), my extended family and my neighbors and friends. Like the Taoist, I want to live in harmony with others and with nature continually balancing the relationship between meeting my worldly needs for sustenance with a deeper longing of loving relationships with each other and the Divine.

I intentionally work fewer hours within a business plan that pursues a goal of income sufficiency: having just enough income to meet the basic needs for the good life. For my family this means buying groceries from local farmers' markets or the market owned by our neighbor. We live with only one vehicle instead of two, and I ride my bike, summer and winter, to the places I meet with clients and friends. I have eliminated all debts so that I have more discretionary income and ultimately more time available for pursuing the things that make life worthwhile. I have learned that while material possessions and luxuries are nice, having too many material possession means too much maintenance, too much dusting and too much time fixing things when they break down. I am now at a place I call the "maintenance stage" where, with most of my material needs having been realized, I can spend my life energy maintaining the integrity of our home (built capital), my relationships with my wife, children, parents, grandparents and friends (social capital) and taking time to connect with my inner spirit and teacher (human capital). The result has been that I have more time for my passions outside of my work and more time with my life partner, my children, my grandparents, my neighbors and my friends.

Like any journey, mine has had many twists, turns, detours, train wrecks and epiphanies. My good friend, Orest Andre, a spry 80-year-old who survived leukemia, reminds me that waking up each morning is itself a miracle; therefore we have no excuse but to celebrate every breath we take. Faced with our own mortality, Orest says that we need to live "an attitude of gratitude."

My grandfather Peter Mitterer, who lived to 95 years of age, used to say "just live it up." Peter worked hard during his life as a gardener for people with financial and material wealth. He experienced the economic pains of the Great Depression which reminded him throughout his life to be grateful for the gifts of life and providence and to live frugally. Together with his wife, my grandmother Catherine, they taught me important lessons of living with enough, with an attitude of sufficiency as genuine stewards of the earth and community. They taught me the importance of sharing, of giving and receiving and ultimately of abundance. I think about Peter and Catherine's example almost every day; they remind me to be thankful for life's little pleasures and to celebrate the gift of life with every breath I take. I only hope that I can remind our daughters to live life with gratitude for abundance.

Some may ask what all this has to do with sustainable living? Everything. I see the journey of sustainability as a deeply spiritual experience. Sustainability is about genuine stewardship of the land and our relationships with each other. We cannot deny our spiritual nature just as we cannot deny our intellect and our intuitions. I find it curious that so many of us who live and work on intellectual planes often long to talk about our spiritual nature, about God and about the true meaning of life. This is because we are spiritual beings, and being human means to be in touch with that attribute. Living sustainable lifestyles means being attuned to the truths of nature — of nature's abundance as epitomized in the abundance of sunshine. I believe that living a life of moderation and sufficiency is a virtuous action: being good stewards of the land, of our bodies, our families, our co-workers and our communities just as the Greek definition of economics reminds us.

Your story

What's your story of Genuine Wealth? What are you thankful for? Are you living your life with an attitude of gratitude for the abundance of genuine wealth that you have? What have you to celebrate today? What changes would you like to make in your life, now or tomorrow? If we are going to live authentic and genuine lives, each one of us must get in touch with our inner teacher. Who are you? Why are you here? What are your dreams? If we begin to live more authentic lives, true to our inner nature and in a way that our souls and hearts are glad, then we can be more fully available to others in service. Most importantly we begin to enjoy the happiness that comes in both giving and receiving and appreciating the abundance of our common wealth.

The Genuine Wealth of
Communities and Nations

W HAT WOULD A COMMUNITY built on Genuine Wealth and an economics of happiness and well-being look like? How can Canada, the United States or any other nation move towards a sustainable economy? How do citizens become actively engaged in genuine democracy to shape well-being policy in their communities, to ensure that what counts as progress is what matters most to people? In this chapter we will travel from Leduc, Alberta to Nunavut in Canada's Arctic, from Santa Monica, California to the Italian region of Emilia Romagna and to China. Communities in many parts of this world are beginning to recognize and celebrate their genuine wealth in a pragmatic way that complements conventional systems of governance and planning.

I believe the future belongs to communities who are wise to the truths of sustainability, who understand the spirit of Robert Kennedy's challenge and are ready to celebrate Genuine Wealth aligned with the values of their citizens. We must measure and manage the things that make life worthwhile. I have had the good fortune of working with many who carry this vision in their minds and hearts. They recognize that traditional ways of measuring progress must change and that opportunity belongs to those who embrace a new stewardship covenant and desire to live their lives genuinely. While each community and application of the Genuine Wealth model is different, there are certain things they share. They all have a strong sense of belonging to their community and a strong relationship with the land and nature.

The UK-based New Economics Foundation's *Well-being Manifesto for a Flourishing Society* provides a compelling and clear vision: a flourishing society needs vibrant, resilient and sustainable communities. The Foundation suggests that key ingredients of a flourishing society include:

- Measuring what matters
- Meaningful work
- Reclaiming time
- Flourishing schools
- Complete health for the nation
- Investing in the very early years
- Authentic advertising
- Community contribution: being actively engaged in community[1]

Many communities in the UK are experimenting with these principles, managing their communities intentionally based on well-being outcomes.

In Canada, the Federation of Canadian Municipalities (FCM) has articulated clear goals and operating principles for a sustainable and smart community. According to the FCM a sustainable smart community achieves economic, environmental and social health by:

- Making the most efficient use of resources
- Generating the least amount of waste
- Providing high quality service to residents
- Living within the carrying capacity of natural resources — land, water and air (i.e. an ecological footprint which is in harmony with nature's capacity to provide natural capital goods and services)
- Preserving or improving quality of life while minimizing impact on the environment

All of this should be managed using an integrated systems approach. The goal is to increase the environmental and economic efficiency of municipal governments.[2] Donella Meadows, one of the great champions of sustainable communities, defined sustainable development for communities very simply: good lives for all people in harmony with nature.[3]

Finding genuine wealth in Leduc, Alberta

The City of Leduc is a community of over 16,000 people just south of Edmonton in the Canadian province of Alberta. It was here in 1949 that Alberta's first oil well struck black gold. The city is part of the larger Alberta's International Region (which includes Leduc County, some of the most fertile agricultural land in the province comprising 645,933 acres of beautiful aspen parkland and prairie landscape) with a population of roughly 40,000 people in all. It is home not only to productive farms but to the Nisku Industrial Business Park, western Canada's largest business and industrial park with over 400 companies employing more than 6,000 highly skilled trades and professional workers who are benefiting from the billions of dollars being invested in Alberta's oilsands development north in Fort McMurray. The Edmonton International Airport is also a key entity in this economically prosperous region. My GDP estimates suggest that Leduc enjoys the third-highest GDP per capita in the world, after Luxembourg and Bermuda!

Why would such a prosperous community be interested in measuring its genuine wealth, quality of life and state of well-being? My work captured the attention and imagination of Pat Klak, executive director of the Leduc-Nisku Economic Development Authority. Pat was inspired by Robert Kennedy's remarks about the GDP and dreamed of a project that would use the emerging Genuine Wealth Assessment to measure the true wealth of this prosperous region of Alberta. She sensed there was more to life in Leduc than tracking an increment in the GDP from Alberta's oil boom, more industrial output and more spending. She worried that a community so economically successful might lose sight of intangible things that contribute to its quality of life. She sensed a need to celebrate things that actually make life worthwhile in this small, close-knit, cohesive community where a sense of belonging and trust run deep. The Mayor of Leduc and Leduc City council wanted to know "why do people choose to live, work and stay in Leduc?" and "why are our kids leaving the community?" A one-year Genuine Wealth Assessment was launched in June of 2005 with financial support from the Federation of Canadian Municipalities, The Edmonton Community Foundation, the City of Leduc and the Leduc-Nisku EDA.[4] The Genuine Wealth model (Figure 5.5) guided the Leduc Genuine Wealth Assessment project.

The goals of the project were three-fold. First, we asked citizens simple quality of life questions: what do you love about your community, what works, what doesn't, and what would you like to see change or improved? I used various instruments including on-line surveys, personal interviews and conversation with a number of social and community groups including high school kids and seniors. The quality of life inventory took six months to complete. People loved to talk about these questions. Early results suggested that people love to live, work and raise their families in a small community atmosphere. They love their parks and play areas and feel Leduc is a safe place to walk after dark. Perhaps most importantly, people feel a strong sense of belonging and neighborliness.

The second goal of the project was to assess the five community capital assets (human, social, natural, built and financial capital) using a host of indicators of physical and qualitative conditions. This gave me a strong sense of the strengths and weaknesses of the community relative to the province of Alberta as a whole, and in comparison with other larger centers like Edmonton and Calgary. We conducted an Ecological Footprint Analysis of the households in the region to assess how their economic life-style is in harmony with the natural environment they occupy. Finally, my goal was to align the indicators of well-being with the values citizens expressed, creating a Genuine Wealth checkup.

The final objective of any such project is to apply the assessment results in local municipal governance and decision-making. The City of Leduc will be using these results to develop its long-range municipal plan and guide its annual strategic-business planning process.

This first 2005 Genuine Well-being report for the city of Leduc showed that there are many things in this community to celebrate. Indicators pointed to these strengths or assets:

- A vibrant, growing and competitive economy (measured in terms of GDP), supported by a diverse, vibrant and close-knit business community and households with above average incomes
- A flourishing community that prides itself in a strong sense of belonging, high quality of life, being a relatively safe place to live, and great place to work and enjoy recreational opportunities with family and friends
- A very happy population of all ages which self-reports being very satisfied with life. However, adults were generally happier than children. Over 80% of adults who responded to the Genuine Wealth survey reported being either very happy or somewhat happy with their personal quality of life while over 82% said they were either very satisfied or somewhat satisfied with the overall quality of life in their community. However, only 61% of grade six students surveyed reported being very happy or somewhat happy
- Abundant green space, trails and recreational facilities

- Abundant, fertile agricultural land that surrounds the city, as part of Leduc County

However, some indicators point to areas for improving well-being through future actions:
- Shortage of affordable housing, particularly for younger workers whose wages may be insufficient to pay rent and stay in the community
- Persistent demand for food bank donations from low income households
- Higher than average levels of childhood asthma, relatively high levels of smoking, a dramatic increase in suicides and relatively high rates of deaths from heart disease and stroke
- Rising property crime rates and drug crime cases
- Challenges in achieving a clean and sustainable environment: relatively high ecological footprint by households, higher than average household and industrial waste to landfills including large volumes of contaminated soil being landfilled and relatively low recycling rates by households. Unfortunately, many environmental conditions, such as water quality, are unknown due to lack of data

These were the survey results:

Why do you like living in Leduc?
When asked to list the key attributes that contribute most to their quality of life, respondents identified the following: a) small town atmosphere or feeling (15.2%); b) the convenience of shopping and other retail needs being met locally (14.1%); c) friendly and caring people (11.2%); d) parks and green space (6.7%); e) sport activities and recreational facilities (6.7%); f) family (6.3%).

How could quality of life be improved?
When asked what their vision for future improvements to the well-being of their community, respondents noted the following top four priorities: improved recreation/sports facilities (22.1%); improving the road infrastructure and solving traffic congestion problems (9.0%); programs for teens/youth (7.6%) and public transit (5.5%).

When asked what they would like to improve in their personal lives the top four priorities of respondents includes: more quality time alone (slowing

down) or with family (26.5%); improving personal health, levels of energy
and fitness (13.3%); more money and financial independence (12.2%); more
leisure and recreation (6.1%).

Sense of belonging
When asked to rate their sense of belonging to their community, 84.8% of respondents said they felt either a very strong or strong sense of belonging to
their community. When asked to rate their sense of belonging to Alberta,
83.3% felt either a very strong or strong sense of belonging. When asked to
rate their sense of belonging to Canada the highest percentage, 89.9% of respondents, said they felt a very strong or strong sense of belonging to Canada.

Trust in others
When asked to rate their trust in others, 74.7% of respondents felt that others could be trusted.

Sense of community and neighborliness
When asked about their sense of community and connection with neighborhood, 15.9% of respondents said they knew most of the people in their neighborhood, 37.5% said they knew many people in their neighborhood, while
42.0% said they knew only a few people in their neighborhood and 4.5% said
they did not know anyone in their neighborhood. This is a very high level of
sense of community.

Leduc Genuine Well-being indicators and indices
The report examined 117 statistical and perceptual indicators of well-being
organized according to 22 well-being themes, each represented as a petal in
the Genuine Well-being Index Flower (Figure 7.1). The more complete or
full each flower petal, the better the overall conditions of well-being for that
well-being theme (e.g. economic vitality, trust and belonging are in optimum condition). A short, wilted or stunted petal (e.g. ethnic diversity, population density) points to weakness or areas that may need attention or
improvement. For Leduc, most economic well-being indicators are robust
while there are challenges in health and wellness, ethnic or cultural diversity,
income equity and fairness and resource conservation. The image of the Genuine Well-being Flower shows both the strengths and weaknesses of the
community.

Genuine Well-being Index Flower was created using numeric scores for each of the well-being themes; Figure 7.2 shows each score in the right column; figures in brackets in the left column represent the number of indicators per theme.

Genuine well-being indicator results

For each of the 117 indicators, the well-being condition of the city of Leduc was compared against an appropriate benchmark, usually the Alberta provincial or Canadian national average or data from the cities like Edmonton or Calgary. The higher the well-being score the better the condition of well-being relative to the benchmark. Character faces were also assigned to each indicator to reflect the condition of well-being relative to the benchmark:

☺ well-being condition is very good to excellent; 10% better than the benchmark

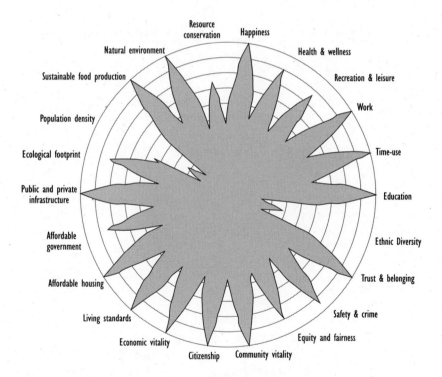

FIGURE 7.1 Leduc Genuine Well-being Index Flower

Credit: Anielski Management Inc. *City of Leduc 2005 Genuine Well-being Report*, p. 11.

☺ well-being condition is moderate to good; 10% +/- (above or below) the benchmark

☹ well-being condition is fair to poor; more than 10% below the benchmark

Out of 117 possible indicators 39 scored a ☺ (great condition!), 36 scored a ☺ (good or average condition), 36 scored a ☹ (poor condition) and 6 indicators lacked data to assess its condition. These results are useful for citizens and decision makers since they point to areas of both strengths and weaknesses in well-being conditions.

Leduc's ecological footprint

Ecological footprint measures the ecological sustainability of a community's lifestyles. It measures how much land and sea space a human population re-

Figure 7.2. Well-being Themes and Scores

Well-being Theme	Well-being Theme Composite Index
1. Happiness (2)	100.0
2. Health and wellness (19)	89.9
3. Recreation and leisure (4)	86.6
4. Work (7)	98.4
5. Time use (4)	99.2
6. Education (5)	104.1
7. Ethnic diversity (2)	38.1
8. Trust and belonging (5)	100.1
9. Safety and crime (7)	93.8
10. Equity and fairness (3)	89.4
11. Community vitality (3)	100.0
12. Citizenship (1)	110.5
13. Economic vitality (6)	123.4
14. Living standards (12)	104.8
15. Affordable housing (6)	99.9
16. Affordable government (3)	84.9
17. Public and private infrastructure (9)	178.3
18. Ecological footprint (2)	81.9
19. Population density (1)	32.1
20. Sustainable food production (2)	100.0
21. Natural Environment (8)	117.6
22. Resource consumption and conservation (7)	73.8

Credit: Anielski Management Inc. *City of Leduc 2005 Genuine Well-being Report,* p. 12.

quires to produce the resources it consumes and to absorb its wastes (under prevailing technology). It puts local consumption into a global perspective and helps identify areas for improvement such as reducing resource use, finding greater energy efficiencies and reducing wasteful practices. By measuring the ecological footprint, we can assess a community's ecological overshoot: the amount by which consumption exceeds nature's biological carrying capacity.

The analysis conducted by my colleague Jeff Wilson showed that the average ecological footprint of citizens of Leduc was 21.0 acres per capita in 2004, roughly 4.1% higher than the Alberta average of 20 acres per capita and higher than Edmonton's footprint of 19.5 acres per capita. By comparison, the average world citizen has an ecological footprint of only 5.4 acres. This means a resident of Leduc has an EF 3.9 times larger than the world's average. If we were to take the average footprint per Leduc citizen multiplied by the 2005 population, it would take 332,034 acres of land to meet the current renewable resource demands of Leduc's citizens. However, as the City of Leduc occupies only 9,309 acres, its total area footprint area is 35.7 times larger than the actual land area of the city. This means that citizens of Leduc are incurring an ecological deficit or shortfall. Leduc's ecological deficit is higher than the rest of the world where a global citizen's footprint averages 5.4 acres per capita with available global biocapacity of 4.4 acres per world citizen.

Yet Leduc is blessed with abundant, highly productive, arable agricultural land. There are an estimated 240,489 acres of prime agricultural farmland suitable for growing food in Leduc County; this is roughly 37% of the total area of Alberta's International Region of 661,209 acres. Despite this wealth of agricultural land suitable for growing nutritious, organic food for local markets in Leduc and Edmonton, there seems to be little appreciation of the land's potential as an asset and opportunity. There is no formal inventory of the amount of food sold in Leduc and other communities in the region that is being produced or grown locally. Local food production would provide local food security, self-sufficiency and food sustainability. As citizens eat more locally produced food, they become less dependent on external inputs and they reduce pollution and greenhouse gas emissions related to transporting food long distances. Food safety increases because farmers can communicate more directly and personally with urban households. And despite growing demand for fresh produce and organic meat, poultry and dairy at Edmonton, Calgary and other local farmer's markets, there are only a handful of organic farmers (roughly seven organic producers of vegetables, poultry and other livestock)

Figure 7.3. Leduc Genuine Wealth Accounts and Genuine Well-being Indicators

Genuine Wealth Capital	Well-being Theme	Genuine Well-being Indicators	Well-being Condition	Well-being Score
Happiness	Self-rated happiness	Self-rated happiness (adults)	☺	100.0
		Self-rated happiness (children)	☺	100.0
Human Capital	Health and wellness	Population	☺	**
		Population growth (2005–2001)	☹	73.3
		Median age of population	😐	100.5
		Life expectancy	😐	100.5
		Mortality rate (all causes of death, all age groups per 100,000)	😐	94.3
		Premature mortality rate (death before 75 years of age)	😐	109.0
		Deaths due to heart disease and stroke	☹	85.0
		Deaths due to cancer	😐	100.8
		Infant mortality (death per 1000 live births)	😐	97.0
		Low birth weight babies	😐	108.8
		Childhood asthma rate (per 100,000)	☹	58.2
		Teen birth rate	☺	151.9
		Overweight and obesity	☹	74.6
		Perception of being overweight or obese	☹	87.9
		Do not smoke	☹	76.2
		Suicide rate per 100,000 population	☹	53.0
		Auto crash mortality rate	☹	23.8
		Number of family physicians per thousand people	☹	83.8
		Access to hospitals	☺	139.6
	Recreation and leisure	Physical activity	😐	96.1
		Leisure-related activities	☹	54.1
		Perception that recreational facilities are affordable	☺	111.5
		Walking or biking to work	☹	84.8
	Work	Work force	☺	100.0
		Employment growth	😐	95.7
		Labor force participation rate	😐	103.0
		Employment rate	😐	103.5
		Unemployment rate	☺	123.8
		Ratio of part-time to full-time employment	😐	108.7
		Percent of residents who work in their community	☹	54.4
	Time use	Unpaid work (persons reporting hours of unpaid work)	😐	99.9
		Unpaid household work (persons reporting hours of unpaid housework)	😐	100.1
		Unpaid parenting (persons reporting hours looking after children, without pay)	😐	106.2
		Unpaid eldercare hours per person per year (persons reporting hours of unpaid care or assistance to seniors)	😐	90.7

Figure 7.3. (continued)

Genuine Wealth Capital	Well-being Theme	Genuine Well-being Indicators	Well-being Condition	Well-being Score
	Education & learning	Educational attainment: percentage of population with some post-secondary education or university degree	🙂	101.5
		High school drop out rate	🙂	94.6
		Grade 3, 6, and 9 achievement scores	🙂	97.5
		Average class sizes (primary and secondary schools)	😊	123.0
		Access to libraries	😊	300.0
Human Capital Well-being Index				**99.1**
Social Capital	Diversity	Ethnic diversity index (visible minorities and aboriginal population)	☹	31.2
		Population that is foreign-born	☹	45.0
	Trust and sense of belonging	Self-rated sense of belonging to the community	😊	100.0
		Self-rated trust of neighbors	😊	100.0
		Neighborliness: number of neighbors you know	😊	100.0
		Citizens who lived at the same address for five years or more	🙂	100.3
		Community organizations, clubs and groups	😊	100.0
	Safety & crime	Violent crime against persons	😊	184.7
		Property crime rate	😊	119.9
		All crime cases per capita	😊	121.6
		Drug crime cases	☹	9.9
		Perception of personal safety regarding crime	😊	115.2
		Unintentional injury death rate	☹	65.8
		Motor vehicle collision rate	☹	39.8
	Equity and fairness	Income gap between top income households and the lowest earning households	😊	121.3
		Ratio of female earnings to male earnings, working full-time.	☹	83.0
		Number of women on municipal/civic councils	☹	64.0
	Community vitality	Attendance at Economic Development Authority Partnership breakfasts	😊	100.0
		Number of festivals, community and cultural events	😊	100.0
		Attendance (visits) at recreation centers and registration in recreation programs per citizen per annum.	😊	100.0
	Citizenship	Voter turnout at elections.	😊	110.5
Social Well-being Index				**91.1**

Figure 7.3. (continued)

Genuine Wealth Capital	Well-being Theme	Genuine Well-being Indicators	Well-being Condition	Well-being Score
Economic & Financial Capital	Economic vitality	GDP per capita	☺	113.7
		GDP annual growth rate	😐	101.8
		Businesses per 1000 citizens	☹	88.3
		Building permit value per capita	☺	163.6
		Economic-Occupational Diversity Index	☹	89.1
		Housing starts per 1000 citizens	☺	183.7
	Living standards	Median total income of persons 15 years of age and over	😐	105.3
		Average earnings per worker working full-time	😐	102.6
		Median household income	☺	115.4
		Average total household expenditures	😐	103.0
		Average household expenditures (2004) as a percentage of median household income (2001)	☺	112.0
		Incidence of low income (poor) households	☺	191.7
		Dependency on government safety net (government transfers as a percentage of income)	😐	106.9
		Individuals whose income is less than a living wage	😐	104.0
		Hours required to meet basic needs at minimum wage, single employable person	😐	100.0
		Food bank usage: number of families (FTE) receiving food bank donations per annum	☹	9.5
		Lone-parent families (as percentage of all families)	😐	106.7
		Ease of access to stores and other services	😐	100.0
	Affordable housing	Average value of a dwelling (average housing price)	☺	118.4
		Net municipal property taxes per person	☺	67.7
		Ratio of median household income average housing price (%)	☺	136.6
		% of households who spend more than 30% of their income on rent	😐	101.3
		% of households who spend more than 30% of their income on a mortgage and taxes	☹	75.5
		Demand for subsidized housing (waiting list, Leduc Community Foundation)	😐	100.0
	Affordable and efficient government	Municipal government expenditures per citizen	☺	116.5
		Municipal tax rates (residential), percentage	☹	45.4
		Municipal tax rates (non- residential), percentage	😐	92.6
Economic Well-being Index				**105.6**

Figure 7.3. (continued)

Genuine Wealth Capital	Well-being Theme	Genuine Well-being Indicators	Well-being Condition	Well-being Score
Built Capital	Public and private infrastructure	Private dwellings (owned and rented)	☺	100.0
		Growth in number of dwellings per 100 people	☹	77.4
		Percentage of dwellings requiring major repairs	😐	97.0
		Municipal government spending on transportation infrastructure and public utilities	☹	24.7
		Recreation facility venues	☺	100.0
		Recreation visitation rates (number of visits per person per year)	☺	100.0
		Bike and walking trails (km) per 1000 people	☺	1,055.3
		Public transit expenditures by municipal governments per capita	☹	0
		Public transit options for youth and seniors	☹	50.0
Built Capital Well-being Index				**178.3**
Natural Capital	Ecological footprint	Ecological footprint: household demand on natural capital vs. nature's supplies	😐	96.1
		Ecological deficit: ratio of ecological footprint to total regional land area	☹	67.7
	Population density	Population density (people per sq km), a measure of the human population pressure on the land	☹	31.5
	Sustainable food production	Prime agricultural land per person	☺	100.0
		Percentage of food grown and sourced locally	?	
	Natural environment	Green space and parkland	☺	310.7
		Forest (tree) cover	?	
		Water quality	?	
		Air quality	☹	17.2
		Greenhouse gas emissions	?	
		Noise pollution	?	
		Pesticide use	?	
		Contaminated soil volume to landfills	☹	25.0
	Consumption and conservation	Water consumption	☺	128.3
		Water storage capacity per citizen	😐	100.0
		Residential waste generated per capita	😐	102.9
		Total solid waste disposed to landfills	☹	36.6
		% of domestic waste recycled (diverted from landfills)	☹	74.9
		Residential energy use (GJ per capita)	☹	73.2
		Percentage of energy sourced from renewable energy sources	☹	1.0
Environmental (Natural Capital) Well-being Index				**83.3**
Leduc Genuine Well-being Index				**109.6**

Notes: ** no index score is given to human population figures.
? means that there was no data available for this indicator at the time of reporting.
Credit: Anielski Management Inc. *City of Leduc 2005 Genuine Well-being Report*, pp. 14–18.

operating in the Leduc region. Typically, these farmers are more financially healthy and sustainable than most conventional farmers, particularly on a per acre of production basis.

Adult Genuine Wealth Stories

"Having moved here from Yellowknife just over five years ago I wasn't sure about the change. However, Leduc has been so good to me the moment I got here. Right from the apartment I wanted when I first moved here to the house that was perfect for me when I decided to make Leduc my permanent home. As with most of Alberta, it's a growing community with tons of potential. Unless I was filthy rich, I honestly can't think of a better place that I could have ended up. I've felt at home as soon as I set foot into Leduc; Leduc is definitely home."

"I grew up in Leduc, finished school here, worked here 35 years, have all my friends and family here nearby, watched Leduc grow and still proud of our growth and developments. Great people living in Leduc."

"We hear so much about young people and problems but I can't get over that I have never gone into a store or place where young teenagers haven't helped open the door for me or helped me out. I think young people are wonderful and most parents in Leduc can be proud of their children. You don't hear this on the news about how good the young people are."

"We have what we need and much more, though I worry about future generations if we keep going this way with the consumerism and the lack of involvement of people today in community; when it [the economic times] is this good people don't think much. They are too busy with their material possessions."

"I think what you folks are doing [Genuine Wealth Assessment] is important; trying to figure out what's happening and why it's happening from both urban and rural is critical to increasing our collective awareness. It makes for a stronger community and stronger businesses."

What's next?

The Genuine Wealth Assessment has provided a baseline of well-being information upon which the community can now chart a sustainable path towards the goals of a flourishing economy of well-being. By establishing both a foundation of citizen values along with a new balance sheet of the conditions of the community's five capitals, Leduc can build on its strengths, address potential risks to future well-being and act on the vision of many of its citizens.

What I learned from Leduc

The Leduc project was the first true test of my Genuine Wealth model. My intuition that citizens desire a meaningful opportunity to express their values, opinions and dreams was proven right. People love to share their feelings about life and to celebrate the many gifts of genuine wealth. I found that youth and seniors in particular were overjoyed that someone would come simply to listen to their stories. I realized that this research provided an opportunity for

Children's Genuine Wealth Stories

"What I like most about the community is how nice people are and there is not a lot of graffiti. Leduc rocks. Leduc is the best."

"What I like about my community is the size. I like how small it is and how you can know people almost everywhere you go. I also enjoy it because my parents can feel safe about letting me and my friends go places. I hope Leduc doesn't get too much bigger because I love the size of it. I also like the outdoor pool because I can go there and spend lots of time outside doing something I enjoy. I also like everything Leduc has to offer and all the fun stuff they let people have access to."

"We are called trailer trash but that isn't true. Everyone I live around is nice and kind to each other. What I like about my community is when I first moved there neighbors invited us over for dinner and I immediately made friends. One problem is our park, though. It is old and falling apart. Other than that it is pretty peaceful."

revitalizing democracy through what we might call "listening seasons": a time
to reflect, celebrate and give thanks for our true wealth through engagement
with each other. I caught a glimpse of a more civil society in which each citizen, each child and each elder has a voice that is respected and heard.

I found in Leduc a great sense of belonging to community, of trust in
one's neighbors and the importance of family. I got a sense of the importance
of relationships and the joy of being a small, cohesive community. Yet, I also
found a community caught up in the economic storm of Alberta's booming
oil economy. I found many adults caught up in whirlwind of capitalism, making money and satisfying an almost insatiable hunger for the services Leduc's
many businesses provide to Alberta's oil-based economy. The Genuine Wealth
survey revealed that in spite of high incomes and high GDP, most longed to
slow down and enjoy more quality time with their families, proving that
time is our most precious asset.

I also learned the limitations of measurement. I learned that too often so-
called objective measures of well-being pale in comparison to personal stories
and subjective impressions of well-being. The project demonstrated the challenges we face, trying to measure the joy that comes from engaging in meaningful conversation. People want to develop new and sustainable economies
focused on well-being, quality of life and happiness as ultimate ends. There is
a genuine hunger for these changes. We have the data, the tools and skills.
Now we only need the will to act.

The wisdom and genuine wealth of the Inuit of Nunavut

In the late summer of 2002 I was invited to Iqaluit, Nunvaut in Canada's
Eastern Arctic by Derek Rasmussen, a policy advisor to the Inuit and to the
Nunavut Tunngavik Inc. (NTI), to help develop the 2002–2003 *Annual Re-
port on the State of Inuit Culture and Society*.[5] This report would be based on Inuit
values and not simply monetary or economic measures of progress like the
GDP. Rasmussen had read my Alberta GPI work and felt that I was the right
person to develop a more genuine well-being assessment for Nunavut. One of
NTI's responsibilities is to prepare and submit, in accordance with Article 32
of the Nunavut Land Claims Agreement, an annual report on the state of the
Inuit culture and society in the Nunavut Settlement Area to the Leader of
the Territorial Government for tabling in the Nunavut Legislative Assembly,
as well as to the Minister of Indian Affairs and Northern Development for
tabling in the Canadian House of Commons.

I journeyed from Edmonton across Canada's vast northern landscapes with David Pollack, former executive director of the Pembina Institute. During my six day visit to Nunavut, I worked closely with the Social and Cultural Development Department of NTI to develop a new framework for measuring the state of Inuit well-being and culture in accordance with Inuit values. My brief encounter with the Inuit and the dramatic landscape of Baffin Island confirmed my intuition that any Genuine Wealth model must be founded on values expressed by the people: elders, children and other adults. Meeting with Inuit elders in Iqaluit, the capital of Nunavut, and in the tiny coastal fishing village of Kimmirut on the edge of Baffin Island, provided a glimpse of the wisdom of this ancient culture. We listened to the stories of the elders to gain an appreciation of the core values and the wisdom that have allowed these people to flourish in the harsh climate of the far north. The Inuit sense of relationship to their place, Nunavut (meaning "our land"), is profound; literally every natural feature (every hill, valley, lake or stream) has a unique name based on its location and importance. What did I have to offer this ancient people whose entire experience of well-being was experiential, not scientific or focused on measurement?

I proposed a unique set of Inuit Genuine Well-being Indicators to paint a portrait of well-being that would resonate with core Inuit values, life principles and goals. This framework would answer the following questions regarding well-being in Nunavut:

- What makes life worthwhile for the Inuit in Nunavut today? What is the core set of quality of life values for Inuit?
- What meaningful indicators of quality of life would provide a portrait of well-being (economic, social, environmental) in accordance with these values?
- What would these indicators reveal about the current and historical conditions of well-being and quality of life? What and how has the quality of life changed? What are the key drivers of this change?
- Is Nunavut on a sustainable course or are there threats to well-being that need attention? How should the Inuit respond to these changes?

The document we drafted was the first of its kind in Canada to report on quality of life indicators that actually align with the unique cultural values, dreams and goals of an indigenous or First Nations people. This report provides full accounting of the unique human, social, natural and produced capital of Nunavut that could ensure that governance and decision making are oriented towards sustainable stewardship of all assets, founded on a principle of sufficiency versus conventional western economic growth paradigms.

For example, the Inuit might measure quality of life by the degree of sharing of country food, snowmobiles or other household assets, or by the feeling of joy for one's family. Instead of celebrating individualism as is the norm in southern cultures, the Inuit measure the strength of society in terms of sharing meals together or the lack of physical barriers like fences. The Genuine Wealth of these communities is defined according to the conditions of well-being of the family as well as the strength of relationships of family members, of interrelationships between families in communities and the relationship to the land. It is the mental, physical and psychological capacities of individuals, families and communities to flourish in the face of environmental and external cultural challenges that have made the Inuit way of living sustainable.

Inuit Elders whom we consulted during this process described core and unique elements that define and contribute to their community social capital and quality of life including:

1. Inuit Qaujimanituqangit (IQ) values and governance
2. Illinniarniq Avatimik (University of the Land): the quality of knowledge transferred by IQ versus reliance on academic credentials
3. Incidence of sharing (cooperative usage of food, assets, and equipment)
4. Local abundance and high levels of reliance on local food sources, harvested collectively
5. Multi-generational proximity
6. Non-monetized recreation and entertainment (hobbies, dancing, singing)
7. Outdoor skills and capacity to flourish in nature
8. Number, range and diversity of Inuktitut skills (mechanical, navigation, safety, hunting, midwifery) and social competencies

In consultation with elders, young Inuit philosophers Joelie Sanguya and Jaypeetee Arnakak identified six core Inuit guiding principles they call Inuit Qaujimanituqangit (IQ).[6] These principles represent fundamental values or operating principles of Inuit society.

Pijitsirniq — The principle of being of service or being useful to others
This value, one of the fundamental expectations in Inuit culture, was taught

to Inuit children in the traditional setting from an early age. To be considered mature, complete and well-formed an Inuk has to be useful to family and community. In today's society, those that profess to be leaders — those that create and administer policy and programs — must demonstrate and practice pijitsirniq, the concept of service, to the communities to be taken seriously.

Aajiiqatigiingniq — The principle of dialogue or communication
This quality is needed to coordinate tasks and finite resources so that they will be used well and in the best interest of the group. A person should seek advice, consensus and understanding by engaging him/herself with the rest of the group, either individually or as a group. That person may have a tentatively set agenda in the beginning, but it changes and improves through meaningful dialogue with others.

Pilimaksarniq — The principle of learning by doing or the process of acquiring skills and knowledge
Pilimaksarniq allows Inuit parents to pass on culture, knowledge and skills to their children. The main features of this principle are: a) learning by

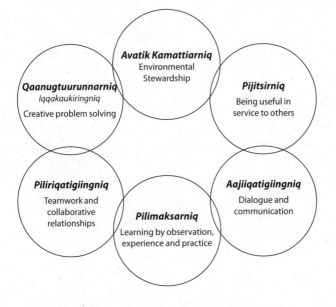

FIGURE 7.4. Inuit Quajimanituqangit Values and Principles
Credit: Nunavut Tunngavik Inc. *2002–2003 Report on the State of Inuit Culture and Society*

observation; b) learning knowledge and skills from experience, experimentation and innovation; c) practicing to perfect a skill, and actually doing the craft.

Piliriqatigiingniq — The principle of teamwork or collaborative relationships
This principle is foundational for the Inuit culture, where communal values are emphasized.

Qaanuqtuurunnarniq or Iqqakaukiringniq — The principle of adaptation and problem solving
One uses any and all resources available in any situation. This term can apply in an emergency situation that calls for immediate action, or in seeking a well-thought-out solution to a problem. When a snowmobile breaks down in the middle of nowhere, one has to be able to fix it with whatever tools and equipment one has; giving up is not an option. Or, one may also qanuqtuuq by seeking to improve or innovate a tool or way of thinking by reflection and contemplation.

Avatik Kamattiarniq — The principle of environmental stewardship
The Inuit mind sees human beings as part of the physical environment; as such, people are subject to its dynamics. Inuit do not believe in the Western notion of ownership of land. Since the environment "owns" us; we cannot "own" it.

Basic life competencies
In Inuit culture, an individual or a society are considered fully formed when they are endowed with a full set of core competencies or skills. A group or individual has integrity, health and wealth when they have the knowledge or skills to practice these core competencies fluently.

Social competencies
In addition to individual core competencies, there are also social skills or competencies critical for a healthy community and cohesive society which were mentioned in Chapter 6.

Inuit Genuine Well-being Indicators (IGWI)
The IGWI is more than a system of performance measures; the IGWI is a

framework for aligning Inuit well-being indicators with a core set of Inuit values commonly shared by the community. The IGWI is also a system for accounting for the capacity of the community to achieve well-being (individual skills and social competencies). The IGWI provides one of the first genuine quality of life reporting systems of its kind in Canada, describing the well-being of Inuit culture and society in accordance with Inuit values, core life and social competencies along four well-being themes: community, individual, economic and nature. NTI along with the Nunvaut Bureau of Statistics and Statistics Canada have begun developing a set of community well-being indicators using the IGWI framework; this work is still in process.

Santa Monica: A sustainable city in the making

In the spring of 2004 Dean Kubani, Environmental Programs Division Manager for the City of Santa Monica, asked me to help develop an integrated sustainability measurement and reporting system to evaluate Santa Monica's Sustainable City Program. Using the Genuine Wealth Accounting model,

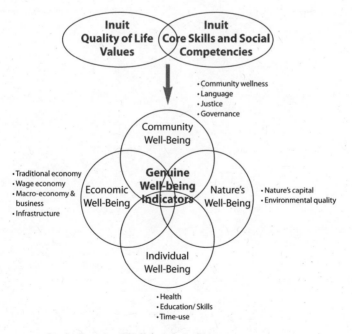

FIGURE 7.5. Inuit Genuine Well-being Indicators

Credit: Nunavut Tunngavik Inc. 2002–2003 *Report on the State of Inuit Culture and Society.*

we created the Santa Monica Sustainability Indicators Reporting System and the Sustainable City Progress Report.[7] I aligned the eight goal areas from the city's Sustainable City Plan into relationship with the five capital accounts of the Genuine Wealth model as follows:

1. Resource Conservation (natural capital)
2. Environmental and Public Health (natural and human capital)
3. Transportation (built capital)
4. Economic Development (financial capital)
5. Open Space and Land Use (natural capital)
6. Housing (built capital)
7. Community Education and Civic Participation (social capital)
8. Human Dignity (human and social capital)

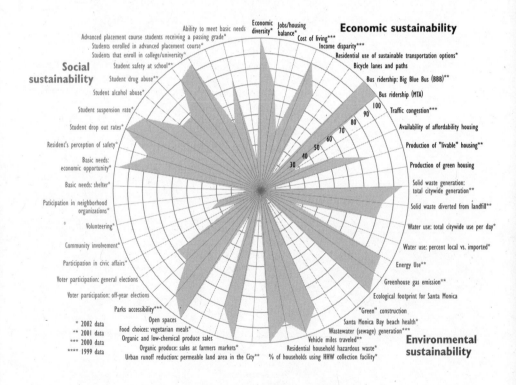

FIGURE 7.6. Santa Monica Sustainability Index for 2003

Credit: Mark Anielski, Anielski Management Inc. Santa Monica's Sustainability Reporting System. April 22, 2004.

For each goal specific sustainability indicators were developed. Two types of indicators were used: 1) system level indicators measuring states, conditions or pressures on a community-wide basis for each respective goal area, and 2) program level indicators measuring the performance or effectiveness of specific programs, policies or actions

The Santa Monica Sustainability Index in the shape of a flower or spider graph shows the conditions of all 66 sustainability indicators, an integrated diagnosis of economic (blue text), environmental (green text) and social (red text) conditions from a 360-degree perspective. An indicator which scores 100 points (a point on the outermost edge of the diagram) suggests an optimum condition of either well-being or sustainability. An indicator scoring less than 100 points (i.e. closer to the center of the circle) suggests an area of weakness requiring investment of resources to improve well-being or performance. The image also reveals the relationships between various economic, environmental and social indicators illustrating clearly how some assets may be robust while others are lagging. This unique sustainability portrait allows decision makers, citizens and media to quickly identify where a community is flourishing and where more work is required. If each sustainability indicator were assigned a performance target, anyone could tell how close or far the community was from a desired sustainable future.

In addition to the Sustainability Index, I developed a comprehensive spreadsheet that contained all of the data for each of the 66 sustainability indicators. A summary table, the *Santa Monica Sustainability Indicators Performance Report,* provided a more detailed report card summary of the state of Santa Monica's sustainability indicators. Composite triple-bottom-line indices for economic, environmental and social sustainability were created by clustering indicators according to these three themes. Finally, a composite Santa Monica Sustainability Index (similar to Dow Jones Industrial Average or the consumer price index) was generated by adding up all 66 indicator scores, giving them equal weighting (in the absence of priorities or value weights) and deriving a composite index. Santa Monica's Sustainability Index for 2003 scored 64.9 points out of a possible 100 maximum points.

Santa Monica is using this system now to report the progress of their sustainability plans. With regular reporting and goal setting, Santa Monica's sustainability measurement system will improve over time. Regular consultation with citizens will ensure that indicators are meaningful and relevant to the lives and values of all who call Santa Monica home.

132   THE ECONOMICS OF HAPPINESS

China's *xiaokang* society: An economy of moderation

Since November 2004, I have been traveling to China along with colleagues
Peter Bartelmus (one of the fathers of green accounting at the United Nations)
and Laszlo Pinter (a sustainability measurement expert with the International
Institute for Sustainable Development based in Winnipeg). We are providing
strategic economic council to the Chinese Academy of Social Sciences regarding China's efforts to adopt green GDP accounting and develop new indicators of progress towards the goal of a harmonious *xiaokang* society.

In his October 12, 2006 address to the Communist Party of China,
China's president Hu Jintao advocated the doctrine and construction of a "so-
cialist harmonious society" — specifically a *xiaokang* or "moderately well-off"
society. A harmonious society, in essence, is one that respects the rights of people and abides by the principles of human civilization and the laws of nature.
Guided by the science-based view of development, the whole country — from
the top authorities on down — intends to build such a harmonious society.

Why would China, which represents 4% of the world's GDP and has
boasted annual GDP growth of over 8% per annum for the past 25 years, intentionally adopt a society of moderation? The reasons are varied and complex. China's torrid economic growth has been driven by a voracious appetite
for natural capital; China is consuming 30% of the world's steel production,
40% of the world's cement production, is now the second largest consumer
of oil after the US, and contributes 31% to the world's SO_2 emissions. This
economic growth is coming at a growing ecological and social cost. Chinese
officials are increasingly concerned about the negative impacts of their consumption of natural resources on air quality, water quality and general environmental integrity, but also on China's social cohesion. This latter issue is
perhaps the most important motivation for a doctrine of harmonious society.
A growing gap between rich and poor and particularly between rural and
urban incomes is fraying China's social fabric, and the country is losing societal harmony.

A harmonious *xiaokang* society does not simply mean achieving a certain
level of GDP per capita. It means that human well-being will be fairly distributed across China, alleviating the current disparities between rural and urban
households and between coastal and inland households. A harmonious *xiaokang* society not only denotes material comforts but harmonious development
in all aspects, including urbanization, promotion of education and reshaping
the social strata. It is a key condition that human and economic development

does not undermine China's natural resource base and ecosystems; without these, the sustainability of human well-being itself will deteriorate. In other words, a *xiaokang* society will improve and sustain economic, social and environmental well-being of all citizens and the country as a whole. Balance between these three domains and moderate balance between material and immaterial aspects of well-being characterize a harmonious *xiaokang* society.

Is this Asian economic giant, an emerging rival to global US hegemony, embarking a path founded on principles of moderation and harmony with nature? Can China make a radical shift from materialism and the growth-maximization mantra of capitalism? China is now engaged in one of the most important economic experiments on the planet: seeking to balance and integrate economic development with environmental stewardship and maintain social cohesion. The experiment includes exploring green GDP accounting by measuring the environmental costs of economic growth. Preliminary estimates of a green GDP for China suggest that roughly 15% of China's GDP is tied to environmental damage. We propose developing a comprehensive suite of progress indicators (balancing the economic, environmental and social attributes of progress) that will be used to measure, evaluate and reward the performance of local municipal governments in China.

If China is genuinely committed to this new path of so-called harmonious development, green GDP accounting, and developing new measures of well-being and progress, this would represent a seismic shift in neoclassical economic development philosophy dominated by British-American capitalism. Indeed, I felt this irony most poignantly at a meeting in August of 2005 held at Chengde, the former 18th century (Qing Dynasty) imperial summer villa and mountain resort area just northeast of Beijing, which Emperor Qianlong built. It was at Chengde in 1793 that the Emperor Qianlong rebuffed the British emissary Lord Macartney from the British East India Company in his attempts to open trade with China. Qianlong dismissed the emissary, saying that China possessed all things and had no need for foreign goods or trade. This rebuff eventually led to the British engaging the Chinese in trade wars. It was at Chengde that I had the good fortune of introducing my Chinese colleagues to alternative measures of progress, the GPI and Genuine Wealth accounting. These new models seemed to resonate with my Chinese hosts. I would later be asked to contribute a chapter in a book written for President Hu Jintao on how the GPI and the Genuine Wealth model could be adopted in China.

Harmonious *xiaokang* society, like Western notions of sustainable development, requires economic development that meets the needs of the present without compromising the ability of future generations to meet their own needs. Yet, while many Western nations talk about how to incorporate the principles of sustainable development into national policies, most nations continue operating on a model of continuous economic (GDP) growth and increasing materialism. China has an opportunity to pioneer a new model of economic development. In this model, sufficiency of basic life needs for all Chinese citizens — not the mere accumulation of material possessions — is the fundamental objective.

President Hu Jintao, in his speech to the November 2004 APEC conference in Santiago, Chile, challenged the world to work together on what he called a "win-win cooperation and sustainable development."

> We should optimize the economic structure, change the way of achieving economic growth, pay closer attention to the conservation and comprehensive utilization of resources, advocate an environment-friendly way of production, life and consumption and bring about a virtuous cycle in both our ecological and socio-economic systems. We should put in place a conservation-oriented management system throughout the process of exploitation, processing, distribution and consumption of resources with a view to building a resource effective national economy and a resource effective society. A well-protected eco-system underpins the growing productive forces and better lives for the people. On the one hand, we must respect laws of nature and plan our economic and social development according to how much nature could sustain. On the other hand, we should actively go for protecting the natural environment, minimizing pollutant discharge, increasing wastes recycling, accelerating pollution control and ecological rehabilitation, preserving bio-diversity and resolutely stopping all practices that are detrimental to nature.

Emilia Romagna: An economy of cooperation

Can we find active honoring of genuine wealth and the good life in today's world? In October 2003, my wife and I journeyed to the northern Italian region of Emilia Romagna to celebrate our tenth wedding anniversary. Emilia Romagna is renowned for its food, vibrant culture and quality of life. Emilia

Romagna is the heart of Italy's fertile bread basket, a region blessed with fertile soils and the life-giving Po River. It is home to Italy's finest cuisine, made from local products including Parmigiano Reggiano (Parmesan) cheese from Parma, prosciutto ham, Modena's famed balsamic vinegar, Lambrusco (a frizzante red wine) and Nocino, a sumptuous walnut liquor made by the people of the little castle-village of Castell'Arquato. The region also produces some of the finest ceramics in all of Europe and is the birthplace of Verdi and Pavarotti. Bologna, the regional capital, is located one hour north of Florence and two hours southwest of Venice. In Emilia Romagna genuine wealth is revealed in the people's love food and the land, a strong sense of community and reciprocal business relationships. Whether it is the first cappuccino in the morning, the two-hour sumptuous lunches at a Bologna bistro or a three-hour dinner in an ancient castle-village, these Italians know how to pause and celebrate life, food and relationships.

The so-called "Slow Food" movement is best experienced in Emilia Romagna. The snail is a fitting symbol of the Slow Food movement, which espouses the philosophy that slowness is an essential virtue for enjoying life. This is slowness in terms of prudence, moderation and solemnity — not sloth. The Slow Food movement calls us to celebrate rest through food, to listen to the rhythm of our own lives and possibly adjust it; to go slowly, to take your time, have a break and find a friend who can provide food and hospitality. This is what I experienced and witnessed each day of our visit to Emilia Romagna.

The people of Emilia Romagna are hard working. Typically, the work day begins at 8 or 9 A.M. and lasts until noon. Then they break for a long meal (sometimes two hours) followed by a siesta: a time to rest and re-create oneself. Restaurants and bistros are filled with lively, long debate and discourse over the pasta from finest local ingredients and fine local wines. Then there is time for a leisurely walk or a rest before returning to work around 3:00 P.M. The sharing of food and wine with friends and colleagues helps renew relationships and to invest time in individual and community genuine wealth. Most stores close from around 1:00 P.M. until about 3:00 P.M. when they reopen for another three or four hours of commerce. In the evenings, time is spent with family and friends, perhaps over fine local food that was purchased at one of the many delis located in the heart of Bologna. Later in the evening, the downtown piazza (town square) is filled with people of all ages. Even on a cold October evening, my wife and I were warmed by chestnuts roasted by a local vendor and by scenes of joy in the piazza.

Emilia Romagna is economically prosperous, with the highest GDP per capita in Europe. It is a world-renowned model of a cooperative economy. The cooperative economic model and philosophy of Emilia Romagna uniquely balances the principles of competition (efficiency), equity (fair distribution) and solidarity or cooperation (sharing and reciprocity). The success of this cooperative economy is its entrepreneurial nature (there is one enterprise for every ten citizens) and cooperative business culture (there are over 15,000 businesses enterprises that are networked through cooperative business associations producing everything from cheese, balsamic vinegar and wine to ceramics).

Professor Stefano Zamagni, former dean of economics at Europe's oldest university, the University of Bologna (established in 1087), is one of the key architects of the Emilia Romagna's cooperative economic model. During our visit to Bologna, my wife and I enjoyed an evening at Stefano's and his economic historian wife Vera's modern condominium. Both Zamagnis said that Emilia Romagna has achieved unparallelled quality of life because all citizens share responsibility for a balanced economy that encourages entrepreneurship and efficiency while recognizing the inherent strength of cooperation in matters of both commerce and social welfare. In other words, *true competition means cooperation.* Indeed, cooperation is evident wherever you turn in Emilia Romagna; there is strong sense of belonging, of shared stewardship of the land, of trust, of joy, a zest for life and ultimately happiness.

How should we measure this social capital and the attributes of cooperative economy? I posed this question to Emilia Romagna's Finance Minister, Flavio Del Bono. He said "we are not explicitly measuring social capital in Emilia Romagna" and instead encouraged me to "see and experience Emilia Romagna for yourself; the food, wine and our hospitality." Indeed, we did without measure. Living in this region for even a brief time was all the evidence I needed to be convinced that Emilia Romagna is a modern economy of well-being, a society dedicated to working hard to build genuine wealth in a business climate of cooperation. An economist schooled in the doctrine of economic efficiency, productivity and growth, I was shown a vibrant, local and living economy of well-being concerned more with stewardship, reciprocity, redistribution, equity, public welfare, strong relationships, social entrepreneurship and cooperative enterprise than the maximization of GDP, profits and competitiveness. It was a tangible sign of hope for that we can build economies of well-being and happiness.

Bhutan's Gross National Happiness

Imagine an economy of happiness or an economy of love. What might the values, virtues and policies of such an economy look like? What if a society were founded on altruistic economics, taking account of all factors of well-being, including a genuine "declaration of happiness"?

The kingdom of Bhutan, situated in the Himalayan mountains bordered by India, Tibet and China, is a nation of a mere 672,425 people,[9] with GDP per capita of $US3,921 in 2005 (ranked 117th in the world).[10] By conventional economic measures Bhutan is a relatively poor, developing country with a resource-based economy that relies on forestry, animal husbandry, subsistence agriculture and now increasingly hydroelectricity, cash crops and tourism. Yet Bhutan is far beyond "developed" countries as its physical environment is beautiful. It is also closer to being sustainable than nearly any other country. Comparing Bhutan to the US, Frank Dixon, Managing Director of Innovest Strategic Value Advisors (New York) observed "whereas our (the US) environment is polluted and unsustainable, our culture is based on materialism, indicating many in the US are unhappy"[11] Bhutan has the highest species density in the world, the highest fraction of land in protected areas and the highest proportion of forest cover of any Asian country.

Bhutan has adopted an official policy (passed by parliament) of Gross National Happiness (GNH) whereby the pursuit of happiness takes precedence over economic prosperity and gross national product (GNP). This isolated Tibetan Buddhist nation, led by its young king King Jigme Singye Wangchuck, is the only country in the world to measure well-being by Gross National Happiness instead of GNP. The concept of GNH was introduced by the leaders of Bhutan as a means of placing Buddhist spiritual principles at the heart of economic life. GNH measures and manages what matters most in people's lives: quality of life, happiness of people and good stewardship of the earth. Furthermore, GNH is intended to not only measure what matters but to encourage discussions about how altruism, spiritual and moral beliefs can be integrated into current economics. In essence, GNH focuses public and policy debate on well-being and the pursuit of happiness rather than the mere acquisition of material things, consumption and production.

At its heart GNH is based on Buddhist philosophy. In Buddhism, happiness is not determined by what we have and own but rather by the qualities of being. Being means being fully human and alive to our individual and shared knowledge, our living skills and our imagination. Compassion and cooperation are as important to achieving happiness as competition. The fourteenth Dalai Lama, Tenzin Gyatso, supports Bhutan's movement for happiness and the GNH. In a letter of support to an international conference in Bhutan on Gross National Happiness, he wrote:

> As a Buddhist, I believe the purpose of our lives is to overcome suffering and cultivate happiness. But by happiness, I do not only mean the temporary pleasure that is derived from material comfort alone. I am thinking more of the enduring happiness that results from the thorough transformation and development of the mind that can be achieved though the cultivation of such qualities as compassion, patience and wisdom. At the same time, on national and global levels we need an economic system that enables such a pursuit of true happiness. The purpose of economic development should be to contribute to rather than obstruct this goal.[12]

Sander Tideman, a Dutch banker, economist and Chairman of the Spirit in Business Network, points out that the GNH makes the qualitative distinctions that are lost in measuring progress quantitatively: "Economic calculations ignore the value of things such as fresh water, green forests, clean air, traditional ways of life" he says, merely because they cannot be easily quantified. Economics has limited itself to measuring only things which can be measured monetarily; this is economics' weakness as well as its empirical strength. Tideman notes that Gross International Happiness could be the next level of evolution in our economic thinking. Tideman says that "everyone wants to be happy. It's a common aspiration of humanity. What if happiness was really possible? In Himalayan cultures, the whole society's economy was meant to serve the quest for happiness. There's a need for a new movement that talks the language of economists and tries to expand their horizons. Since the Enlightenment we stopped seeing the divine in everything, and the West created economic models that say that if we have enough material goods we will be happy. Now that is completely invalidated." He argues that western culture has narrowly defined well-being and the objective of life in purely material terms and that we need a model that embraces the totality of life including, emotions, feelings, water, earth, sunshine, all those softer values that don't show up in current economic and business models. "Once you do that you can create true value. That's the way forward" says Tideman.[13]

This unorthodox approach to measuring progress is a serious attempt to question the values of capitalism and neoclassical economics and shift towards a more balanced, harmonious and altruistic economics. What Sander Tideman suggests is that initiatives like Bhutan's GNH "point us to the need to base development on spiritual values, transmitted through culture, rather than merely material values." Tideman supports distinguishing between means and ends and between needs and wants for the good life. Material development and the accumulation of money should only ever be seen as a means for people to devote themselves to spiritual development. In this kind of Buddhist economics, accounting for material factors should be relative to the amount of time they allow people to develop their minds and inner spiritual selves. The Dalai Lama endorses Tideman's opinions, noting: "I have discovered in my travels around the world that people in wealthy countries are often not nearly as happy as I had expected them to be, considering their material affluence. Seeing deep poverty side by side with conspicuous consumption in both wealthy and poor countries also indicates that all is not well."[14]

Ronald Colman, founder and executive director of GPI Atlantic based in Halifax, serves as an international advisor to Bhutan and hosted the second international conference on Gross National Happiness in June 2005 in Antigonish, Nova Scotia. Colman says that the GNH is not simply a fairy tale or utopian dream, but a real development strategy. Colman notes that "the Bhutanese use of the term 'happiness' is quite different than the way we generally use it in the west (often to equate it with 'pleasure')."[15]

GNH, which is meant to guide governance and policy and decision making, is based on four pillars:

1. Sustainable and socio-economic development or economic self reliance
2. Preservation and promotion of cultural heritage
3. Preservation and sustainable use of the environment
4. Good governance

These are further articulated by specific policy objectives and targets, both medium-term, five-year plans (2002–07) and long-term plans (2020). The long-term objectives articulated in a document titled *Bhutan 2020: A Vision for Peace, Prosperity and Happiness*[16] include:

• Providing electricity to 50% of the rural population by 2012
• Achieving a three-fold increase in real income of farmers by 2012

- 100% rural electrification by 2020
- Ensuring that 75% of the rural population live within half a day's walk from the nearest road
- Maintaining 60% of Bhutan's land area under forest coverage in perpetuity

These objectives are supported by a Declaration on Gross National Happiness which was adopted at the first international GNH seminar February 2004 in Thimphu, Bhutan.

How does Bhutan intend to measure the GNH? According to the Prime Minister of Bhutan, Lyonpo Jigmi Y.Thinley, "We have not been overly concerned with this. No serious attempts have been made to determine the nature or elements of what constitutes individual or gross national happiness. We have also not developed qualitative or quantitative indicators. Until very recent times Bhutanese were not inclined to mention GNH outside the country. It was a staple for us alone. One could not help suspect that foreign experts found it to be a utopian idea, not to be taken seriously. However, in 1998 the UNDP [United Nations Development Program], which devised the Human Development Index, invited Bhutan to speak on GNH at its Asia-Pacific Millennium Summit in Seoul. Though the subject was presented there with some trepidation, the response gave us reasons to be less coy about the way we are undertaking our development."[17]

The thorny task of quantifying the unquantifiable aspects of happiness, life and wealth remains. I don't believe that solutions lie using monetized metrics but rather in the Genuine Wealth approach where, for example, self-rated happiness combined with non-monetary indicators based on the determinants of well-being are sufficient. Altruistic economics, with an important spiritual dimension, may be possible, but presently Gross National Happiness remains an ideal, not a quantifiable economic system. Yet, Bhutan's leadership demonstrates the possibility of developing and implementing a new economic system based on happiness and well-being.

A vision of an economy of Genuine Wealth for Canada

In the spring of 2003, I was invited along with other Canadian visionaries including Elizabeth May to Vancouver by David Suzuki and his Foundation to contribute to a new vision and road map for a sustainable Canada. Drafted by environmental lawyer David Boyd, the blueprint released in the spring of

2004 was called *Sustainability Within A Generation: A New Vision for Canada.*[18] The document, which was presented to Prime Minister Paul Martin, proposed that by 2030 Canada would be a world leader in sustainable living and environmental protection. The report proposed two bold new priorities for Canada: (1) that Canada should set a goal of achieving sustainability within a generation (i.e. 20–25 years) and (2) that Canadians should focus national efforts on generating genuine wealth, rather than measuring progress by the narrow and inherently flawed yardstick of economic growth. The concept of Genuine Wealth as a practical tool captured the imagination of the David Suzuki Foundation. The report noted that Genuine Wealth encompasses the five key capital assets. Genuine Wealth "embraces the full range of qualities that make life worth living — things like vibrant communities, meaningful work, good housing, high quality education and health care, functional infrastructure, outstanding recreational opportunities, clean air, clean water, healthy relationships with others, and dynamic economic prospects."

The two national priorities of setting goals for sustainability and generating Genuine Wealth go hand in hand. The report notes: "Our quality of life is fundamentally dependent upon the environment. Clean water, fresh air, a stable climate, and ecological processes such as pollination and soil regeneration are prerequisites to healthy communities and a vibrant economy. At the same time, it is only by broadening our societal objectives from the narrow goal of economic growth toward the more comprehensive concept of genuine wealth that we will achieve sustainability. Although governments use changes in Gross Domestic Product (GDP) as a surrogate for progress, Canadians want much more from life than economic growth. A recent study of Canadians in 40 communities revealed that economic development ranked eighth among the nine most important quality of life issues, with the environment ranked fourth after democratic rights and freedoms, health, and education, respectively. By setting our sights on achieving sustainability and generating genuine wealth, we are much more likely to improve our overall quality of life."

This vision for a sustainable Canada identifies nine critical challenges and establishes a practical game plan, including strategies, targets and timelines for achieving the vision of sustainability for Canada by 2030. These nine critical challenges are:

1. Generating Genuine Wealth: Supplementing the narrow goal of economic growth with the objective of genuine wealth

A Declaration by Participants in the Seminar on
GROSS NATIONAL HAPPINESS

We, participants, in the International Seminar on Operationalizing Gross National Happiness, held in Thimphu, Bhutan, from 18th to 20th of February 2004, and attended by some 400 individuals, including senior professors, research fellows, journalists, lawyers, medical professionals, religious leaders, managers, environmentalists, economists, social activists, financiers, civil servants and students from around the world, after intense deliberations, wish to declare:

I. Our deep appreciation to His Majesty, Jigme Singye Wangchuck, the King of Bhutan, and to the Government of Bhutan, for having adopted over the past two decades the enlightened strategy of Gross National Happiness as the cornerstone of Bhutan's national development policy, articulated in His Majesty's statement, "Gross National Happiness is more important that Gross National Product."

II. Our great satisfaction with the quality of the seminar's written and oral presentations, which have provided a wealth of information and a number of valuable ideas concerning the strengthening and the operationalization of the concept of Gross National Happiness.

III. Our understanding that, notwithstanding the necessity of devoting further time to review all the diverse contributions of the seminar participants in order to synthesize them into a general expression of the opinions expressed at the seminar, some common threads and conclusions can be set forth as follows:

1. Happiness is and always has been a fundamental human quest and has been acknowledged as such in countries and cultures as diverse as the Bhutan and the United States of America.

2. Happiness may be understood as a state of physical and emotional well-being and inner contentment, founded on principles of sociality and of not harming other sentient beings or the environment.

3. Happiness thus should not be seen as a distant goal, provided by others; happiness is the path, in the here and now, which primarily depends on self-responsibility and self-fulfillment in sharing with others. Happiness is an immediate, proximate, goal that depends on the responsibility of both society and the individual and on the recognition that no individual can be completely happy in the presence of the unhappiness of others.

4. The materialism and competition that characterizes the dominant civilization in the world today have not been conducive to the pursuit of happiness,

and, in many respects, actually has led in the opposite direction. "Gross Domestic Product," the monetary value of national economic activity, which has become the theoretical and de facto measure of national economic and developmental policies, reflects this dominant paradigm. Therefore, we recognize the need for major reform to take into account other policy dimensions and objectives, such as social and environmental well-being, which the concept of Gross Domestic Product does not address; happiness is being sacrificed on the altar of statistical economic growth based on run-away consumerism.

5. The operationalization of Gross National Happiness (GNH) should fully take into account national, regional and local considerations. Likewise, it should to take into account the interactive and interrelated dimensions of the particular needs and views of diverse cultures, age groups, genders, occupations and families; which coming together in the context of the common human identity and the search for unity in diversity.

6. The operationalization of GNH should be facilitated by the development of indicators that address human physical and emotional well-being. They must be capable of use for self-evaluation, so that individuals and groups may gauge their progress in the attainment of happiness. In addition, indicators should facilitate full accountability, good governance, and socially constructive business practices, both in day-to-day life and in long-range policies and activities.

7. Further reflection and research on the discussions and proposals that emerged from the Seminar may contribute to policy development both on the social and governmental levels. In this regard, the Seminar welcomed the proposal of the Royal Government of Bhutan to the Seminar on Gross National Happiness on an annual basis in order to further explore the concerns and policy considerations expressed in this first Seminar. This may include meetings in various locations around the world, and the development of a variety of initiatives, including research, publications, experimental work with indicators, and policy proposals.

8. Finally, we pledge ourselves, as a matter of individual and collective human responsibility, to advocate actively and fully the goal of genuine happiness as the cornerstone of national policy everywhere in the world, to be fully socially engaged, and to advocate policies and measures that uphold the great objective of happiness for all.

Thimphu February 21st, 2004
LUNAR NEW YEAR[19]

2. Improving Efficiency: Increasing the efficiency of energy and resource use by a factor of four to ten times

3. Shifting to Clean Energy: Replacing fossil fuels with clean, low-impact, renewable sources of energy

4. Reducing Waste and Pollution: Moving from a linear "throw-away" economy to a cyclical "reduce, re-use, and recycle" economy

5. Protecting and Conserving Water: Recognizing and respecting the value of water in our laws, policies and actions

6. Producing Healthy Food: Ensuring Canadian food is healthy, and produced in ways that do not compromise our land, water or biodiversity

7. Conserving, Protecting and Restoring Canadian Nature: Taking effective steps to stop the decline of biodiversity and revive the health of ecosystems

8. Building Sustainable Cities: Avoiding urban sprawl in order to protect agricultural land and wild places, and improve our quality of life

9. Promoting Global Sustainability: Increasing Canada's contribution to sustainable development in poor countries

The vision established a clear set of targets and timelines for generating genuine wealth between 2004–2010. These include:

1. Canada makes a concerted effort to educate its citizens about the concept of Genuine Wealth

2. Canada creates a national Genuine Wealth Index that measures the annual change in the things that Canadians values most, i.e. "that which makes life worthwhile." Wherever possible, these indicators should be made relevant to different communities or regions

3. Canada enacts a law such as the proposed Canadian Well-being Measurement Act, and the federal government publishes quarterly and annual reports on changes in the Genuine Wealth Index that are sent to all Canadian households

4. Canada's Auditor General reviews the impacts of federal laws, policies and programs on Genuine Wealth Index indicators on a regular basis

5. The provinces, territories, and First Nations of Canada adopt the Genuine Wealth Index to measure changes in quality of life

6. Canada assists other countries in developing their own national and regional statistics based on the Genuine Wealth Index

While *Sustainability Within A Generation* generated some national attention, the vision and goals of this sustainability road map have not yet been adopted by any Canadian political party as part of its mandate or agenda.

Canadian Index of Well-being: Measuring what matters

The idea of a national Genuine Wealth Index or a national Genuine Progress Index has taken on new life through the Canadian Index of Well-being (CIW). The CIW, which has been sponsored by the Atkinson Foundation of Toronto (Joseph Atkinson was the publisher of the *Toronto Star* newspaper), is an effort by some of the world's experts in measures of sustainability, well-being and quality of life, including Ronald Colman (GPI Atlantic), myself, and many others with support from Statistics Canada and the Honourable Roy J. Romanow, to tell Canadians how we are doing as a country and to measure definitively what matters most to us.[20]

This new index will use powerful indicators that count and measure the extent to which we are realizing our values and goals as a society and whether we are leaving the world a better place for our children. The CIW national team is creating an integrated index composed of headline indicators from seven well-being domains:

1. Living Standards: Secure and meaningful employment, adequate income, low-income rates, gap between rich and poor, food security, and affordable housing

2. Time Allocation: Balance between paid work, unpaid work and free time, the capacity to make choices about the use of time and the stress of overload

3. Healthy Populations: Self-rated health, functional health, disability-adjusted life expectancy, infant mortality, low birth weight, mortality and morbidity due to circulatory diseases, cancers, respiratory diseases and diabetes, rates of depression and suicide, body-mass index, smoking and physical activity

4. Ecosystem Health: Good air and water quality, healthy forests, soils and marine environment, greenhouse gas emissions, waste diversion and environmental sustainability

5. Educated Populace: Literacy, numeracy and indicators of educational attainment and quality

6. Community Vitality: Safe communities, cohesion, equity, diversity,

identity, culture, arts and recreation and inclusion of all communities in our vision for a better world.

7. Civic Engagement: Including meaningful participation

How can we report to Canadians on such a broad subject as well-being in ways relevant and meaningful at the community level? This is one of CIW's many challenges. Nevertheless, we hope that CIW will help redefine progress and what it means to be prosperous so imaginatively that we capture Canadians' imagination and inspire discussions in the coffee shops, at the water coolers and the dinner tables of the nation.

Conclusion

These are a few examples of communities and nations redefining progress towards a more altruistic economics of sustainable well-being and happiness. There are undoubtedly hundreds of other similar initiatives that we could celebrate. In many parts of our world there are declarations, policies, models and tools which are beacons of hope, charting new courses for genuine progress.

Genuine Wealth for Business
and Organizations

A<small>N ENTERPRISE IS ANY BUSINESSES</small> or organization that, operating either for-profit or not-for-profit, takes on risky, daring and courageous ventures that involve confidence and initiative. How can enterprises that are committed to the principles of sustainability, corporate social and environmental responsibility use the Genuine Wealth model to build sustainable and vibrant enterprises and communities? Can corporations and other businesses account for their performance using the integrated five-capital asset Genuine Wealth accounting and reporting model? How would they begin to account for the full environmental and social costs of their actions? What is the role of business in an economy of well-being, and what is the future of the publicly traded corporation? Can businesses become genuinely competitive — that is cooperative, striving together like trees and other species in a forest ecosystem? These are subjects I discuss with MBA and business students each January to April in a course dedicated to business ethics, corporate social responsibility and social entrepreneurship at the University of Alberta.

Accounting has undergone important changes with new measurement innovations like the balanced score-card, triple-bottom-line measurement (financial, social and environmental) and the new Global Reporting Initiative sustainability accounting and reporting guidelines for the global business community. These are positive signs that the consciousness of business is shifting towards accepting greater responsibility for their impacts on society and the environment. The Genuine Wealth accounting model, with its holistic perspective, provides help accounting for these impacts.

The Genuine Wealth model measures and reports on the sustainability and financial, social and environmental performance of any enterprise in an economy. It can be applied to any of what John Pearce calls the three main systems that make up our economy:

1. Private Sector or private, profit oriented system: This is small, medium and large businesses and corporations (including multinational) whose primary objective is to maximize financial returns to individual owners called shareholders or investors. Here efficiency is the primary economic principle guiding the enterprise.

2. Social Economy or the self-help mutual social purpose system: This includes social enterprises, fair trade companies, co-ops and credit unions, non-profit organizations, volunteer associations and service associations, involving citizens taking action, collaborating to satisfy their needs and pursuing social goals that include caring for people and the environment. These values are given a higher priority than maximizing profits.

3. Public Service Sector which includes governments from the community or neighborhood (community league) level to local authorities, municipal governments, national and regional governments and global governments (e.g. United Nations): This sector provides public goods and services with the central economic goal of seeking greater equality and equitable distribution of wealth in society.[1]

What is the purpose of an enterprise or business?

Before applying the Genuine Wealth model to an enterprise, we need to ask fundamental questions: what is the purpose of the enterprise? What is it responsible for? To whom? What is its legal mandate: the fundamental reason for its existence both under law and for taxation purposes? How is the enterprise held to account for its actions and for the impacts (both positive and negative) on the economic, social and environmental well-being of society?

I have been discussing the purpose of business in society with Dan Rubenstein, a former senior auditor with the Auditor General's Office of Canada, for years. It's generally believed that business exists to make money, to maximize profits or create value for its shareholders. It could be said that a business takes risks in taking on new ventures, using resources from the community and nature to innovate, create and produce goods and services for the improvement or sustained well-being of society. I believe that in practice most businesses are simply trying to flourish, trying to become profitable while being conscious and possibly responsible for their actions in relation to the community and the environment. Dan claims that to this day that there is no agreed upon definition of the role of business. While we have many beliefs or even myths about the purpose of business, we have no definitive statements in law. Given this tautology, we can say that the role of a business (its responsibility to community) is whatever its owners, directors and shareholders define it to be. It could be said that a corporation is devoid of values or principles to guide its behavior; nothing explicitly exists against which we can hold its actions to account.

If we agree that in a market economy making a profit is the core purpose of a business, then how is profit defined in accounting terms? The term profit has never been adequately defined in the accounting world — even in Luca Pacioli's day. In the age of guilds and cooperatives, any residual or surplus left over after all expenses was paid out to the guild members. The residual was equitably distributed. In other words, there effectively was no surplus — what we now call a profit — because everything balanced out. But one of the first corporations, the British East India company created by Queen Elizabeth I, had a special charter to appropriate wealth (material possessions such as furs, natural resources, land) from other nations for the benefit of the British Crown. It was clear though not written in law that the profit (excess, plunder of resources) accrued to the benefit of a single shareholder, the Queen.

The word corporate comes from the Latin, *corporatus* meaning "united in one body." Corporation can refer to a church, a business or any kind of unit of many members with a common set of principles or with a common mission. Though distinct from a natural person, a corporation is a legal entity which often has similar rights in law to those of a person. Critics view this "corporate personhood" as a fundamental flaw in the nature of corporations. Joel Bakan, author of the book and movie *The Corporation*,[2] argues that the corporation is a legal entity (a person) required by law to make decisions and take actions that are solely in the interest of its shareholders. Most interpret this interest as maximization of profits or returns to shareholder equity. Bakan argues that the corporation's legally defined mandate is to pursue relentlessly and without exception its own economic self-interest regardless of harmful consequences on nature, people or community. He argues that if the corporation were psychologically analyzed for personality and mental disorders it would exhibit psychopathic characteristics: a) callous unconcern for the feelings of others; b) incapacity to maintain enduring relationships; c) reckless disregard for the safety of others; d) deceitfulness (repeated lying and conning others for profit); e) incapacity to experience guilt; f) failure to conform to social norms with respect to lawful behaviors.[3]

One of the captains of corporate America, Ray Anderson CEO of Interface the world's largest commercial carpet manufacturer based in Atlanta, has begun to regret the impacts of corporations on societal well-being. He concurs with Bakan's diagnosis of the corporate personality. Indeed, neither the private or publicly-traded corporations nor businesses in general are held to account by society or the law for the negative impacts of their actions. Anderson has adopted a new credo of corporate social responsibility; the new motto for Interface is "doing well by doing good." Anderson believes that one day corporations will be held accountable for regrettable impacts on the well-being of society and that CEOs like himself may one day find themselves in jail for plundering the natural wealth of the earth.[4]

The emerging movement called corporate social responsibility (CSR), which includes voluntary environmental, social and sustainability accounting and performance reporting by some progressive businesses, seems promising. But some, like Bakan and many of my business students, are suspicious that virtuous actions by corporations are motivated by economic self-interest to maintain profitability and market share without a genuine regard for the well-being of others. In other words, many see CSR as corporate yellow and green washing to mitigate potential loss of political and social capital with community and governments. Bakan argues that this new creed of corporate social responsibility is a self-conscious corrective to earlier greed-inspired visions of the corporation. Despite this new shirt, he argues, the corporation itself has not changed. It remains a legally designated person designed to valorize self-interest and invalidate moral concern. It remains to be seen if tinkering with corporate image and voluntary social and environmental reporting will be sufficient to redeem the soul of business without completely restructuring the very legal description and charters which give every business enterprise birth and license to operate in society.

The late economist Milton Friedman challenged the premise of CSR, arguing that a corporation is the property of its stockholders and that its interests are their interests. He asked whether a corporation can spend the stockholders' money for purposes which it regards as socially responsible, but which it cannot connect to its bottom line. The answer, he said unequivocally, is "no." The late business management guru Peter Drucker, in conversion with Joel Bakan, noted that executives who try to act morally by choosing social and environmental goals over profits are, in fact, immoral. Drucker said, without reservation, "If you find an executive who wants to take on social responsibilities, fire him. Fast!"[5]

The key premise is that a business's primary obligation is to ensure maximum profits for its shareholders, also known as maximizing shareholder value. But are corporation or a business *legally responsible* for maximizing profits or is this mythology? For example, the legal incorporation document for my own corporation (Anielski Management Inc.) includes not a single clause or phrase requiring our corporation to maximize profits to the corporations shareholders. I am not required to report such performance in the annual renewal of our corporate license with the Alberta or Canadian governments. As a director, I am only required to report any changes in the directors of the corporation and changes in the distribution of shares. The only other obligation is an annual filing of Anielski Management Inc.'s financial statements to Canadian Customs and Revenue Agency showing either a surplus (profit) or deficit, upon which our corporate taxes are assessed.

Bryan Redd is a Portland-based lawyer and CEO of Upstream 21, the first corporation in Oregon history which has explicitly written into its charter that its performance responsibilities extend to multiple stakeholders (employees, suppliers, the broader community and the environment). He notes "I would disagree that as a matter of law corporations are compelled to maximize shareholder value. I am not aware of a single legal case in all of the US states that elevates shareholders above the best interest of the company." 21."[6] Redd points out that while there are expectations that directors of corporations use their best business judgment in what is in the best interests of the corporation there are no clear legal statements which define "best interests." In other words, the very incorporation papers that give birth to the business enterprise are silent on any area of responsibility. Redd argues that the pressure to narrowly define the "best interests" of the corporation to mean looking only at shareholder entitlements or benefits came from Wall Street beginning in the 1970s, not from a compelling body of US case law. Redd believes it was Wall Street's short-term and somewhat irrational focus on quarterly performance results (earnings) which ultimately led investors, corporate managers and directors to exercise judgment only in short-term interests.

More importantly this Wall Street culture led to a new generation of investors who, unlike Warren Buffett, became speculators in a market which behaved like a casino. For investors like Buffett (Berkshire Hathaway) being a shareholder meant being a part owner of the corporation; one had the long-view and the hope that your company would flourish. Instead, both investors and corporations began to lurch from one quarterly earnings report to the next without a long-term view of the sustainability of the corporation or the market, in general. By contrast Bryan Redd has modeled Upstream 21 on Buffett's Berkshire Hathaway, focussing on long-term investment rather than short-term results. The Upstream 21 model also recognizes that accountability for performance extends to multiple constituents including shareholders, employees, suppliers, the community and stewardship responsibility for the environment. Upstream 21 thus sets an important precedent; it establishes a new corporate charter that clearly defines responsibilities extending to multiple stakeholders as well as imposing an accountability structure that considers the impacts of its business actions on all of its constituents.

If the legal charters which give businesses license to operate provide no clear direction on financial, social or environmental responsibility, then we are dealing with a serious void in accountability. But there is opportunity as well. We can literally write new corporate charters where accountability and responsibilities for the common wealth are clearly spelled out. What if citizens and households had a role in defining the purpose, roles and responsibilities for businesses and corporations (both private and publicly-traded) in their communities? What if a citizen panel could regularly scrutinize corporate charters to assess whether these enterprises were contributing to improved well-being conditions in their community? If an economy is defined as the science of the stewardship of households, their life conditions and the nature of their interrelationships, then a business could be defined in terms of how enterprise, innovation and entrepreneurship contribute to genuinely improved or sustained well-being conditions (the five capitals) of households and the community at large. If this were the definition of business, granting a legal license to operate in any community would depend on the ability of the business to demonstrate contributions to the five capitals of the community, improving well-being conditions of households and the environment. Fundamentally, businesses would be required to have integrity which means the "quality or state of being complete; unbroken; wholeness, unimpaired, perfect condition; soundness; morally principled; uprightness; honest and sincere."[7] Integrity is closely aligned with the original definition of the word wealth. This is my vision of the new world of business.

Applying the Genuine Wealth model to business

I have tested the Genuine Wealth model with two corporate clients and presented the model to several non-profit organizations including the United Way of northern Alberta. Many progressive companies and organizations are adopting the ideas and practices of corporate social responsibility and are being challenged with measuring performance and impacts beyond conventional financial indicators. This generally includes adopting new performance and measurement systems such as sustainability accounting (using the Global Reporting Initiative guidelines for sustainability reporting), triple-bottom-line accounting, social (community) accountability reports, and outcome-based performance measurement. Some of the business leaders who have developed such reports are Suncor Energy, BC Hydro, Vancity Savings Credit Union, Starbucks, Interface and Nike. I have had the pleasure of working on the integrated five-capital Genuine Wealth model with Suncor Energy and EPCOR. Suncor has adopted the GRI guidelines for sustainability reporting and is considered one of Canada's leading CSR and sustainability reporting corporations. Vancity is also a leader in CSR and social reporting.

When the Genuine Wealth model is applied to enterprises one views all five capital assets (human, social, natural, built (fixed) and financial) as a whole — complementary, ideally balanced or in harmony. For example, the human capital conditions of an enterprise are no more or less important than the relationship of the enterprise to nature (as a source of raw materials and as a sink for waste or pollution). Capital can be either tangible (monetary) or intangible (non-monetary) in nature. For example, a firm's employees are a form of non-monetary human capital, as is the goodwill a firm may have with a community. An enterprise which manages all of its capital or its total wealth in a manner that ensures their physical and qualitative conditions are sustained over time should, in theory, result in a vibrant and flourishing enterprise. The Genuine Wealth accounting model also encourages a full cost-benefit accounting of an enterprise's activities. This means measuring the human, social and environmental costs of creating products and providing services, but also measuring the returns on all five capitals of the enterprise. These returns are expressed generally in monetary terms but also count important factors like employee satisfaction with the workplace, community goodwill and trust.

For those enterprises that have already begun to adopt environmental and social accounting, sustainability reporting or triple-bottom-line reporting, the Genuine Wealth model may represent the next step towards a total wealth measurement and management system. To manage for sustainability requires that the physical, qualitative and monetary conditions of all five capital assets be taken into account in the daily operations of any organization.

Financial Assets
- Current financial assets: cash, accounts receivable, inventories
- Capital assets

Financial Liabilities
- Debt (short and long-term borrowings)
- Accounts payable

Shareholders' Equity
- Preferred securities
- Share capital
- Retained earnings

- People (employees, contractors, suppliers)
- Intellectual capital: educational attainment, knowledge, skills
- Employment rate
- Labor participation rates
- Full-time, permanaent job rate
- Benefits including workplace interventions
- Creativity and entrepreneurship
- Capabilities
- Motivation

- Productivity
- Happiness (self-rated)
- Time use balance (work, family, leisure, community)
- Health (disease, diet, overall health)
- Physical well-being (fitness)
- Mental well-being
- Spiritual well-being
- Addictions (drugs, alcohol, gambling)
- Workplace safety
- Training and professional development
- Personal self-development

Financial Capital   **Human Capital**

Built Capital   **Social Capital**

- Infrastructure: roads, pipelines, transmission lines, other structures
- Buildings
- Machinery and equipment
- Technology
- Patents
- Brands
- Intellectual property (ideas, innovations)
- Management processes
- Production processes
- Databases

Natural Capital

- Environmental goods and services
- Natural resources (stocks and flows): land, minerals, oil, gas, coal, forests (trees), fish and wildlife, water, air, carbon sinks
- Ecosystem integrity
- Energy (by type, source, and end-use)

- Customer relationships (value, loyalty and commitment by customers)
- Supplier relationships (value and commitment by suppliers)
- Reputation
- Workplace relational capital: employee interrelationships, workplace climate (e.g., stress, excitement, joy), social cohesion (teams and team spirit), workplace climate (happiness with work)
- Equity (incomes, age-sex distribution, women in management)
- Employee family quality of life
- Networks
- Friendships amongst workplace colleagues
- Membership in professional associations, clubs, and other organizations
- Social events with colleagues
- Family outings with workplace colleagues
- Financial investment/giving/donations to the community

FIGURE 8.1. Genuine Wealth Account Attributes for Business
Credit: Anielski Management Inc.

Such accounts inform directors, shareholders and communities about the effective rate of return to investment in all five capital assets and analyze the efficiency and effectiveness of total capital management. This includes evaluating the integrity or condition of capital for sustained flows of benefits as well as the annual depreciation or depletion rate of capital. Total capital management identifies risks to sustained economic, social and environmental viability that result from the depreciation costs, depletion or degradation of the five capital assets.

Just like a community well-being check-up, the Genuine Wealth model offers businesses a full check-up using progress or performance indicators drawn from the five capital accounts for the enterprise.

The Genuine Wealth model for business integrates all financial accounting, human resources, environmental performance and other corporate information into four domains.

Integrated five-capitals balance sheet

This balance sheet brings all of the enterprise's performance information together within a consolidated and integrated accounting system. Quantitative, qualitative and financial information for various ledgers or sub-accounts within the five capital accounts reveal the conditions of the five capital assets of the firm, using sustainability performance indicators. These accounts reveal both strengths (assets) and weaknesses (liabilities) of the enterprise which contribute towards a sustainable and flourishing business.

Full cost-benefit sustainable income statement

Full human, social and environmental costs of an enterprise's business, production or services are accounted for. This includes, for example, proxy estimates for the environmental costs of production such as the value of carbon emissions from production. This may also include a full accounting of contingent (unaccounted for or unfunded) environmental or societal/community liabilities. The result is a modified income statement, similar to the GPI, that attempts to reveal sustainability of the enterprise's performance expressed in monetary (full cost) terms.

Sustainable progress indicators

Sets of performance indicators serve as proxies for the conditions of the enterprise's five capital assets and the enterprise's performance in being a good steward of its capital assets. Raw performance data is converted into indexed data by normalizing the data set. The results create flower or spider graph images of the enterprise's overall performance. Figure 8.2 provides a hypothetical sustainability performance index or scorecard for an oil company showing the performance of a number of human, social, environmental and financial indicators. Performance is reported using indexed raw data and targets, budgets or benchmarks where a score of 100 implies performance is either on target or possibly ahead of target. This figure provides an integrated total performance portrait for the enterprise. The sustainability web shows the interrelationships of various performance indicators, ideally in line with the values and operating principles of the enterprise. It graphically illustrated the balancing act between financial profitability, healthy relationships with employees, customers, shareholders, other business partners and the environment in which the business operates. This portrait of performance is comprehensive and integrated.

The indicators can also be clustered according to each of the five capital accounts, to create either separate portraits or a composite index for each of the five capitals. This is done using the indexing system in the Genuine Wealth model converting raw data to a normalized data set based on benchmarking using either performance targets or historical data. Some enterprises may prefer a triple-bottom-line report where the indicators are clustered according to financial-economic, social (community) and environmental themes.

In addition to reporting sustainability indicators, the Genuine Wealth accounting system can also reveal how efficiently capital is managed or used. For example, by mixing and matching financial, social and environmental performance information, indicators of how efficiently total wealth is managed can emerge. Indicators might include: net revenues or total expenditures per employee, operating costs per unit of production, productivity or yield indicators for resource extraction (e.g. energy and water input per barrel of oil), energy and water intensity, carbon and ecological footprints, employee turnover rate and satisfaction and community investment as a percentage of earnings.

Genuine progress or sustainability report

The enterprise's progress during any fiscal operating period can be analyzed. This report summarizes how well the enterprise has managed all five capitals assets. Sustainability performance indicators, as proxies for returns or improvements to the total wealth of the enterprise, can be complemented with stories of successes or challenges the enterprise experienced. Finally, such a report includes full cost and benefit financial accounting in a unique income statement. This statement can, for example, show estimates of unfunded human, social and environmental liabilities and the depreciation costs of the five capital assets and estimate the true and full costs of running the enterprise, including things such as the value of environmental externalities like pollution or carbon emissions. The result is a comprehensive report on the sustainability of the enterprise, its contribution to society and ultimately to the common good.

The Genuine Wealth model provides a unique tool, creating integrated performance measurement and management that shows the delicate balance required to achieve genuine sustainability. The model is by no means perfect; it is a work-in-progress. It will take years to develop common standards for measurement and reporting in these new ways, just as the Generally Accepted

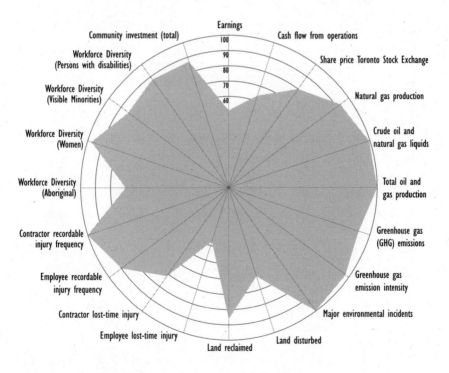

FIGURE 8.2. Sustainable Performance Index for a Firm
Credit: Anielski Management Inc.

Accounting Principles (GAAP) and the GRI Guidelines for sustainability reporting have taken years to develop. I believe that each enterprise must voluntarily develop its own systems through experiment and continuous refine-
ment. Like sustainability, this new accounting practice is a journey. I hope
that the Genuine Wealth model will be useful to any enterprise, no matter its
size, which wants to be a better and wiser steward of society's common wealth.

The future of business that builds Genuine Wealth

Businesses today have an important opportunity — indeed a responsibility
— to make their actions contribute to the well-being of communities. The
future belongs to business leaders who understand, at the heart level, the
need for social and environmental responsibility for the common good. There
are many business leaders who are waking up to this truth, and many new
business students from the University of Alberta School of Business and the
Bainbridge Graduate Institute in Washington state are learning the importance of business ethics, sustainability, social and environmental responsibility and the nature of genuine competition through cooperation. I have hope
for the future of business and corporations. Here are some progressive businesses that are leading the way to a Genuine Wealth economy.

ShoreBank Pacific
David Williams, President and CEO of ShoreBank Pacific based in Ilwaco,
Washington, is a leader in the financial community who understands the
essence of the Genuine Wealth model. ShoreBank Pacific, a Washington state
chartered FDIC insured bank, is the first commercial bank in the United States
with a commitment to environmentally sustainable community development. ShoreBank Pacific was formed in 1997 as a joint project of ShoreBank
Corp. Chicago (the nation's first community development bank) and Ecotrust
(an environmental non-profit). ShoreBank believes that long-term community prosperity goes hand-in-hand with a healthy environment. ShoreBank
Pacific helps borrowers use energy efficiently, reduce waste and pollution,
conserve natural resources and plan for the long term. David makes the point
that in order to help support the creation of sustainable and living economies
of well-being, we need different criteria to assess the possibilities. He suggests two key standards be adopted: 1) Will the current residents be better off
with this company here?, and 2) Is the business activity sustainable in the
community or economic region over a 100-year period?[8]

Vancity Savings Credit Union

Vancity Savings Credit Union is Canada's largest cooperative financial institution and credit union. Vancity is a cooperative bank where each member is a shareholder (one share, one vote). Formed in 1945, it now manages over $10.5 billion in assets and has more than 340,000 members and 42 branches throughout Greater Vancouver, the Fraser Valley and Victoria, British Columbia. It has developed a number of innovative financial products and services including the first values-based credit card (EnviroCard VISA); the first self-reliance loans to businesses without collateral; the first socially responsible mutual fund and financial products (such as discounted car loans for purchasing hybrid vehicles) that allow its members to invest according to their personal values. Vancity uses its business and financial resources to help non-profits and co-operatives find innovative ways to build and leverage assets for long-term sustainability.

Vancity is guided by a commitment to corporate social responsibility and to improving the quality of life in the communities where its customers live and work. It operates on a clear statement of values, operating principles and commitments. Vancity's mission is: "To be a democratic, ethical, and innovative provider of financial services to our members. Through strong financial performance, we serve as a catalyst for the self-reliance and economic well-being of our membership and community." Its values include integrity, innovation and responsibility to its members, employees and communities.[9] Vancity reports its performance in an Accountability Report every two years; this report is also externally verified. Vancity uses its own customized performance indicators that are consistent with the GRI guidelines as well as the A1000 social accountability, auditing and reporting standards developed in England. Their social audit process helps Vancity set new targets and action plans. Vancity is unique as a bank because it is a values-based organization that balances financial responsibility with making a contribution to the communities and broader society in which it operates, especially with community members not adequately served by mainstream financial organizations.

Interface

Ray Anderson, the charismatic founder and current chair of the board of Interface Inc., provides a poignant personal story of the new generation of corporations that have adopted ecological industrial principles. Interface, headquartered in Atlanta, is the world's largest manufacturer of modular and broadloom carpet with manufacturing locations on four continents and offices in more than 100 countries. In 1994 Ray had an experience he describes as a "spear in the chest" after reading Paul Hawken's *The Ecology of Commerce*.[10] This catalyst led Ray to examine his own conscience about manufacturing carpets which, after being bought, used and disposed of in landfills, would cause multi-generational environmental liabilities for which Interface and its customers took no responsibility. He embarked on journey that took Interface from a giant externalization-of-pollutants-enterprise to one operating on principles of sustainability. Instead of selling the physical carpet to customers, Ray's Interface dream-team and employees designed a new carpet that would be made of recycled carpet returned to Interface after its useful life. Moreover, no longer would you purchase carpet outright, but you would lease the service or utility of the carpet from Interface.

> For the first twenty-one years of Interface's existence, I never gave one thought to what we took from or did to the Earth, except to be sure we obeyed all laws and regulations. That is, until August of 1994. At that time, our research division organized a task force with representatives from all our worldwide businesses to review Interface's environmental position and [I was] asked to give the group an environmental vision. Frankly, I didn't have a vision, except "comply, comply, comply." I had heard statesmen advocate "sustainable development," but I had no idea what it meant. I sweated for three weeks over what to say to that group. Then, through what seemed like pure serendipity, somebody sent me a book: Paul Hawken's *The Ecology of Commerce*. I read it, and it changed my life. It was an epiphany. I wasn't halfway through it before the vision I sought became clear, along with a powerful sense of urgency to do something. Hawken's message was a spear in my chest that remains to this day. In the speech, I borrowed Hawken's ideas shamelessly. And I agreed with his central thesis: while business is part of the problem, it can also be a part of the solution. Business is the largest, wealthiest, most pervasive institution on Earth, and responsible for most of the damage. It must take the lead in directing the Earth away from collapse, and toward sustainability and restoration.... I believe we have come to the threshold of the next industrial revolution. At Interface, we seek to

become the first sustainable corporation in the world, and, following
that, the first restorative company. It means creating the technologies of the future-kinder, gentler technologies that emulate nature's
systems. I believe that's where we will find the right model. Ultimately, I believe we must learn to depend solely on available income
the way a forest does, not on our precious stores of natural capital.
Linear practices must be replaced by cyclical ones. That's nature's
way. In nature, there is no waste; one organism's waste is another's
food.... Literally, our company will grow by cleaning up the world,
not by polluting or degrading it. We'll be doing well by doing good.
That's the vision. Is it a dream? Certainly, but it is a dream we share
with our 5000 associates, our vendors, and our customers. Everyone
will have to dream this dream to make it a reality, but until then, we
are committed to leading the way.[11]

Interface sees sustainability as more than token environmentalism but rather
living and working in ways that don't jeopardize the future of social, economic and natural resources. "In business, sustainability means managing human
and natural capital with the same vigor we apply to the management of financial capital. It means widening the scope of our awareness so we can understand fully the 'true cost' of every choice we make."[12]

The story of Interface is described in Ray Anderson's book *Mid-course
Correction,*[13] and in *The Natural Step for Business* by Brian Nattrass and Mary
Altomare.[14] In 1996 Interface, following other corporations like IKEA of
Sweden, was the first American company to adopt The Natural Step as a tool
for guiding its journey towards sustainability.

According to the The Natural Step framework, sustainability occurs
when four system conditions are fulfilled.

In a sustainable society, nature is not subject to systematically increasing:
1. concentrations of substances extracted from Earth's crust;
2. concentrations of substances produced by society;
3. degradation by physical means
   and, in that society
4. people are not subject to conditions that systematically undermine their capacity to meet their needs.[16]

Guided by these four system conditions Interface, like IKEA, completely re-thought their business and manufacturing processes including purchase of materials, manufacturing, transportation, construction of facilities, maintenance and waste management. Anderson notes "The Natural Step has become a compass, a reference point, something to recognize and be consistent with."[17]

I have come to personally know Ray Anderson as a person of great integrity and principle. He gives hope to a new generation of business leaders who will create companies like Ray's — operating with integrity, innovation and responsibility. While the journey towards genuine sustainability is a long one for Ray and Interface, the important point is that it has begun and evolves with a sustained commitment and transparent accountability for its failures and its victories.

Upstream 21

Leslie Christian is president of Progressive Investment Management, a Seattle- and Portland-based financial services corporation that since 1982 has offered socially responsible portfolio management services to individuals and institutions. Leslie is a chartered financial analyst with more than 30 years of experience in the investment field, including nine years in New York as a Director with Salomon Brothers Inc. Progressive Investment Management is actively involved in the socially responsible investment community, promoting corporate responsibility through social screening and shareholder activism. In 1999 Progressive established Portfolio 21, a no load global equity mutual fund investing in companies throughout the world that are incorporating environmental sustainability into their business strategies. In 2004 Leslie, along with others like lawyer Bryan Redd and with some of my input on the Genuine Wealth accounting model, co-founded a new company, Upstream 21, which is directing financial capital to small businesses supporting environmental sustainability in local economies.

Upstream was conceived by Leslie to address a fundamental shortcoming of financial services, particularly opportunities for individuals to invest in their local economy. In most publicly traded corporations and many private corporations, the majority of the shareholders are absentee owners who have purchased shares in the secondary market, are passive investors and expect that the company will place their interests above all else, including the employees who work to provide profits, the communities that support the businesses and the ecosystems that sustain them. Upstream 21 was designed with a mandate, supported by its legal structure, charter, bylaws and culture to serve the common good. Moreover, it is a financial services model that questions the fundamental economic imperative for more growth. Short-term financial growth, as practiced today, is not only one-dimensional but also dangerous and misleading. According to Leslie, Upstream 21 is shifting the priorities of investment from short term profit maximization to long term value creation, ultimately to sustainability.[18] Upstream wants to grow true wealth: healthy communities, fair and equitable business practices, regenerative ecosystems, personal well being and security for the future.

Upstream 21 provides investors an opportunity to invest in local ecomonies by purchasing shares in Upstream 21, which has itself acquired locally-owned businesses committed to sustainability, environmental stewardship and building vibrant communities. Upstream 21 acquires companies that are committed to sustaining their communities, their natural environment and long-term economic vitality, and seek investors who are committed to this mandate. Upstream seeks to become a long-term owner of already successful

> I don't believe that the solutions in society will come from the left or the right or the north or the south. They will come from islands within those organizations; islands of people with integrity who want to do something.
> — KARL HEINRIK ROBÈRT[15]

companies known for their integrity and respect for their employees, environment, and community. By purchasing these progressive companies, Upstream 21 will become a catalyst for advancing these community values. In this role, it will strengthen the activities of its portfolio companies by providing synergies between partners, access to capital, greater operating efficiencies and management practices that serve the common good. Companies will be included in the Upstream 21 portfolio if they share the vision, values and operating principles of Upstream 21.

There are several things that makes Upstream 21 unique. First, it is the first corporation in Oregon legal history to have been incorporated with a charter explicitly stating that its responsibilities extend to due consideration of its subsidiaries' social, legal and economic effects on their employees, customers and suppliers, and on the communities and geographic areas in which these companies operate. Long-term as well as short-term interests of Upstream and its shareholders and the effects of both Upstream and its subsidiaries on the environment are also considered. Second, in local economies, investments will continually redefine the corporate mandate. Risk to the investor will be managed by carefully selecting a diversified group of well-established companies with proven track records. The hope is that investors will realize a reasonable long-term financial return, while contributing to the betterment of local communities. Third, Upstream 21 is organized to redefine, redistribute and renew real or genuine wealth, not only financial wealth. By redefining wealth as well-being, meaningful work and family life and security rather than money only, Upstream 21 expands the scope of normal business thinking.

By acting locally, Upstream 21 can build more personal relationships between investors and the businesses they invest in. A more direct relationship is created between the household as a purchaser of goods and services and local enterprise. Now, as investors have a direct personal interest in the success of the businesses they invest in, they support themselves and others by purchasing life needs from these businesses. Money should stay in the community. This gives new meaning to the adage "buy and live locally while thinking globally."

Upstream 21 expects to drive demand for societal well-being outcomes like fair and equitable compensation for employees, company investment in renewable and sustainable practices (including renewable energy and purchasing of local produce), local procurement of goods and services and environmental practices which are restorative of land, air and water while still providing shareholders a reasonable — but not excessive — financial return.

Leslie Christian believes that Upstream 21 models a new capitalism which advances local economies by building — rather than eroding — their natural, social and economic capital. In principle, the model can be replicated in any community and virtually at any population or geographic scale.

Corporation 20/20

Corporation 20/20 is a multi-stakeholder initiative that seeks to answer the question: What would a corporation look like that is designed to seamlessly integrate both social and financial purpose? "Its goal is to develop and disseminate corporate designs where social purpose moves from the periphery to the heart of future organizations." Corporation 20/20 exemplifies the process of system redesign. Its advocates argue that the existing corporate form — directors duties, capitalization, liability, accountability — are in urgent need of redefinition. These designers believe that it is no longer enough to ask, "What is the business case for social responsibility?" but rather "What is the social purpose case for business?"[19]

Six principles of corporate redesign are proposed, as a guide towards the Corporation 20/20 vision:

1. The purpose of the corporation is to harness private interests to serve the public interest.
Corporations are unique as private organizations. They are created to serve general welfare by people motivated to create wealth and rewarding livelihoods for themselves as they produce goods and services. Corporate actions must be consistent with the public interest.

2. Corporations shall accrue fair returns for shareholders, but not at the expense of the legitimate interests of other stakeholders.
Stakeholders have legitimate claims because they provide human, natural, social and financial capital to corporations.

3. Corporations shall operate sustainably, meeting the needs of the present generation without compromising the ability of future generations to meet their needs.
Corporations are stewards. They should not abdicate long-term responsibility to the public in the pursuit of private short-term gain.

4. Corporations shall distribute their wealth equitably among those who contribute to the creation of that wealth.
Corporations should consider issues like paying living wages, employees sharing ownership and profits, trading and procuring fairly and equitably, paying tax based on consumption of public resources as well as fair returns to shareholders.

5. Corporations shall be governed in a manner that is participatory, transparent, ethical, and accountable.
New governance structures should openly involve all stakeholders or affected parties.

6. Corporations shall not infringe on the right of natural persons to govern themselves, nor infringe on other universal human rights.[20]

While this initiative attempts to redefine the nature of the corporation and definitions of wealth and shareholder values, I believe that without fundamental legal restructuring of corporate charters, which would explicitly imbed social and environmental responsibility into the DNA of a corporation in the way Upstream 21 has done, there is little hope that such principles will be taken seriously.

The cooperative business enterprise

What if businesses practiced according to the real meaning of the word competition: to strive together? How could businesses cooperate rather than fight for apparently scarce financial and other resources? Could this lead to more meaningful relationships and indeed more efficient use of resources?

During my tenure as a professor at the University of Alberta School of Business, I have become fascinated in the cooperative business model as a framework for business in North America and internationally. There are many examples of cooperatives: farm cooperatives, housing cooperatives and even automobile cooperatives like the American and Canadian Automobile Associations. Cooperatives operate by the principle of shared responsibility; each member has only one vote. Important principles of reciprocity and sharing wealth characterize cooperative businesses.

Mountain Equipment Co-op

One of my favorite business cooperatives is Canada's Mountain Equipment Co-op (MEC). Established in 1971 in Vancouver, British Columbia MEC is one of Canada's most successful business cooperatives providing products (gear) and services to over 2.3 million Canadian members (one in 15 Canadians are members of MEC) for the purpose of self-propelled wilderness-oriented recreation. I have been a member since the early 1980s. MEC, with annual sales of $197 million in 2005 (a 10% increase over 2004) and more than 1,120 employees, is an enterprise wholly owned by its members, established to provide inexpensive outdoor gear to its members and not to maximize profits.[21] MEC is owned by its members, the people who shop at its stores. It is democratically controlled by members: each member of MEC has one lifetime share (at a cost of only $5.00) which gives that member a single vote in the cooperative. So the share gives each member the opportunity to purchase and rent quality outdoor gear as well as having a say in how the cooperative operates through voting for the next Board of Directors.

MEC is a retail consumer cooperative, meaning that it purchases selected merchandise and makes it available to its membership at the least possible
cost. MEC operates as a not-for-profit enterprise, dispersing earnings by providing retail space for members to shop, donating to selected wilderness and
community oriented causes and occasionally paying dividends to members. If
there is a surplus left over after all costs and community investments are
made at the end of the operating year, it is a tiny cushion to ensure long-term
financial sustainability.[23]

MEC's strategic advantage over its for-profit competitors is that it operates on the principles of cooperation and the pooling of resources. Cooperatives differ from corporations in many ways. Ownership is dispersed equitably among members in a coop, whereas ownership within the corporation

MEC is guided by a clear mission and values.

MEC's Purpose
To support people in achieving the benefit of self-propelled wilderness-oriented recreation.

MEC's Vision
MEC is an innovative, thriving co-operative that inspires excellence in
products and services, passion for wilderness experiences, leadership
for a just world, and action for a healthy planet.

MEC's Mission
MEC provides quality products and services for self-propelled wilderness-oriented recreation, such as hiking and mountaineering, at the
lowest reasonable price in an informative, respectful manner. We are a
member-owned co-operative striving for social and environmental
leadership.

MEC Values
We conduct ourselves ethically and with integrity. We show respect for
others in our words and actions. We act in the spirit of community and
co-operation. We respect and protect our natural environment. We
strive for personal growth, continual learning, and adventure.[22]

is concentrated in shareholders who own the largest percentage of the company. Rick Kohn, former Chief Financial Officer of MEC, once told me that he prefers the word "care-holder" over shareholder in reference to MEC members. Dispersed and equitable ownership translates into several principles of cooperative ownership that MEC upholds. Membership is open and voluntary. Member control of the coop is democratic: members elect the Board of Directors and can propose and vote for direction-setting resolutions. Member service drives MEC's operations. Member participation is important for decision-making, which is aimed at meeting member needs and interests. Coops are naturally community committed because ownership is community based.[24]

MEC's first Accountability Report sets a high standard. It provides a very simplified financial performance statement. In 2005, with $197 million in purchases by members, 5.6 cents on every dollar was given back to members based on their patronage. In addition 2.1 cents ($4 million in 2005) on every dollar of sales went to community organizations that support MEC's vision. Only a small surplus, 0.2 cents on every member dollar, was retained for future discretionary investment. The report contains unique performance indicators assessing MEC as a cooperative structure, its successes and failures in new sustainable product design (including maximizing product life through gear swaps), greening their operations, the energy and transportation footprint of their products, staff and member satisfaction as well as how they are supporting their community. MEC used the GRI sustainability reporting guidelines and the AccountAbility 1000 (AA1000) Standards to guide their reporting along with being consistent with the International Co-operative Principles, the Global Compact and the Fair Labor Association (FLA) principles. MEC admits openly that it isn't perfect and has room to improve upon its successful model. For example, while members and staff may feel satisfied and happy, MEC's surveys indicate that there is room for improvement. MEC also admits that there is a long way to go before the products it sells are truly food-for-nature (that is truly sustainable), benign (non-toxic in nature) while providing optimum utility.

MEC is a model medium-sized corporation that provides high quality, low cost, efficiently and ethically produced goods and services to support the economy of well-being I envision. This is why I challenge my business students at the University of Alberta to imagine the next opportunity for a MEC-type business enterprise to produce things that help make life worthwhile.

Mondragón Cooperative Corporation (MCC) in Spain

Another successful cooperative business is the Mondragón Cooperative Corporation (MCC) based in the Basque Country and extending over all of Spain. MCC is the world's largest worker cooperative, made up of manufacturing and retail companies. This large integrated business cooperative is now the largest corporation in the Basque Country and 7th largest industrial group in Spain, with over 11.9 billion euros (US$14.8 billion) in annual sales in 2005 and a workforce of roughly 78,455. MCC's ventures include six financial enterprises (credit unions and community banks), 67 industrial enterprises manufacturing everything from refrigerators to bicycles, eight retail and distribution businesses, cultural centers and three universities. Estimates for 2002 suggest that MCC contributed 3.7% towards the total GDP of the Basque Country.[25]

MCC is founded on core values that include education, democracy, solidarity and hard work. These are values which the Italian region of Emilia Romagna shares. MCC also believes and practices the fair distribution of wages. For example, no one person working within MCC is allowed to earn more than six times what another person earns; for most of the enterprises within MCC this ratio is 4:1 or less. I often compare this policy with US corporate wage inequality. In 1997 I estimated that the president of Safeway (with corporate headquarters in California) earned roughly 700 times more than the check-out clerk at my local Edmonton Safeway store (roughly $14.00 an hour with benefits): a clear and gross inequity.

> "To build cooperativism is not to do the opposite of capitalism as if this system did not have any useful features... Cooperativism must surpass it, and for this purpose must assimilate its methods and dynamism."
>
> — FR. JOSE ARZIMENDI

Another unique attribute of MCC is that it operates, like MEC, by a set of principles:

- Open membership
- Democratic organization
- Primacy of work
- Capital as a means
- Participation in management
- Wage solidarity

- Inter-cooperation
- Social transformation
- Universal mission
- Education

It is useful to contrast the traditional corporation and the cooperative corporation:

As Greg MacLeod, Canada's leading expert on cooperative corporations and sustainable community economic development, notes, "I believe the commentators from a traditional economic point of view have missed the point. They have ignored the fact that the key to all of these community-based economic developments are the values rooted in a particular society, not neutral ideas and techniques claimed to be independent of social context."[26] This sentiment was echoed by Emilia Romagna's finance minister, Flavio del Bono, when I met him in Bologna. While these models of cooperative economies and enterprise may not be readily transferable to another society or culture, there are attributes that could find a good fit, aligned with an emerging consciousness of shared responsibility for stewardship of our common wealth.

BALLE: Business Alliance for Local Living Economies

Imagine a network of small and medium size businesses and entrepreneurs working in genuine cooperation based on similar principles as MEC and MCC. This is BALLE: the Business Alliance for Local Living Economies. Originally inspired and founded by sustainable business pioneers like Philadelphia's Judy Wicks (White Dog Café)[27] and Laury Hammel with support from David Korten, a former Harvard business professor from Bainbridge Island, Washington. BALLE was born at the Fall 2001 Social Venture Network conference to address the concerns a group of investors, entrepreneurs, economists and authors were feeling about increasing wealth inequalities and the worsening environmental destruction of our planet.[28] BALLE was established to build a network of business people committed to local, living and sustainable economies. There are now chapters across the United States (e.g. Seattle)[29] and Canada (e.g. Vancouver[30] and recently Toronto). BALLE comprises 35 such business networks with more than 11,000 business members overall. BALLE is guided by a series of objectives that direct resources, organizing tools and sustainable economic development models to local networks and encourage:

- Local ownership of businesses
- Creation of a sense of community and place
- Structuring business ownership for community accountability
- Appropriately scaled production for regional and renewable (zero-waste, closed loop) production
- Changing consumers to customers through education
- Community investment: financing socially and ecologically responsible businesses and the retention of capital within a community
- Public policies that support independent, local businesses

Figure 8.3. The Traditional Corporation versus the Cooperative Corporation

Capitalist Model: Traditional Corporation	Cooperative Model: Cooperative Corporation
1. Priority of the financial, meaning the highest and most rapid return on investment.	1. Priority of persons, professionalism, excellence of products, satisfaction of clients. Viability is not a primary objective rather it is a consequence.
2. Persons are considered as means and are expendable.	2. Persons form part of the enterprise. They are part of the purpose and participate in management.
3. The contract is with a worker and the commitment is to a task. The relation is one of confrontation between labor and capital.	3. The contract is with society and the commitment is to the development of the business. The tendency is to lifetime employment with cooperation between workers and capital.
4. Priority of technical training with no attention to other types of education.	4. Education is considered an investment in a human, social and technical sense. It is capitalization through professional competence.
5. Policies are short term and directed to short term profits.	5. Policies tend to a long term and social good.
6. The enterprise is available for sale to the highest bidder — which usually means down-sizing.	6. Priority to growth through self development of the enterprise.
7. Ease of access to external capital markets.	7. Difficulty in accessing external capital markets.
8. Power lies mainly in the hands of the financiers.	8. Power is shared between the various departments: technical, commercial and financial.
9. The profits are privatized and the losses are socialized and externalized.	9. The profits and losses are shared amongst all proportionally.
10. Personnel policy considers employees as entities with a capacity for work.	10. Personnel policy is oriented to men and women as persons invested with dignity.

Credit: Greg MacLeod. *From Mondragon to America: Experiments in Community Economic Development*. University College of Cape Breton Press, 1997, p. 96.

- Economic democracy
- Linking local living economies through online international market-place of independently-owned, community-based businesses
- Organizing events that bring these business owners together
- Connecting capital to living economy enterprises
- Supporting national and local public policies that strengthen independent local businesses and farms, promote equity and protect the environment[31]

BALLE hopes to create an intricate web of locally focused, fairly trading economies all over the globe. Its members believe in healthy and vibrant economies for everyone. As local business leaders directly improving the livability of their communities and bio-regions, they work to increase the production and purchasing of local, sustainable products.[32]

BALLE is a model for building economies of well-being and happiness where relationships are key. While not as formal as MCC, BALLE is an informal and organic network not unlike a forest where all living beings must co-exist to flourish. It is important that not only business people, but also other citizens, students and our children, gather together to talk, share ideas, be collective entrepreneurs and begin to understand how our economic decisions (purchasing and selling) and networks can be strengthened when we genuinely cooperate with each other. These are opportunities to break down the myth of competition and realize the strength of genuine cooperation and shared responsibility for our common wealth. I have found that when you begin to have such conversations, you realize the treasures that lie in each of us, in our skills, capacities, dreams and visions for the good life.

Ways forward

There is no perfect model for a business enterprise that fully embraces the ideals that the Genuine Wealth model represents. But the examples in this chapter — and there are many others — afford us hope that innovations and entrepreneurship may lead all enterprise to its rightful and virtuous place in society.

I envision cooperative, innovative and entrepreneurial modeled businesses. Could we design a business like my friend Janine Benyus[33] envisions: inspired by nature's elegant, functional, efficient and beautiful design? I believe businesses can be guided by new sets of principles like The Natural Step

(TNS) principles where production of goods and services is benign to nature and human health and where products are designed to be food for nature.

I envision a world of business where there may be no employees, simply individual artisans working together like the Amish do when they build a new barn; each contributing her or his own personal talent, skills and passion. I envision a world where entrepreneurial spirit is alive and where people are having fun in the reality of abundance not stuck in a model of artificial scarcity. In this space there is joy in cooperating together building beautiful things and innovating new products that contribute to genuine improved well-being.

My hope lies in good people currently working within large corporations waking up to the reality that much of what they do within a corporation is inconsistent with their values and actions at home with their families. Many who are feeling this catharsis are leaving their employment and finding a more meaningful way. There are many like Leslie Christian, Dave Williams, Ray Anderson, Karl Heinrik Robèrt, David Korten, Bob Williams, Raffi, Joey Hundert, and many others who are leading the way to a new more compassionate and responsible business world.

I envision a day when each corporate leader will wake up in the morning and ask: how will what I do today (my actions and decisions) contribute to an improvement in the well-being of all the children of this earth? I imagine a day when presidents, prime ministers and corporate captains will simply ask of their economic decisions: how do the decisions I make contribute to the life, liberty and happiness of all people? To what end and to whose benefit do I produce goods and services, if not for the well-being our children, then for whom? I imagine a business day beginning with a genuine reflection on Raffi Cavoukian's "Covenant for Honouring Children." Living and acting according to this covenant means considering the well-being of children in all we do and living according to the principle of "first, do no harm." Raffi explains that the Covenant takes "a 'children first' approach to healing communities and restoring ecosystems; it views how we regard and treat our young as the key to building humane and sustainable world."[34] If we were to govern our businesses in this manner, then we can say at the end of the day, what we did today we did for the well-being of all the children.

A Covenant for Honouring Children

Raffi

We find these joys to be self-evident: That all children are created whole, endowed with innate intelligence, with dignity and wonder, worthy of respect. The embodiment of life, liberty and happiness, children are original blessings, here to learn their own song. Every girl and boy is entitled to love, to dream and belong to a loving "village." And to pursue a life of purpose.

We affirm our duty to nourish and nurture the young, to honour their caring ideals as the heart of being human. To recognize the early years as the foundation of life, and to cherish the contribution of young children to human evolution.

We commit ourselves to peaceful ways and vow to keep from harm or neglect these, our most vulnerable citizens. As guardians of their prosperity we honour the bountiful Earth whose diversity sustains us. Thus we pledge our love for generations to come.[35]

CHAPTER 9

Money and Genuine Wealth

Money is capable of doing what we want it to do, rather than (as at present) making us do what it wants us to do. Money is capable of reflecting reality and conveying the policy we want. The true worth of money as an invention, frankly, has never been fully explored. The range of reform facing us, once we decide to correct the overbearing mathematical defect of debt, are as rich as the diverse opportunities and material benefits our economies can possible offer. In fact, in a sense they are the one and the same thing.

— MICHAEL ROWBOTHAM[1]

THIS CHAPTER IS DEDICATED to the many people who have sought to understand the genuine nature of money, our relationship with it and how it commands the living capitals of modern societies. This chapter is addressed to all of us who have no idea what money is, particularly our children in which my hope lies to redefine the nature of money and how it is created so we may all return money's power to us-the-people for a genuine pursuit of life, liberty and happiness.

The lights go on

The more I delved into the nature of economies the more I began to realize that the nature of money and its creation were veiled in mystery. I realized that very little is written or taught about how money is created in our modern economies yet it is the most important driver of human behavior. One of my favorite authorities is Vicki Robin's and Joe Dominguez's book *Your Money or Your Life* which provides an important plain-language approach to understanding money and our relationships with it. The authors remind us we spend much of our life trading our life energy or time in exchange for money. Ironically, however, while time is genuinely real and limited (we will all die), money on the other hand is an illusion in that has no basis in real wealth. Robin and Dominguez offer a simple calculation to determine how many minutes and hours you expend each day, month or year to earn an income; this includes adding up the value of unpaid hours spent related to working, including the time spent dressing and getting ready to work, time commuting, time worrying and stressing about deadlines and time recovering from a stressful day and commute from work. In addition, they help us account for the value of transportation, clothing, lunches, child care, education, entertainment, taxes. Based on this fuller cost accounting you can more honestly assess whether you receive a genuine return to happiness and your life energy in exchange for your work for money.[2]

The truth is that we often compromise the pursuit of happiness and the good life in the mere accumulation of material things and most importantly money. We confuse money with real things; instead of a medium of exchange we treat money as a store of value. Few of us realize that money is no longer backed by anything real, whether gold, land or heads of cattle. Nor do we realize that governments don't control or create money; money comes into existence when banks make loans. More than 95% of the money supply in the United States is based on interest-bearing bank loans. Most importantly, the power to create money no longer resides with us but rather is increasingly concentrated in the hands of a few private banks who compound interest and issue loans using the common banking practice called fractional reserve banking. Banks issue more money, in the form of loans to customers, than they hold in their reserves. As a result financial wealth becomes increasingly concentrated in the hands of an elite few. We have failed to uphold the teachings of most world religions which forbid usury — the charging of interest on loans. We have, as Thomas Jefferson warned, become unwittingly indentured or wage slaves to the money power. We have also lost our imagination about how we can meet our deeper needs (e.g. spiritual or worldly) without money. In our collective ignorance of how money is created we fail to see how this usurious system actually aids the cancerous overconsumption and overproduction that we are witnessing today. It's time to reclaim our power over money creation by redefining it and redesigning our economic systems so that money is created to support the stewardship of our genuine wealth.

> If the American people ever allow private banks to control the issue of their currency, first by inflation, then by deflation, the banks and the corporations which grow up around them will deprive the people of all property until their children wake up homeless on the continent their fathers conquered. The issuing power of money should be taken from the banks and restored to Congress and the people to whom it belongs. I sincerely believe the banking institutions having the power of Money are more dangerous to liberty than standing armies.   — THOMAS JEFFERSON[3]

I have examined constitutional amendments that might alter how the US Federal Reserve and Bank of Canada operate, alternative local currencies created by citizens at the local level and interest-free banks like the Swedish JAK Members Bank. My vision is a money system that is no longer based on debt and no longer charges interest (e.g. eschews usury) but where money is created to support the conditions of the five capitals in a Genuine Wealth accounting system from the national to the local community level. Money creation can help to support the conditions for genuinely sustainable and flourishing economies rather than cannibalize living capital as debt-based systems currently do. I have come to the conclusion that without a fundamental redesign of how money is created and who governs its creation, the pursuit of sustainable economies of life, liberty and happiness are impossible.

> I see in the near future a crisis approach that unnerves me and causes me to tremble for the safety of my country. Corporations have been enthroned, an era of corruption will follow, and the money power of the country will endeavor to prolong its reign by working upon the prejudices of the people, until the wealth is aggregated in a few hands, and the republic destroyed... The Government should create, issue, and circulate all the currency and credits needed to satisfy the spending power of the Government and the buying power of consumers. By the adoption of these principles, the taxpayers will

be saved immense sums of interest. Money will cease to be master and become the servant of humanity.[4] Money is the creature of law, and the creation of the original issue of money should be maintained as the exclusive monopoly of national government.... The monetary needs of increasing numbers of people advancing towards higher standards of living can and should be met by the government. Such needs can be met by the issue of national currency and credit through the operation of a national banking system. The circulation of a medium of exchange issued and backed by the government can be properly regulated and redundancy of issue avoided by withdrawing from circulation such amounts as may be necessary by taxation, re-deposit and otherwise. Government, possessing the power to create and issue currency and credit as money...need not and should not borrow capital at interest.... The financing of all public enterprises, the maintenance of stable government and ordered progress, and the conduct of the Treasury will become matters of practical administration... Money will cease to be the master and become the servant of humanity. Democracy will rise superior to the money power.   — ABRAHAM LINCOLN[5]

Any system which gives so much power and so much discretion to a few men, (so) that mistakes — excusable or not — can have such far reaching effects, is a bad system. It is a bad system to believers in freedom just because it gives a few men such power without any effective check by the body politic — this is the key political argument against an independent central bank... To paraphrase Clemenceau: money is much too serious a matter to be left to the Central Bankers.   — MILTON FRIEDMAN[6]

I presented some of these ideas at the Canadian Economics Association conference at the University of British Columbia (UBC) in 2000. I began to gain insights into why the achievement of a genuinely sustainable economy was impossible without redressing the nature of money and returning the power of money creation back to the people.[7] Since that time — like Thomas Jefferson, Abraham Lincoln and Milton Friedman — I have challenged Canadians and Americans to return money power back to the people so that we can become each others bankers, sharing our financial wealth as needed.

Our relationship with money

Our relationship with money is one of the most important social phenomenons of our age. Almost everyone talks about their relationship with money. We stress about not having enough money or how to make more money. The rich often stress about what to do with their money or with the label of being rich. Some people have asked me personally how they can "get more of it" as if I am an alchemist of money creation. Many dream about winning the lottery to get ahead and realize their real dreams. Students in universities and colleges are increasingly fixated on making their first million dollars when they graduate; indeed many expect it. We live in a money-centric-valued world where everything that is produced or purchased or consumed is transacted with what we call money. Everything, it would seem, revolves around money. We have come to believe that we won't survive without money, that it is necessary to fulfill our needs, yet have forgotten that money is a tool we invented, a form of an agreement that it would serve as a medium of exchange, and which we have the power to change.

Lynne Twist, a successful US fundraiser and author of *The Soul of Money,* argues that we live in a time where the planet and humanity everywhere has gone crazy over and about money. We experience both individual and communal anxiety, dilemma, confusion and shame about money. We have been taught that money is chronically scarce; there is never enough to go around. Money is viewed as something deeply personal; something we are encouraged not to talk about openly with others. If you are poor you don't want to talk about how little money you have; if you are rich you don't want your neighbors to know you are flush with financial assets. This collective anxiety over money has paralyzed us collectively. Twist notes that we need to come to the place where we no longer fear money and can demystify the mythology of money that has dominated our human societies for thousands of years.

Our relationship with money is confusing and complex. As in many relationships, we actually give money its power and authority! We give power to money when we accept it in exchange for material things. Few understand that money is nothing but coins or paper that was created virtually out of thin air. We have forgotten that the power behind money lives with us, not with the central bank or private banks who currently issue money. Twist challenges us to wake up to the reality that we, as sovereign individuals, can reclaim our power over money. Taking back the power over money means returning our own sovereignty as citizens (repudiating the economic concept of "consumer"), so that money is returned to its rightful place as a legitimate medium of exchange for the stewardship of our common wealth. Money should no longer be a store of value.

Twist identifies other mantras we hear constantly in our communities such as "there isn't enough of this or that" and "I don't get enough done" which again is reinforced by advertising compelling us to consume more stuff since we don't have "enough" already. Instead of money being a tool to facilitate exchange and healthy relationships between people, it has become a pathological object that divides us and is often used to dominate and marginalize. Instead of ensuring money flows freely and is indeed ubiquitous throughout society, people hoard it, fearful that they will not have enough today, tomorrow or in their old age. Twist notes that we have now made money more important than human life, the natural world and our own spirituality. Twist calls us to move money away from fear, violence and the illusion of scarcity. We are called to return to a more authentic and genuine life not commanded by money and the pursuit of material possessions but the creation of genuine wealth, meaningful relationships and genuine stewardship.[8]

When I ask people about the importance of money, most say that money is less important than being loved and having loving relationships. Most of us when on our death bed wouldn't say "if I only had more money to take with me;" we would long for peace and loving memories. Most of us are making a dying, not a living. We do horrendous things in the name of money. We will kill for money. We will go to war for money. We will compromise meaningful and loving relationships and meaningful work for money. Some might even sell their souls for money. Strangely, our culture actually fosters this obsession with money and materialism. We live in a gambling culture where the majority of people play games of chance — buy lottery tickets, play VLTs, bingo or gamble in casinos — in the hope of getting rich. Most who do win the lottery are not any happier; indeed many become lost in their excess.

Instead of being defined as citizens we have allowed ourselves to be defined by economists and politicians as consumers. But we are not simply utility maximizing machines that feed the insatiable GDP calculator; we are human beings and citizens. A citizen is someone who is responsible for the good of the whole of the community. By contrast a consumer is the equivalent of a cancer cell, someone who consumes, destroys and depletes without any apparent limit to its appetite for more.

What is money?

> The monetary system...promotes competition and short-term thinking...like a treadmill [the monetary system] requires continuous economic growth...it undervalues care, education and tasks crucial to maintaining a society.   — BERNARD LIETAER[9]

One of the words for money in the Hebrew language is *mammon. Mammon,* a word of Aramaic origin, means riches. It is used in the Christian Bible when Jesus says "No one can serve two masters: for either they will hate the one, and love the other; or else they will hold to the one, and despise the other. You cannot serve God and *mammon.*"[10]

What is money? Where does it come from? Why is money always scarce? What evidence is there that the current monetary system is leading to unsustainable outcomes and erosion of overall societal and ecological well-being? These are questions I debate with my university business students; most students as well as economists, business people and average citizens have no idea what money is or where it comes from let alone who creates it. John Kenneth Galbraith once noted that "The study of money, above all fields in economics, is one in which complexity is used to disguise truth, or evade truth, not to reveal it."[11] How is it that we weren't taught this in primary school or high school?

If you look up money in a dictionary you will find that money is a current medium of exchange in the form of coins and banknotes. Economists explain more precisely that money is now defined by its

Money is intrinsically worthless; it has no inherent value.

functions in trade as a medium of exchange, store of value and unit of account. Money is one of the most ingenuous inventions of our time. It is useful as a medium of exchange since it prevents us from having to trade one concrete and inherently valuable thing for another. In reality money is not a thing and has no inherent value; it is not real or tied to anything of real substance or genuine wealth.

Because money may be used to obtain any material good, in a materialistic society it can take the place of God (the Divine) because it represents possession and enjoyment of all possible goods. Money can lead to judgment of others: those who have money or material possessions are admired and those who are materially poor are often scorned or forgotten. In such a society —

which is what our post-modern Western society is rapidly becoming —
humankind worships money (be it currency, gold or mortgages) as the Jewish
people literally did when they worshipped a golden calf in the time of Moses.
Indeed, God forbid Jews to worship the golden calf and forbid usury (lending
money with interest charges): "Thou shalt not lend upon usury to thy brother; usury of money, usury of victuals, usury of any thing that is lent upon
usury."[12]

Bernard Lietaer, professor of international finance at the University of
Leuven in Belgium, economist, former banker, one of the architects of the euro
and someone *Business Week* magazine proclaimed as the world's best currency
dealer, describes money as an agreement — like a marriage, a business contract or an agreement within a community — to use something as a means of
payment. According to Lietaer, it is important to realize that money is not a
living thing.[13]

Countries use a system of "fiat money" when they print paper currency or
mint coin. The Latin word *fiat* in Latin means "let it be made." Therefore fiat
money is literally created out of nothing or created by decree (usually by governments) to be something of value to be used as legal tender for the purpose
of exchange of goods and services. So money itself has no inherent or genuine
value but only has power in our economic system because we have collectively agreed to use it as a medium of exchange.

Most people think that governments control the creation of money.
However, the truth is that only a tiny fraction of today's money is in the form
of currency or minted coin, created at almost no cost by governments. Bernard
Lietaer reminds us that almost all money is created in the form of a debt or
loan; dollars, pounds, euros or yen are created through bank loans. Today over
98% of the US and Canadian money supply is in the form of debt. Few appreciate what this collective mountain of government, business, household and
foreign debt (now over US$42 trillion in the US) means; it represents a moun-
tain of debt that can never be repaid.

Nobel Prize winner in chemistry Frederick Soddy noted that money represents a claim against real wealth[14] or what we might call life capital —
human, social and natural. Soddy wrote that "wealth is the positive quantity
to be measured and money as the claim to wealth is a debt, a quantity of
wealth owed to but not owned by the owner of the money."[15] Herman Daly
supports Soddy's contentions noting that "the fundamental error in economics is the confusion of wealth, a magnitude with a physical, irreducible di-

mension, with debt, a purely mathematical or imaginary quantity."[16] Because a human being cannot alone amass the physical requirements to survive, he or she converts non-storable surplus of capital into a lien against future income ("future sunlight" in Frederick Soddy's words). We trade money today for the right to consume tomorrow.[17]

The obligations to pay the interest on this collective mountain of debt gives the economy as a whole a basic growth bias. Since the accumulated outstanding debt is unrepayable out of current production by factories, businesses and household labor, the economy must expand through increasing output in order to feed the insatiable appetite of a debt-based money system. Real wealth, as Soddy and Daly see it, is subject to the limits of nature and the force of entropy; Soddy saw true wealth as income/revenue (living capital) just like sunlight. Because real income from real wealth is insufficient to repay the mathematically growing mountain of fictitious money (debt), we are creating a protracted and vicious circle of debt financing and repayment from the depletion of human capital (labor) and natural capital (resources, land). This is why the system is like cancer: if compound interest is left unchecked the accumulated debt will consume its host, the life economy. This process of compound interest is assumed to be normal in our age yet in reality it is pathological. Frederick Soddy noted that this could not go on without ultimate system bankruptcy: "If wealth cannot be created *ex nihilo* then how can we allow money (debt) to be created *ex nihilo* (and just as easily destroyed)?"[18]

Therein lies the great paradox about economic growth, export-import trade regimes and debt-based money systems. Firms and households are caught in a perpetual motion machine required to produce more output and trade their labor (life's energy) to repay debts which are mathematically unrepayable. Even if firms and households wished to pursue sustainable living or voluntary simplicity, the burden of debt precludes them from pursuing such desired outcomes. Debt-based money is the lifeblood of the economy, and the banking system is its heart. Without debt money expansion, the entire system would collapse.

Many believe that the exponential growth of debt in most countries could lead to an economic apocalypse. There is increasing evidence that many households are facing a debt time bomb in Canada and the US. According to a Canadian study, household debt levels may now exceed disposable income by 105% or more. Debt is increasing faster than the economy's fundamentals can support; personal or household borrowing to support our lifestyles is unsustainable and cannot be supported by our incomes. Many households are vulnerable to higher interest rates and thus potential bankruptcy.[19] Over the last 50 years of our economic progress, our entire economic prosperity has been financed by debt: mortgages, personal loans, credit card debt, government debt and business debt which thanks to the power of compounding interest has soared exponentially. Virtually everything we purchase these days is purchased with credit while savings have declined to all-time lows.

Why do we want money so badly?

Instead of being a simple medium of exchange money has itself become a store of value. As a result of interest there is an incentive to hoard money. We want money so badly partly because it is in limited supply and other people want it too. People want money because they believe it gives them the power to purchase goods and services they need. Our collective consent over its purchasing power is the only thing that gives money power over us. If money is the true opiate of modern society, who are the powers which control its creation and destruction and how is it created?

How is money created?

> The process by which banks create money is so simple the mind is repelled. Where something so important is involved, a deeper mystery seems only decent.   — JOHN KENNETH GALBRAITH[20]

The late economist John Maynard Keynes once noted that he knew only three people who understood money: a professor at another university; one of his own students and a rather junior clerk at the Bank of England.[21] The current money systems — whether private banks or national banks — create money in parallel with debt and literally with no relationship to the actual life conditions or needs of a community. In short, all money is effectively in the form of a loan, a debt which commands interest payments and is ultimately a permanent claim on the genuine wealth of individuals, families, businesses, governments and society. This process of money creation was confirmed by England's former central banker (Chancellor of the Exchequer) the Rt. Hon. Reginald McKenna: "I am afraid that the ordinary citizen would not like to be told that banks or the Bank of England, can create and destroy money. The amount of money in existence varies only with the action of the banks in increasing and decreasing deposits and bank purchases. Every loan, overdraft or bank purchase creates a deposit and every repayment of a loan, overdraft or bank sale destroys a deposit."[22]

In other words all money is literally created out of nothing when a private bank issues a mortgage, a student loan or a business loan or the government prints money and issues a government debt bond. This means that citizens and governments are left out of the potentially significant benefit of minting coins and printing currency at a miniscule cost to taxpayers. Instead, we collectively pay interest on all that we buy and sell and on a growing mountain of debt that was initially created by private bank corporations and held widely by individuals and businesses.

In the US between 1950 and 2005, for example, the total outstanding debt (household, business, government, and foreign) has increased 86 times compared with a 40 times increase in GDP. How dramatically the debt load is outstripping economic growth! In 2005, total outstanding debt (excluding the unfunded liabilities) as a percentage of GDP was 326% and growing. According to the Federal Reserve statistics, as of the fourth quarter of 2006 the total outstanding debt for the entire US economy stood at $44.55 trillion:$14.13 trillion from the domestic financial sector, $12.82 trillion from households ($9.67 trillion in mortgages and $2.43 in consumer credit), $8.99 trillion from businesses, $4.88 trillion in federal government debt, $2.00 trillion in state and local government debt, and $1.72 trillion in foreign-owned debt. This total outstanding debt amounts to $105,369 for every person in America. Add to this unofficial estimates of nearly $25 trillion in unfunded Social Security and Medicare liabilities and you have a debt mountain of roughly $69.55

> "Each and every time a bank makes a loan, new bank credit is created — new deposits — brand new money."
> — GRAHAM TOWERS, former Governor of the Central Bank of Canada[23]

trillion dollars or $232,218 owing per American. If you applied a 5.5% interest rate (a reasonable long-term preferred bond rate) to the total outstanding and unrepayable mountain of debt, including the unfunded liabilities, Americans would be paying roughly $3.82 trillion annually in interest charges alone. This amount continues to increase. If this were not bad enough, consider that an estimated $2 trillion worth of currencies is traded every day around the world, roughly 90% of which is accounted for by speculation that is unrelated to the sale of goods and services. This amounts to an estimated

$730 trillion per year created through currency speculation; the global casino economy amounts to 12 times more than the world's total income or Gross World Product of $65 trillion in 2006.[25]

Most people, including most economists, do not appreciate that, unlike a personal mortgage you can hope to repay, the total outstanding debt of nations is unrepayable out of the current and future production of all of our households and businesses. No matter how much harder we work, how much more efficient we become or how much more we grow the economy, debt obligations remain and indeed grow worse by the day. In essence, entire nations and the world itself are mortgaged. The new money needed just to service the interest on the outstanding debt requires new loans or new debt.

> "Money is created out of nothing (*fiat lux*) when a government prints a number on a piece of paper or a bank issues a loan and credits the amount to an account in its computers. It has no substance or inherent utility, and since President Nixon took the US dollar off the gold standard in 1971, the governments and banks that create it no longer back it with anything of value."
> — DAVID C. KORTEN[24]

This debt-based system of money is, however, only a recent phenomenon. In ancient times money took the form of cattle (our word "pecuniary" comes from the Latin word for cattle, *pecus*), shells or other tokens used in the barter or exchange economy to pay for goods and services (the word pay is from the Latin *pacare* meaning to pacify, to appease, to make peace). In hunting and gathering cultures, food and practical items for living were exchanged in ceremonies like the potlatch (a ceremony of gifting from one family to another; a form of thanksgiving). Eventually money took the form of gold coins; gold was chosen as a medium of exchange because it was incorruptible, scarce, precious, beautiful and useful for making jewelry. There was a time when money was created or issued by the Sovereign (King or Queen) or the Government (Crown), as the basis of paying taxes and as a medium of exchange, not as a store of value. The reigning monarch issued money in the forms of notes and coins based on his or her perceived needs of the community and legitimized the money with a portrait. Throughout much of England's history, for example, there was no debt; instead "tally sticks" were used as the medium of exchange.[26] England used the tally stick as money until 1826; this period in English economic history was one of its most stable. Money was created without debt and thus without a cost to the people. Until modern times "money" had to be a scarce good, of some real or inherent value, or backed up by something valuable like gold or silver.

This changed with the emergence of fiat currencies and then credit financing. Fiat money creation meant that governments could print money without regard to any limiting factors. Benjamin Franklin (1706–1790), who spent several years in England studying their banking system, came to the conclusion that the English colonies in North America could issue their own money (Colonial Script) in proper proportion to make goods pass easily from producers to consumers. In this manner the colonies controlled both the creation and purchasing power of money with no interest charges paid to English bankers. England countered by issuing laws that forbid the colonies from issuing their own money. According to Franklin this was the real cause of the American revolutionary war.

Over time fiat money created free of charge by governments was replaced by credit money created by private banks. Credit money is a byproduct of lending and borrowing money. While strictly speaking debt is not money because debt is not a unit of account, issuing loans or debt-instruments has become the dominant form of money creation in our modern economies.

> This is a staggering thought. We are completely dependent on the commercial banks. Someone has to borrow every dollar we have in circulation, cash or credit. If the banks create ample synthetic money we are prosperous; if not, we starve. We are absolutely without a permanent money system. When one gets a complete grasp of the picture, the tragic absurdity of our hopeless position is almost incredible, but there it is. It is the most important subject intelligent persons can investigate and reflect upon. It is so important that our present civilization may collapse unless it becomes widely understood and the defects remedied very soon.
>
> — ROBERT H. HEMPHILL,
> Credit manager of Federal Reserve Bank, Atlanta, Georgia[27]

In an economy with thousands of mortgages and other household and business loans, the collection of interest by banks results in the concentration of wealth in the hands of those who already have money to lend. At a systems level, this growing mountain of debt forces society into an endless and ultimately unsustainable loop of economic growth where new money must be constantly lent into existence as debt to pay off old loans. In reality, the total amount of outstanding debt is unrepayable out of our current production and labor.

Usury was originally defined as receiving any interest on money, and this practice was deemed a sin by both Islam and by the Catholic Church for centuries. This was, however, forgotten after King Henry VIII of England legalized usury in 1545. One could say that the world is in the midst of a pandemic of usury where all have accepted interest paid on both savings and interest charged on loans. The entire money system is driven by interest payments,

What is a mortgage?

Few people, including loans officers in banks, appreciate what a mortgage is or how it is created. Prior to the 20th century, having a mortgage was equivalent to being gripped not only for your own life but for multiple generations by the price paid for borrowed money to purchase your home (principal plus interest payments on the principal). A mortgage is a form of a loan that banks create through a simple bookkeeping entry. When the bank creates money by providing you with a $100,000 mortgage loan, it creates only the principal when it credits your account. With a 20-year mortgage, the bank expects you to pay back a total of $200,000 in repayment and interest over the next 20 years. If you don't, you will lose your home. It is important to realize that your bank is not creating the second $100,000. Your bank does not create the interest; it sends you out into the world to compete with others to bring back the second $100,000. Because all the other banks do exactly the same thing, the system requires that some participants go bankrupt in order to provide you with your $100,000. In other words, some people must lose money or go bankrupt in order to put others in the position to pay off their loan. When you pay back interest on your loan, you are using someone else's principal.[28] Now consider the effects of this process on a society with thousands of mortgages, car loans, and business loans.

which fundamentally goes against the vision of a sustainable economy. Indeed, this debt-based system actually works against the goals of sustainability and building economies of well-being. It doesn't matter if you are a household with a mortgage or Starbucks with a business loan, no one is capable of escaping the system that compels us to work harder and make a profit today to help pay the interest on our exponentially growing individual and collective debt. The result is that our collective actions remain focused on the short term rather than on long-term sustainable objectives. It means that it is financially beneficial to extract more oil than we need, cut down old growth forests or fish the oceans to extinction even though we know this is both unsustainable and ruinous. Bank interest grows faster than natural capital. The system is also biased against investments in long-term renewable energy infrastructure such as expensive solar panels because our financial calculators (net present value calculus) tell us that these kinds of investments don't pay as well as putting your money in the bank. As Bernard Lietaer explained, in the current monetary system it would make no sense to take 100 years to build a beautiful cathedral even if it were to provide a place of worship for the next 800 years.[29]

> An estimated 30–50% of the costs of all goods and services are imbedded interest costs.

One of the great misconceptions of money is that when we borrow money we only pay the interest on the money we borrow. In fact, interest costs are literally imbedded in everything we buy and sell. German economist Margarit Kennedy explains that, "Every price we pay includes a certain amount of interest. The exact proportion varies according to the labour versus capital costs of the goods and services we buy. This ranges from a capital share of only 12% in garbage collection, (because here the share of capital costs is relatively low and the share of physical labour is particularly high) to 38% in drinking water, up to 77% in public housing. On the average we pay about 50% interest in all the prices of our goods and services. In medieval times, people paid 'the tenth' of their income or produce to the feudal landlord. In this respect, they were better off than we are nowadays, where one half of each Deutsch Mark (DM) or Dollar goes to serve people who own capital."[30]

I have come to the conclusion that if interest charges on all debts were eliminated we would likely have to work at least 50% less since much of our current labor is going to pay for interest charges on the collective outstanding debt throughout the economy. This would require the repudiation of usury. If we forgave debt charges, we could enjoy life more since we would have more free time to devote to things that make life worthwhile. We would have more time to heal our broken relationship with nature and renew the strength of our relationships. Also, we wouldn't have to keep the economy growing at unsustainable rates.

If money is nothing more than an agreement and money is created largely by banks which are businesses chartered to create the money, what would prevent us from no longer believing in the monetary system or withdrawing our consent? The problem is that it's not easy trying to live outside of a ubiquitous system; for the vast majority of people who have limited financial wealth there is no alternative or escape from debt financing our lifestyles. Moreover, there is no escaping from what economists call inflation.

The prevailing view in mainstream economics is that inflation is caused by the interaction of the supply of money with output and interest rates that results in a rise in the general level of prices, as measured against some baseline of purchasing power. It means that there is too little money available to chase the goods available resulting in an increase in what people will pay for these goods. Margarit Kennedy explains that the role of inflation in our economic system is misunderstood and is not natural at all. She notes that inflation is just another form of taxation which governments use to overcome the worst problems of an increasing interest burden. When governments print money to reduce their debts inflation results.[31] I have also challenged the conventional definition of inflation: if most money is created in the form of a debt or loan by private banks, inflation is really an increase in money supply through the issuance of debt. It is not physical assets, labor or natural resources which are inherently scarce but rather it is money which is made artificially scarce. One might agree that this is truly a form of magic or a form of systemic slavery in which we are all collectively participating.

The role of the central bank in money creation

A great industrial nation is controlled by its system of credit. Our system of credit is concentrated. The growth of the Nation and all our activities are in the hands of a few men. We have come to be one of the worst ruled, one of the most completely controlled and dominated Governments in the world — no longer a Government of free opinion no longer a Government by conviction and vote of the ma-

jority, but a Government by the opinion and duress of small groups
of dominant men.   — US President Woodrow Wilson[32]

If understanding the modus operandi of private banks is difficult, understanding the role and functions of central banks adds another layer of complexity. In most nations the central bank controls monetary policy through
adjusting interest rates. Central banks also control the liquidity of private
banks by determining their reserve requirements: how much money banks
must have on hand to meet demand deposits of their customers. While in
principle central banks should be operating in the interests of the people's
happiness and well-being, most are no different than private banks. Interest
rates are adjusted the way the fuel injection system on a vehicle is operated, to
provide just enough new money in the system to sustain economic growth.

  You may believe that central banks are public institutions of the government. However in the United States, the Federal Reserve Bank is a privately-
owned institution consisting of 12 regional banks. It is owned and controlled
by member banks, which are themselves privately owned bank corporations.
The US Fed is the most powerful institution in the country since it controls
monetary policy, interest rates, the issuance of money, the control of reserve
requirements for private bank loans and ultimately the entire economic des-
tiny of every citizen. However, because the Fed is a private corporation, the
constituent member banks receive approximately 6% profit on funds paid
into the Fed, no matter the economic conditions.

  With its establishment in 1913, the seniorage over money creation in
the US fell into private hands. Edward G. Griffin examined the secret meeting on Jekyll Island in Georgia at which the Federal Reserve was conceived.
This meeting created a banking cartel designed to protect its members from
competition; a strategy was also developed to convince Congress and the public that this cartel was an agency of the United States government. Griffin
identifies seven men who were present, representing an estimated one-fourth
of the total wealth of the entire world. They were:

  1. Nelson W. Aldrich, Republican whip in the Senate, Chairman of the Na-
     tional Monetary Commission, business associate of J. P. Morgan, father-
     in-law to John D. Rockefeller, Jr.
  2. Abraham Piatt Andrew, Assistant Secretary of the United States Treasury
  3. Frank A. Vanderlip, president of the National City Bank of New York
     (the most powerful of the banks at that time) representing William

Rockefeller and the international investment banking house of Kuhn, Loeb & Company

4. Henry P. Davison, senior partner of the J. P. Morgan Company
5. Charles D. Norton, president of J. P. Morgan's First National Bank of New York
6. Benjamin Strong, head of J. P. Morgan's Bankers Trust Company
7. Paul M. Warburg, a partner in Kuhn, Loeb & Company, a representative of the Rothschild banking dynasty in England and France, and brother to Max Warburg who was head of the Warburg banking consortium in Germany and the Netherlands

Anthony Sutton, former Research Fellow at the Hoover Institution for War, Revolution and Peace and also Professor of Economics at California State University, Los Angeles, provided insights into the motivation behind the creation of the US Fed. He wrote: "Warburg's revolutionary plan to get American Society to go to work for Wall Street was astonishingly simple. Even today, ...academic theoreticians cover their blackboards with meaningless equations, and the general public struggles in bewildered confusion with inflation and the coming credit collapse, while the quite simple explanation of the problem goes undiscussed and almost entirely uncomprehended. The Federal Reserve System is a legal private monopoly of the money supply operated for the benefit of the few under the guise of protecting and promoting the public interest."[33]

As Congressman Paul describes, the US Fed literally controls the life

A fiat monetary system allows power and influence to fall into the hands of those who control the creation of new money, and to those who get to use the money or credit early in its circulation. The insidious and eventual cost falls on unidentified victims who are usually oblivious to the cause of their plight. This system of legalized plunder (though not constitutional) allows one group to benefit at the expense of another. An actual transfer of wealth goes from the poor and the middle class to those in privileged financial positions.

— US Congressman Ron Paul[34]

blood of the nation by carefully adjusting money supply through its interest rate policies. The Fed unabashedly admits that it purposely tries to maintain the scarcity of money; "Money...derives its value from its scarcity in relation to its usefulness."[35] In other words the Fed maintains a system that is based on the myth of scarcity even if most Americans would affirm the truth of an abundant and loving universe. Yet while the Fed would appear to have the ultimate power over monetary policy and thus money creation it only contributes about 2% to the creation of the US money supply. It is the private banks that, pursuant to the fractional reserve banking authorized by the Federal Reserve Act of 1913, make or create-from-nothing-for-their-private-profit the other roughly 98% of the US money supply. The Fed is thus simply a quasi-governmental central organizing body behind which the real private banking money-creation system operates.

Fractional reserve banking is the practice of issuing paper notes in amounts which exceed the value of the stores of gold, silver or other inherently valuable assets they represent. This means that loans can be issued by private banks that exceed the value or even physical asset which supports the loan. In the United States as in most other nations, issuing paper money in parallel with gold reserves became too limiting. In 1971 US President Richard Nixon relaxed the need to tie money creation to US gold reserves effectively allowing unlimited amounts of debt-money to be created. As Frederick Soddy noted "Money now is nothing you get from something before you can get anything."[36]

Patrick S. J. Carmack and Bill Still together produced an important documentary film "The Money Masters" on the history of money power in the United States since the revolutionary war. In the film they examine the development of a central or national bank in the US that eventually gave rise to the establishment of the US Federal Reserve Bank. They describe how several presidents including Jefferson, Madison, Jackson and Lincoln fought the money power's desire to establish a private national bank. The original stockholders of the Fed included many of the major US national private banks. Today, the most powerful of the 12 Fed Banks is the New York Federal Reserve Bank, once more widely owned by the major New York national banks and dominated by a single New York bank, which according to Pat Carmack is either JP Morgan Chase or Citigroup.[38]

An even broader international money power also exists, a network of central banks that form what is known as the Bank for International Settlements.

How does the Fed "create" money out of nothing? It is a four-step process. But first a word on bonds. Bonds are simply promises to pay — government IOUs. People buy bonds to get a secure rate of interest. At the end of the term of the bond, the government repays the principal plus interest (if not paid periodically), and the bond is destroyed. There are trillions of dollars worth of these bonds at present. Now here is the Fed moneymaking process:

Step 1. The Fed Open Market Committee approves the purchase of US Bonds on the open market.

Step 2. The bonds are purchased by the New York Fed Bank from whoever is offering them for sale on the open market.

Step 3. The Fed pays for the bonds with electronic credits to the seller's bank, which in turn credits the seller's bank account. These credits are based on nothing tangible. The Fed just creates them.

Step 4. The banks use these deposits as reserves. Most banks may loan out ten times (10x) the amount of their reserves to new borrowers, all at interest.

In this way, a Fed purchase of, say a million dollars worth of bonds, gets turned into over 10 million dollars in bank deposits. The Fed, in effect, creates 10% of this totally new money and the banks create the other 90%.

This also explains why the Fed consistently holds about 10% of the total US Treasury bonds. It had to buy those (with accounts or Fed notes the Fed simply created) from the public in order to provide the base for the rest of the money the private banks then get to create, most of which eventually winds up being used to purchase Treasury bonds, thus supplying Congress with the borrowed money to pay for its expenditures.

Due to a number of important exceptions to the 10% reserve ratio, some loans require less than 10% reserves, and many require no (0%) reserves, making it possible for banks to create many times more than ten times the money they have in "reserve." Due to these exceptions from the 10% reserve requirement, the Fed creates only a little under 2% of the total US money supply, while private banks create the other 98%.

To reduce the amount of money in the economy, the process is just reversed — the Fed sells bonds to the public, and money flows out of the purchaser's local bank. Loans must be reduced by ten times the amount of the sale. So a Fed sale of a million dollars in bonds, results in 10 million dollars less money in the economy.[37]

Carroll Quigley, a political history professor at Georgetown University and a person whom former President Bill Clinton considered one of his most influential teachers, provided a succinct description of the goal of the international money power:

> The powers of financial capitalism had a far-reaching aim, nothing less than to create a world system of financial control in private hands able to dominate the political system of each country and the economy of the world as a whole. This system was to be controlled in a feudalist fashion by the central banks of the world acting in concert, by secret agreements arrived at in frequent meetings and conferences. The apex of the systems was to be the Bank for International Settlements in Basel, Switzerland, a private bank owned and controlled by the world's central banks which were themselves private corporations. Each central bank...sought to dominate its government by its ability to control Treasury loans, to manipulate foreign exchanges, to influence the level of economic activity in the country, and to influence cooperative politicians by subsequent economic rewards in the business world.[39]

For most of us this information is simply too much to comprehend. It may leave one to despair about changing a system so entrenched and so powerful. However change is always possible, and there are a few people I know that are raising awareness and offering practical solutions to a system that is clearly unjust and unsustainable. I encourage my students to study the history of banking, money and their nation and come to their own conclusions. We are collectively responsible for raising our awareness of how the system operates and to individually and collective begin to explore, negotiate and design new agreements regarding money and who should have the power to create it. Put simply we need to choose between a system of money that supports life and the pursuit of happiness and a system that is akin to a societal cancer

It is well enough that people of the nation do not understand our banking and monetary system, for if they did, I believe there would be a revolution before tomorrow morning.   — HENRY FORD[40]

whose appetite is so insatiable that it will eventually kill its host. Fortunately, the current money system is both unnecessary and can be changed. Money and its creation can then cease to be our master and be returned to its rightful place as an effective medium of exchange.

The origins of usury: Charging interest on money

There must be no lending at interest.   — PLATO

The trade of the petty usurer is hated with most reason: it makes a profit from currency itself, instead of making it from the process which currency was meant to serve. Their common characteristic is obviously their sordid avarice.   — ARISTOTLE[41]

Banking was conceived in iniquity and was born in sin. The bankers own the earth. Take it away from them, but leave them the power to create money, and with the flick of the pen they will create enough deposits to buy it back again. However, take it away from them, and all the great fortunes like mine will disappear and they ought to disappear, for this would be a happier and better world to live in. But, if you wish to remain the slaves of bankers and pay the cost of your own slavery, let them continue to create money.

— SIR JOSIAH STAMP (Director of the Bank of England in the 1920s
and reputed to be the second wealthiest man in England at that time)[42]

Charging any interest on the use of money is called usury from the Latin *usuria* meaning "demanding in return for a loan a greater amount than was borrowed." Originally usuary was charging a fee for the use of money. This usually meant interest on loans, although charging a fee for changing money (as at a bureau de change) is included in the original meaning. Usury infers a wearing down or diminishing, taking advantage of another and assumes the creation of new wealth that does not exist in reality. Usury was denounced by countless spiritual leaders and philosophers of ancient times, including Plato, Aristotle, Cato, Cicero, Seneca, Plutarch, Aquinas, Muhammad, Moses and Gautama Buddha. Usury was emphatically outlawed by Judaism, Christianity and Islam. It is only in the past 150 years that the strict definition and condemnation of usury was relaxed. A just interest rate on loans was allowed so long as the rate was not considered excessive or even criminal.

Usury is a hidden force in commerce and capitalism, playing constantly in the background. It is a practice that diminishes the real living capital wealth of the needy (those who need money for living) and consumes it to the profit of the lender. The result is the transfer of real wealth from the debtor to the lender. If unchecked, all living capital or real wealth will be absorbed into the hands of money brokers (namely banks) who control or are legally licensed to create money through credit or loans. While cancer kills individuals, usury has the power to kill both nature and destroy societies.

In Judaism, the charging of interest on loans was clearly limited. "Do not charge your brother interest, whether on money or food or anything else that may earn interest."[43] However, an exception is made "You may charge a foreigner interest, but not a brother Israelite, so that the Lord your God may bless you in everything you put your hand to in the land you are entering to possess."[44]

> To take usury for money lent is unjust in itself, because, this is to sell what does not exist, and this evidently leads to inequality, which is contrary to justice. Now, money was invented chiefly for the purpose of exchange. Hence, it is by its very nature unlawful to take payment for the use of money lent, which is known as interest.
>
> — THOMAS AQUINAS (1225–1275)[45]

Christianity until recent times outlawed usury. The Catholic Church has always considered charging of interest on money lent as a sin. In the Doctrine of Usury articulated at the Lateran Council (1512–1517) usury was defined as "receiving any interest on money." This meant that no interest could be charged at all in issuing loans. Over history the Catholic Church upheld these teachings in the encyclical by Pope Benedict XIV On Usury and Other Dishonest Profit promulgated on November 1, 1745. However since the mid 1800s the Church seems to have simply forgotten its own teachings.

In Islam the Qur'an unequivocally condemns usury. "Those who charge usury are in the same position as those controlled by the devil's influence. This is because they claim that usury is the same as commerce. However, God permits commerce, and prohibits usury. Thus, whoever heeds this commandment from his Lord, and refrains from usury, he may keep his past earnings, and his judgment rests with God. As for those who persist in usury, they incur Hell, wherein they abide forever."[46] "God condemns usury, and blesses charities."[47] The Prophet Mohammed is quoted that "Allah has forbidden you to take usury (interest), therefore all interest obligation shall henceforth be waived. Your capital is yours to keep. You will neither inflict nor suffer any inequality. Allah has judged that there shall be no interest and that all interest due to Abbas Ibn 'Aal-Muttalib be waived."[48] These teachings are embedded in Rabiah law; Islamic contract law prohibits trading on credit, and commercial transactions must be made on the spot.

Being anti-usury might be a far more compelling cause for unity among the religions and nations of the world than being anti-capitalist or anti-globalization. Ending interest everywhere simultaneously could be done with sufficient political will and the support of the world's citizens in every community. It would require an increased level of consciousness or awareness of the nature of usury in our world and a reminder of why virtually every religion forbids it. This would require remembering teachings and rediscovering their wisdom. A collective repudiation of usury would start a global revolution against forces which have led to unsustainable and unrepayable debt loads. It would simply require the power of the collective will power of people acting with passion, conviction and integrity, seeking truth and genuine justice.

Towards genuine money and banking

A future without usury — banking without interest — is not beyond our imagination. It is part of my vision for a Genuine Wealth economy. In my vision of the future, I see banks that no longer charge interest on loans but rather provide financial management advice to clients for a legitimate service fee. I envision a network of national, regional and municipal banks which issue currency to support innovation and entrepreneurship and to provide necessary liquidity to maintain the genuine wealth of communities. I envision these banks using Genuine Wealth accounts at various scales from the national to provincial/state and local community scale. Money would be created as a genuine medium of exchange in parallel with what the Genuine Wealth accounts tell us about the conditions of our human, social, natural and built capital assets.

I envision a money system which reflects reality. I picture a day when the Bank of Canada would be a legitimate Genuine Wealth Bank of Canada that makes decisions not based on outmoded measures like the GDP or using interest rates to calibrate an economy but instead where economists use national Genuine Wealth accounts and quality of life indicators to determine how much money is needed to ensure genuine sustainability of the nation, its people and a healthy natural environment. I see each province having its own provincial Genuine Wealth bank that would act in concert with other provincial banks and the federal Bank of Canada.

I see cooperative member-owned banks and credit unions operating locally within a community and replacing the current large privately owned banks whose directors and shareholders are absent. Ownership in these financial institutions would be widely held by citizens in a community in the form of a cooperative business enterprise. I see these new banks and credit unions return to their rightful role in the community, providing households and businesses with financial stewardship services and guidance to help the community at large become more effective and efficient stewards of the money or financial capital in the co-stewardship of the community's genuine wealth. Instead of issuing loans like mortgages, banks would become the facilitators of money sharing between individuals, households and businesses as the JAK Members Bank does in Sweden. I see genuine banking facilitating the sharing of financial capital between those who currently enjoy more (e.g. older adults) with those who are just getting started in life; between mature and sustainable business enterprise and the younger entrepreneur who has a dream or a great idea. This kind of interpersonal lending becomes a more genuine economy of reciprocity, of giving and receiving and of sharing genuine wealth assets. No longer would banks charge interest on loans but simply recover their operating and service costs with a fair service charge. Their social license to operate would be given or taken away by the community or local government based on the satisfaction of their customers. In addition, such banks and bankers can help facilitate investments in the genuine wealth (well-being) of their community, investments oriented towards sustainability of all capital. Their lending decisions could be connected with the Genuine Wealth accounting systems of local government or organizations like the United Way, community charitable foundations or other non-profits. I imagine a day when no longer do we stress about interest rates on mortgages and government debt but rather measure the conditions of our well-being and quality of life — including the health and vitality of our forests, lakes, rivers and air — accurately.

Decisions about how much money is created at the local level could be made by wisdom councils at various scales with members of the community selected from a cross section of socio-economic, cultural, religious, age and gender groupings. I envision the use of many forms of alternative currencies from a national currency that would facilitate inter-regional or inter-community trade to local currencies created by the community and circulated locally amongst households and businesses. I envision a world without usury; such a world would be conducive to an economy of happiness and well-being.

Genuine Wealth banking and money

For several years I have been studying practical alternative banking and currency systems throughout the world that could help to build a new Genuine Wealth banking and money system. Some examples include the JAK Members Bank of Sweden, Local Exchange Transaction Systems (LETS), local currencies (Salt Spring Island dollars, Ithaca hours), complementary currencies, gift and reciprocity economies as practiced by the Inuit of Canada's Arctic or in Bali in Indonesia.

A bank that doesn't charge interest: The JAK Members Bank of Sweden

> Interest causes unemployment, inflation and environmental destruction. Every hike in interest rates means that business has to pay more to service their loans. To counteract this financial strain they must either cut their labour costs, which worsens unemployment; or raise prices, causing inflation; or re-engineer their work to increase output, which leads to increased use of natural resources.
> — OSCAR KJELLBERG, CEO of JAK Members Bank, Sweden[49]

In 2003 I had the pleasure of visiting Oscar Kjellberg, an economist and CEO of the JAK Members Bank in Stockholm, Sweden. Bob Williams, former chairman of Vancity Credit Union in Vancouver, British Columbia, and I spent a week with Kjellberg studying how, explicitly rejecting usury, the JAK Bank operates without charging interests on loans. I wanted to demonstrate that a financial institution like Vancity could also operate on the JAK model without losing customers and indeed increase their market share.[50]

The JAK (which stands for land, labor and capital in Swedish) Members Bank is the first cooperative, no-interest, members-owned-bank in Sweden. The bank is owned and managed by its 25,000 members. JAK is a highly cost efficient enterprise operated by a small complement of 26 professional staff based out of a single office located in Skövde, Sweden, roughly 180 kilometers west of Stockholm. All business is done by telephone, internet or post through a state-of-the-art computer system. The enterprise is supported by 380 specially trained volunteers who support JAK's 24 regional communities. These dedicated volunteers are the "marketing force" which publicizes JAK's benefits and services without any labor cost. So great is the faith in the benefits of the JAK model that bank deposits as of year-end December 2002 totaled about 625 million SEK (C$101 million or US$64 million) and outstanding loans about 534 million SEK (C$86 million or US$55 million). JAK also maintains a reserve of Treasury Bills totaling 97.8 million SEK (C$15.8 million or US$10 million). Operating income in 2002 was roughly 26.1 million SEK (C$4.2 million or US$2.7 million) while operating costs in 2002 were roughly 22.2 million SEK (C$3.5 million or US$2.2 million). Net profits for 2002 were 789 thousand SEK (C$136 thousand or US$85 thousand).

The main purpose of JAK is to provide members with interest-free loans. Members are also able to earmark their savings for selected local enterprises through JAK Local Enterprise bank accounts. JAK is committed to spreading information about the ill effects of the prevailing interest-bearing monetary system (usury). There has been international recognition for JAK's contributions to global monetary reform, including interest amongst Muslims that JAK may provide a model of banking that is consistent with Rabiah law.

JAK is a bank of reciprocity where members share their savings, making no-interest loans available to other members and their families. In essence each member becomes a banker. This cooperative aspect of JAK is a remarkable feature that distinguishes it from all other banks. Moreover, the JAK Bank management takes on a more dynamic role in its community by maintaining a strong relationship with members and a shared interest in the well-being of member households, businesses and the communities that benefit from no-interest loans. JAK's original aim was to counter the way in which established banks are channeling savings from rural regions to urban centers abroad. Now it appeals to a broader spectrum of Swedes across the country.

How does JAK make money? In essence, it doesn't; at least it does not make money from money through interest. More importantly it empowers individuals to realize the power of money as a medium of exchange rather than a store of value or something to be hoarded. Through JAK, all members and their communities are better off by pooling their financial wealth and sharing it with those members most in need. Instead of financial wealth, "real" or "genuine wealth" of households and communities are being improved. JAK is a viable enterprise; I showed this with a full cost-accounting analysis comparing operating costs of JAK with Vancity.

Most banks make their profits from service fees and the margin between the interest rate they pay savers and the much higher interest rate they charge borrowers. JAK is not in the business of making a profit. JAK operates as close to break-even as possible, charging just enough in loan fees and membership fees to cover its operating costs. In 2002 it covered over 90% of its 22.2 million SEK (C$3.9 million or US$3.1 million) in operating costs (which includes 25 paid employees) through these fees. Those costs amount to an average per member operating cost of only C$144 per each of its 25,000 members. All members pay an annual membership fee of 200 Swedish kronor (about US$20 or $25 Canadian) that supports the costs of operating their account and provides them with a magazine that informs them about banks activities and educational workshops it organizes. Other sources of revenue include interest earned on liquid assets, including Swedish Treasury Bills that are held as a safety reserve against member savings.

JAK has several comparative advantages that make its model worth considering, particularly for savings and credit unions in North America. I believe that credit unions could achieve the benefits of the JAK, no-interest banking model with a rather small operational step change. The more challenging educational step would be to educate bankers and citizens so conditioned to paying interest!

JAK operates on these fundamental principles:
- Taking of interest is inimical to a stable economy
- Interest causes unemployment, inflation and environmental destruction — in some combination
- Interest moves money in the long term from the poor to the rich
- Interest favors projects, often large-scale, which yield high profits in the short-term

JAK's ultimate goal is to abolish interest as an economic instrument and to replace it with means which help its members build healthy and sustainable communities.

To achieve this goal, JAK works on two fronts:
1. Ideological: To disseminate information on harmful effects taking interest has on the economy, society at large and the environment and to present and explain alternatives.

2. Practical: To administer an interest-free savings-and-loan system to show that interest-free financing is not only feasible but also quite valuable in helping to liberate people weighed down with heavy interest loans.

JAK does have a positive if indirect effect on unemployment. As JAK liberates more people from interest expenses more money is freed up to buy goods and services. This stimulates businesses so that they can employ more people.

Figure 9.1. JAK Members Bank vs. Conventional Bank Model

Key Attributes	JAK Members Bank	Conventional Banks
Clients	A members-based, cooperative enterprise: one share, one vote.	Conventional corporate model: client-based with major shareholders.
Bank System	100% reserve system: Loans are lent out on the basis of the total liquidity (savings) in the system. Loans are 100% supported by member savings and liquid assets. All money is fully secured.	Fractional reserve system: Whenever a loan is issued, new money is created through two simple bookkeeping entries. The loan is largely unsupported by other member savings; only a small fraction of the loan needs to be secured by the private bank, under law, with a central bank. The reserve requirement of US private banks is currently a mere 0–3% on chequing accounts.
Loans	Loans are issued on the basis of bank liquidity and the member's income capacity to both save and repay the loan. Loan repayment is ONLY the principal of the loan.	Loans are issued on the basis of credit worthiness (assets that support the loan). Loan repayments include principal plus interest charges.
Interest on loans	Does not charge interest on loans but does recover operating costs through an administrative loan fee.	Charges interest on all loans and credit.
Interest on savings	Does not pay interest on savings but does provide a means of earning savings points which are like interest income.	Pays interest on savings, but at current low rates this is minimal.
Returns to investors	JAK operates like a not-for-profit bank enterprise , with its members as "careholders" whose returns include interest cost savings on all loans.	Private banks have shareholders who receive returns in the form of share value and dividends that result from profits earned from interest rate spreads, user fees and other bank profits.

Credit: Mark Anielski. The JAK Members Bank Sweden: an Assessment of Sweden's No-Interest Bank. 2004.

JAK's interest-free savings and loan model has appealed almost exclusively to consumers — especially those purchasing homes (90% of the membership). There are few commercial enterprises using the system.

How does the cost of a JAK loan compare to conventional bank loans? Using the JAK loan calculator developed by Börje Johansson and modified by Bengt Landegren, it is possible to compare the full costs of a JAK loan with a conventional bank loan. This calculation reveals the actual net savings in interest costs realized by a JAK member.

Calculate your savings points			Scroll to get the loan you wish	$20,000.00
Saving factor	0.7		Loan equity deposit	$1,200.00
One single deposit			Loan fee	$2,701.29
Monthly deposit			Loan fee per month	$22.51
Time of Deposit (months)	0		Repayment of loan per month	$166.67
Sum of saving points	0		After savings per month	$166.67
			Payment per month	$355.84
Add existing saving points			Payment per Q	$1,067.53
Repayment period (years)	10		Sum total of after savings	$20,000.00

Comparison between a conventional loan and a JAK loan

Borrowers annual service fee	$40		Size of bank loan	$20,000.00
Estimated interest payment	0.05%		Cost (interest) of bank loan (annuity loan)	$9,308.75
			Cost per month	$77.57
			Payment per month	$244.24
			Cost of bank loan (straight loan)	$8,251.23

Net Savings of a JAK Loan versus Conventional Bank Loan

Cost (loan fee) of JAK Loan	$2,701.29
JAK Annual Membership Fee	$339.27
Subtotal JAK Loan Costs	$3,040.56
Cost (interest) of conventional bank loan (annuity loan)	$9,308.75
Annual service fees	$400.00
Subtotal Conventional Loan Costs	$9,708.75
Net Cost Savings with JAK Loan	**$6,668.18**
Estimated Life Energy (days working) saved	76

FIGURE 9.2. The JAK Loan Calculator: Example: $20,000 loan (JAK vs. Conventional Bank Loan)

Credit: Mark Anielski. *The JAK Members Bank Sweden: an Assessment of Sweden's No-Interest Bank.* 2004.

The JAK loan has no interest charges, however JAK does charge a loan fee and an annual membership fee over the life of the loan. The membership fees over 10 years would total $339.27 while the loan fee (a monthly loan fee payment of $22.51) on a 10-year loan would total $2,701.29. The monthly loan repayment, the amount of principal repaid per month, is $166.67. At the same time the member is required to set aside by saving in JAK the same amount as the monthly principal loan repayment. So, in this example $166.67 per month goes into a savings account, without interest. These savings are meant to ensure there is enough liquidity in the banking system for other members. These monthly savings accumulate over time in the JAK Bank and would, in the case of our example, total $20,000 after 10 years which is fully available to the member three months after the last loan repayment has been made. When you add up all of the costs of this loan, the $10,000 JAK loan would cost the member $3,040.56.

I then compared a JAK loan with the interest and other costs for a conventional 10-year mortgage bank loan (in this example a 10-year, Canadian mortgage at 8.05%). The cost of interest charges alone is $9,308.75 plus an estimated total annual banking service fee (associated with the loan) of $400.00 for a total cost for a conventional bank loan of $9,708.75. This suggests that if you were a JAK Bank member you would save $6,668.18 in interest and other costs to borrow the same amount of money! I converted these cost savings into the number of days that an average worker would have had to work to pay for them if the average living wage (the hourly wage of a full-time worker to meet the needs of a household of four)[51] is $11.00 per hour. At this hourly rate a worker borrowing from JAK would have saved 76 working days that would have been required to pay interest costs on the conventional loan. We can then say that a JAK loan can literally save the most important asset in life — time or life energy — making it available to pursue other more life-giving and meaningful activities.

A Genuine Wealth bank

I can imagine the creation of new bank charters for Genuine Wealth banks. Genuine Wealth banks would be legally licensed to operate in a community's best interests. They would operate much like the JAK Bank, without charging interest, yet recovering their operating costs through member and service fees. A Genuine Wealth banker would facilitate financial wealth exchange within a cooperative banking environment as well as potentially serve as a financial coach or steward to clients. This new bank could also make use of the Genuine Wealth accounting system and well-being inventories maintained by municipal or local governments to determine bank lending policies that help support genuine wealth development in the community. They would operate on a 100% reserve system thereby eliminating fractional reserve banking and ultimately eliminating usury.

Each community would define its own unique set of needs and wants, using the means-to-ultimate-ends lens developed by Herman Daly to assess how real wealth is distributed amongst the community. These local Genuine Wealth banks could form a network of other cooperative Genuine Wealth banks across a region, province, state or nation by sharing information about genuine wealth conditions in other jurisdictions. The Genuine Wealth bank could also work closely with or become an arm of enterprises like Upstream 21 Corporation, owned by local residents who want to advance local economies that build, rather than erode, natural, social and economic capital.

There are other important banking models such as the Banca Ethica in Emilia Romagna, Italy which provides zero or low interest loans to poor households or small businesses and is compensated by the state for the interest in-

Genuine Wealth Bank

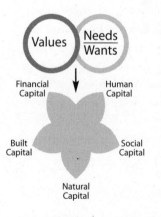

Assets	Using the genuine Wealth Accounts
• short-term	for each community of interests,
• medium-term	Genuine Wealth Banks would
• long-term	operate providing credit/loans
• intrinsic	(creating money) that are directly
	linked to the "genuine wealth" needs
Liabilities	and desires of the community.
• short-term	Genuine Wealth Banks would
• medium-term	operate with a social charter or
• long-term	license given by each community.
• expectations	

Members Equity

Genuine Wealth Accounts
Genuine Progress Indicators

FIGURE 9.3. The Genuine Wealth Bank Model

Credit: Mark Anielski. "The Genuine Wealth Bank: Redefining Banking for Genuine Well-being." January 7, 2004.

come it forgoes. Another model is the Edmonton Community Loan Fund (ECLF), a local bank that provides prime plus 1–2% loans to poor households who need small amounts of financial start-up capital. Other models include ShoreBank Pacific (Portland)[52], Chicago's South ShoreBank and the Grameen Bank in Bangladesh.[53]

The creation of a Genuine Wealth banking system is not utopian. The JAK story proves that banks can legally operate without resorting to usury. What will be required is small and concurrent experiments across the nations. For example in Edmonton, I have spoken with a few Christian church communities about creating a JAK-style trust which would allow members of congregations to give out small or no interest to church members.

National, State or Provincial Wealth banks

I am among a few economists, former bankers, accountants, lawyers and academics who believe that reforms to the US Federal Reserve and the Bank of Canada are possible and feasible within our lifetimes. What is required is the will power to make amendments in the laws and constitutions of nations to return the money power to the people. I acknowledge that the challenge is daunting given the pervasiveness of the current system of central banking. However I would like to hope that vision, with practical steps and conviction, could lead to such a change.

What if accountability for monetary policies of our nations were oriented towards building and sustaining genuine wealth? Imagine US or Canadian Genuine Wealth Dollars facilitating more genuine trade of the nations' comparative advantages rather than supporting the current system of trade which encourages over production and over consumption. Imagine the province of Alberta or the State of Texas using Alberta and Texas Genuine Wealth accounts to guide regional monetary policy and possibly issuing provincial or state currency. Imagine the City of Seattle or the City of Edmonton having a set of municipal Genuine Wealth accounts to guide local banking and credit decision making. Imagine the creation of local complementary currencies — Seattle Bucks or Edmonton Dollars. Money would no longer be created out of thin air but created in proportion to the real life conditions in a community and to improve or sustain the real wealth and quality of life of each community in accordance with its own assets and dreams.

Such a reformed central bank would require that all private banks maintain a 100% reserve against their member deposits, eliminating the ruinous

How would the Genuine Wealth bank operate?

The Genuine Wealth bank would be cooperative, member-owned and non usurious. It would operate on a full cost recovery basis, charging administration fees to members for the financial services provided. The Genuine Wealth bank would operate on the principle of facilitating the pooling of individual financial capital to be then available to those most immediately in need for liquidity. The Genuine Wealth bank would teach people that they are sovereign with respect to money.

Cooperative

The Genuine Wealth bank would be owned by its members, including households, local businesses and entrepreneurs who live and work in the community. These members would pool their financial assets (savings) in a cooperative social enterprise sharing a common vision of the bank as a financial steward. Like the JAK bank, members would be encouraged to save their work income in the bank, earning points which are redeemable in the future as no-interest loans to themselves, their family members or other members of the community. Money and credit are therefore seen as common assets, as services (mediums of exchange) that facilitate efficient stewardship of the community's assets while encouraging entrepreneurship and meaningful work for all in the community, regardless of their capacity (skills or knowledge) to work.

Scale

The scale of the Genuine Wealth bank could range from clusters of 50–500 households or families. Though scale may not be a constraining factor, the closer the bank is to the community, the more effective the relationship between members of that community in relationship to the banks' financial services.

Legal structure

Whether the bank would be chartered under conventional Canadian or US banking laws or established as a trust needs to be worked out. The

Genuine Wealth bank should however be governed through a social license given by the municipal, provincial or state government. This license would specify the principles and terms of services and relationships the bank has with its cooperative members (households). It would be governed by its members, who might serve on the board on a rotating basis with three-year terms.

Use of Genuine Wealth accounts

Credit decisions and policies would be made according to a set of Genuine Wealth accounts. Loans (micro business, mortgages, student loans, etc.) would be extended on the basis of what the Genuine Wealth accounts reveal about the community as a whole and how the individual borrower's needs or dreams align with the need for flourishing and sustainable communities.

The banker's role

The Genuine Wealth bank model returns the banker to a more noble and integral part of the community, understanding the needs, aspirations and assets of its members to build truly sustainable and vibrant communities. I began to imagine this possibility after talking with Oscar Kjellberg of JAK Bank in his tugboat-home in Stockholm in July of 2003. Oscar was concerned for the future well-being of his bank members from the looming crisis of peak oil. This led us to imagine JAK playing a leadership role in Sweden by helping households finance alternative and renewable energy systems, such as solar, wind, geothermal or micro-hydro systems. Oscar imagined a day when Sweden would be free of its dependence on oil. It is fitting that Sweden's Prime Minister has since announced that Sweden would be take concrete measures to become the first nation to be an oil-free society or no longer dependent on oil by 2020.[54] Somehow, I sense Oscar had a role to play in this, and that JAK may help to facilitate it coming to pass.

fractional reserve system that currently leads to compounded mountains of unrepayable debt. Private banks should be left to receive deposits and make loans and charge fees for their services on a full 100% reserve basis so that they do not create any money. Nor would the state make any loans (except for modest ones for temporary situations). It means that the power over money creation returns back to the commonwealth, to *res publica* (a public matter) or the people through their government. These changes would fundamentally alter the current disordered usurious system. US President Abraham Lincoln spelled this out clearly in an address to the US Senate in 1865:

> Money is the creature of law, and the creation of the original issue of money should be maintained as the exclusive monopoly of national government.... The monetary needs of increasing numbers of people advancing towards higher standards of living can and should be met by the government. Such needs can be met by the issue of national currency and credit through the operation of a national banking system. The circulation of a medium of exchange issued and backed by the government can be properly regulated and redundancy of issue avoided by withdrawing from circulation such amounts as may be necessary by taxation, re-deposit and otherwise. Government, possessing the power to create and issue currency and credit as money...need not and should not borrow capital at interest.... The financing of all public enterprises, the maintenance of stable government and ordered progress, and the conduct of the Treasury will become matters of practical administration... Money will cease to be the master and become the servant of humanity. Democracy will rise superior to the money power.[55]

Pat Carmack has drafted a statutory Monetary Reform Act which spells out in sufficient detail some practical steps to return the power of money creation back to the US Congress. The act proposes:

> To restore confidence in and governmental control over money and credit, to stabilize the money supply and price level, to establish full reserve banking, to prohibit fractional reserve banking, to retire the national debt, to repeal conflicting Acts, to withdraw from international banks, to restore political accountability for monetary policy,

and to remove the causes of economic depressions, without additional taxation, inflation or deflation, and for other purposes.[56]

Carmack has provided a legal framework for ending of usury in the United States.

The late economist and Nobel Laureate Milton Friedman recommended reform whereby "Congress shall have the power to authorize non-interest-bearing obligations of the government in the form of currency or book entries, provided that the total dollar amount outstanding increases by no more than 5 percent per year and no less than 3 percent...a Constitutional Amendment would be the most effective way to establish confidence in the stability of the rule...Congress could equally well legislate it."[57] Of Carmack's proposed Monetary Reform Act he wrote: "I am entirely sympathetic with the objectives of your Monetary Reform Act... You deserve a great deal of credit for carrying through so thoroughly on your own conception...I am impressed by your persistence and attention to detail in your successive revisions."[58]

Frederick Soddy recommended restoring honesty and accuracy to the function of money in the economic system through three basic reforms:

1. A 100% reserve requirement for commercial banks
2. A policy of maintaining a constant price index
3. Freely fluctuating exchange rates internationally

Soddy envisioned a monetary system that was connected with real wealth to eliminate the obfuscation prevalent in a chrematistic world. What Soddy advocated was money creation that is tied to the physical laws of nature (e.g. laws of thermodynamics) and the real wealth of communities including natural capital. Soddy noted that the "acid test (for such a monetary system) is that no monetary accountancy be allowed that could not be done equally well by physical counters."[59] Money creation would then be tied to the sustained well-being of all living capital, no longer disconnected from that which makes life worthwhile and no longer leading to the unwitting destruction of real wealth.

Herman Daly and John Cobb Jr. support Soddy's vision stating that "We believe these policies remain very sensible even though the world has changed much in the half century since they were suggested."[60] Soddy's key reform was the adoption of a 100% reserve requirement for private banks. Depression-era economist Irving Fisher (author of 100% Money) was also a

I see us free, therefore, to return to some of the most sure and certain principles of religion and traditional virtue that avarice is a vice, that the exaction of usury is a misdemeanour, and the love of money is detestable, that those walk most truly in the paths of virtue and sane wisdom who take least thought for the morrow. We shall once more value ends above means and prefer the good to the useful. We shall honor those who can teach us how to pluck the hour and the day virtuously and well, the delightful people who are capable of taking direct enjoyment in things, the lilies of the field who toil not, neither do they spin. But beware! The time for all this is not yet. For at least another hundred years we must pretend to ourselves and to every one that fair is foul and foul is fair; for foul is useful and fair is not. Avarice and usury and precaution must be our gods for a little longer still. For only they can lead us out of the tunnel of economic necessity into daylight.

— JOHN MAYNARD KEYNES[61]

strong advocate for 100% government-created, debt-free money. This would preclude private banks from creating and destroying money as they currently do by lending money into existence. Of course, such reform would constrain the current exponential growth and profits that are exhibited in national debt, GDP and stock market statistics.

Consider a potential future scenario. Monetary policy and investment decisions are made based on evidence contained in the Genuine Wealth accounts for the nation, provinces or states which measure the physical and qualitative state of real wealth — natural, social, human and human-made. The majority of the money supply is created by the national government with the central bank in an expanded role which includes the co-stewardship of natural, human and social capital. National currency would be complemented by local time-based currencies where time is the crucial asset and medium of exchange at the individual household level. Private banks would continue to exist but would operate on the JAK Bank model, a 100% reserve or 100% deposit system. Bankers would become intermediaries of exchange between depositors earning an income from the exchange process. Money supply would be expanded or contracted to provide sufficient economic blood flow for the well-being of the households of the community and nation. Evidence of the state of living capital assets would be contained in total real wealth accounts (total wealth balance sheets and full benefit-cost income accounts).

In addition to local cooperative, member-based banks, local currencies and local exchange transaction systems (LETS) could form complementary national currencies. A number of local currencies including Salt Spring Island Dollars, Ithaca Hours and Toronto Dollars are in circulation already. These currencies are created by local citizens and honored within the local economy as a medium of exchange between households and businesses. One of my favorite currency models is Bernard Lietaer's Taoist-based monetary system of dual, Yang-Ying currencies where national currencies (Yang currencies like the dollar or Rupiah) are complemented by Ying (time-based) currencies. He provides an example from Indonesia. The *Narayan banjar* is a time currency in which time is a form of money; each household commits to giving a few hours of their day to community projects and works. The strength of this system is that time is the currency of exchange at the local level of community governance. Community projects are organized through a Banjar (3000 operate throughout Bali) which are decentralized, democratic, cooperative institutions that operate at the local level. Banjars meet once a month and are open to all citizens. Here people discuss, determine and plan for community projects that will sustain or improve quality of life. Democratically elected members of the community, each with one vote, govern the Banjar. Assessing community needs and measuring community assets using Genuine Wealth accounting could help communities like these set priorities.

This transformation of our economic system must begin with a redefinition of money along with the creation of a national well-being accounting system and real-wealth-monetary policies used by governments, communities, households and businesses to guide and manage for the well-being of the people and our natural environment. I believe this can be achieved within our lifetime though there will be challenges and indeed vigorous opposition from some powerful politically entrenched actors. I hold the vision of John Maynard Keynes and the conviction of Pope John Paul II that authentic reform will require a return to principles of religion, such as a repudiation of usury, recognition of our spiritual natures and a renewed appreciation of the moral foundations of genuine and authentic economic development that ultimately leads to an economy and civilization of love.

CHAPTER 10

The Economics of Happiness

Now the goodness that we have to consider is human goodness, since the good or happiness which we set out to seek was human good and human happiness. But human goodness means in our view excellence of the soul, not excellence of the body; also our definition of happiness is an activity of the soul.

— ARISTOTLE, The Nicomachean Ethics[1]

I was raised in an economic classroom to believe that money buys quite a lot of happiness. I have to revise that opinion.

— ANDREW OSWALD, British economist,

pioneer in the economics of happiness[2]

PHILOSOPHERS AND THEOLOGIANS since Aristotle's time have struggled with the definition of happiness and the good life. But only recently have economists begun to weigh in on the debate. There are growing numbers, including Richard Easterlin (University of Southern California), John Helliwell (University of British Columbia) and Andrew Oswald who are beginning to study the relationship between money and happiness; they are learning that more income and money generates far less happiness than we might expect. Carelton University in Ottawa, Canada has opened a $500,000 "happy lab" run by psychologist John Zelenski to study what causes happiness. What is the architecture of happiness, and what are its economic dimensions? Does money buy happiness? If not, why do we persist in making the accumulation of money and material wealth our primary goal?

The monetary value of happiness

Because everything has its price in our current economic system, some of these happiness economists have begun to estimate monetary value of being happy. Based on US figures, Oswald and others have estimated happiness values that come from lifestyle characteristics.

While this kind of analysis might cause us to snicker, placing values on positive and negative attributes of life may help us better understand the full costs of losses in human and social capital. Complete analysis would require cross tabulating happiness survey results with socio-economic impact profile data. But the economic values assigned do confirm what most of us intuitively feel without assigning money value: that having healthy relationships, good and hopefully meaningful jobs and trusting workplaces makes people happier.

Does money buy happiness?

But there is a problem: economists are puzzled that despite rising GDP and increasing levels of material wealth, modern societies are no happier today than in the 1950s. There is increasing evidence that at least in most developed nations, economic progress buys only a small amount of extra happiness. It seems we get used to what we have, and then would like at least as much as those around us or more; we covet our neighbors' material wealth.

According to the old economic adage, *homo economicus* is a model human

Figure 10.1. The Economic Value of Happiness

Life Condition	Economic Value (US$)
High workplace trust	+ $118,000
Married or common-law	+ $100,000
A job that requires skills	+ $70,000
Seeing family often	+ $60,000
Divorce	- $70,000
Unemployment	- $290,000
Widowhood	-$300,000
Illness	- $320,000

Credit: Erin Anderssen. "Come on, get happy." *Globe and Mail*, October 9, 2004, p. F1.

being "who acts to obtain the highest possible well-being given available information about opportunities and other constraints, both natural and insti-
tutional, on ability to achieve predetermined goals."[3] In this view, humans
are assumed to be both rational in the choices they make about what they
want and insatiable in wanting material goods. One increases the welfare of
such creatures by providing ever-greater goods and services, as measured by
their market value. For *homo economicus,* there is no end to desiring more income, spending more and accumulating more material wealth; it is assumed
all of this will lead to greater welfare or well-being. The logic of this model
extends to the larger scale of a society or national economy so that unending
economic growth is not problematic; indeed it is seen as rational.

Traditionally wealth and economic performance (GDP) have been the
most important indicators to measure the goodness of society at all levels.
This has been based on the assumption or belief that by increasing the level of
economic output (i.e. producing more goods and services) society is truly better off. GDP indicators of progress may provide measures of the means to the
good life (e.g. material possession), but they do not measure the ends, such as
happiness, love or spiritual enlightenment. This is most poignantly reflected
in the US Declaration of Independence, drafted by Thomas Jefferson, which
affirms that the pursuit of happiness is the ultimate desired outcome of life:
"We hold these truths to be self-evident, that all men are created equal, that
they are endowed by their Creator with certain unalienable Rights, that among
these are Life, Liberty and the pursuit of Happiness."[4]

Human beings are not consistently rational in our decisions about what
we want. Nor do we necessarily distinguish between our wants and our needs
and between means and ends. This is particularly true when it comes to our
relationship with money, material wealth and the pursuit of happiness and
the good life. Aristotle wrote more than 2000 years ago that the activity of
pursuing wealth for the sake of wealth accumulation is not natural nor is it
the ultimate goal we search, but a means to reach more transcendental goals
such as happiness and love. Aristotle proposed that people's happiness was
the highest good, and his understanding of happiness embraced living and
doing well, not just feeling good.[5] The Greek word for the ultimate end is
telos, and the word *eudaimonia* is usually translated as happiness. But a closer
translation of *eudaimonia* would be spiritual well-being.[6]

Some economists as well as economic think-tanks like the UK-based
New Economics Foundation are beginning to measure the relationship

between money, income and objective and subjective measures of happiness or well-being. Many are realizing that objective measures of well-being like income, wealth or GDP per capita are inadequate unless they are juxtaposed with measures of subjective well-being — how each person feels and thinks about his or her life. This includes how people experience relationships, love and spirituality.

In *The (un)Happy Planet Index* published in 2006, the New Economics Foundation noted how many surveys reveal what people really value in life is their health and the happiness of themselves and their families. Diener and Scollon, who research subjective well-being on an international scale, have found that in importance rankings on a range from 1 to 9, happiness comes out on top with a global average of 8.0 followed by health (7.9), love (7.9), meaning (7.3), wealth (6.8) and attractiveness (6.3).[7]

John Helliwell, professor emeritus at the University of British Columbia, is delving into the economics of happiness, teaming up with others like Dr. Robert Putnam, Harvard professor, guru in the science of social capital and author of *Bowling Alone*. Putnam has argued, using extensive empirical evidence, that the social fabric (i.e. social capital) of the United States has been unraveling since the early 1960s as family, friends, neighbors and democratic structures are increasingly disconnected. Helliwell, studying the relationship between social capital and suicide, has found that across most nations more social capital and higher levels of trust are associated with lower national suicide rates and higher levels of subjective well-being.[8] He found a strong negative correlation between national average suicide rates and the measure of life satisfaction; the higher life satisfaction the lower the suicide rate.[9]

Evidence suggests that once we have met most of our basic material needs for life, more money doesn't translate into either more objective or subjective well-being or happiness. Empirical research into happiness has shown that in industrialized countries well-being appears to rise with the national income, but then reaches a threshold at a certain level. Above this level an increase in well-being is so small as to be almost undetectable .[10]

Princeton University economist Alan Krueger and Daniel Kahneman, a psychologist and winner of the 2002 Noble Prize in economics, teamed up to study whether more money or income buys more happiness. Their conclusion was that "the belief that high income is associated with good mood (happiness) is greatly exaggerated and mostly an illusion." The two researchers studied how people of different income levels spend their time and which activities they find enjoyable. They found that, while the wealthiest households (those earning $100,000 US or more) felt about twice as "very happy" than the poorest households (those earning $20,000 US or less), on a moment-to-moment basis both groups spend about the same time on things that made them happy or unhappy. Kahneman notes that as long as people are not battling poverty they tend to rate their own happiness in the same range as those with higher incomes. They did, however, find that that rich people spend more time in high stress activities than people with modest resources or poor people. Those with the highest incomes spend more time working, worrying, shopping, taking care of the kids and exercising and less time relaxing with a book. They note that "people with above-average income are relatively satisfied with their lives but are barely happier than others in moment-to-moment experience and tend to be more tense and do not spend time in particularly enjoyable activities." They concluded that as income rises, so too do our expectations, and that ultimately we adjust to whatever income we have.[11]

Dr. Richard Suzman, associate director of behavorial and social research at the US National Institute on Aging, said that surveys like those conducted by Kahneman and Krueger should give policy makers improved measures of well-being and ultimately "help us set up a national well-being account, similar to the gross national product, that would give us a better understanding of how changes in policy, or social trends, affect quality of life."[12]

When we examine the relationship between GDP and life satisfaction across 178 countries (see Figure 10.2), we see diminishing returns to life satisfaction with incremental increase in GDP per capita. The graph clearly shows that there is a relationship between income and life satisfaction, but that after a surprisingly low level of GDP per capita is reached, the increment in life satisfaction is marginal. The graph shows that people in countries like Luxembourg, the US and Norway, while enjoying the highest GDP per capita, are no more satisfied with life than the average person living in Costa Rica or Bhutan. Denmark and Switzerland enjoy the highest level of life satisfaction (8.2 out of 10) with relatively high GDP per capita while Burundi, Zimbabwe and the Congo have both low life satisfaction and GDP per capita.

Comparing life expectancy with GDP shows that the rich tend to live longer than the poor, and the slightly richer may live longer than the rich (see Figure 10.3). But here too we see a diminishing rate of return. For example, while a Swiss person may live to be 80.5 years and enjoy a GDP per capita of US$30,677, the average Costa Rican or Cuban will live to 78.2 years and 77.3

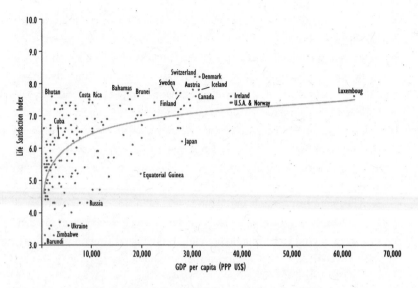

FIGURE 10.2. Life Satisfaction and GDP per capita of 178 Nations, 2003

Credit: New Economics Foundation and Friends of the Earth. *The (un)Happy Planet Index.* 2006.

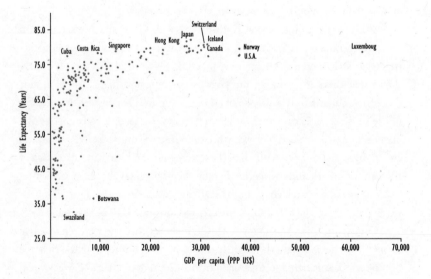

FIGURE 10.3. Life Expectancy versus GDP per capita for 178 nations

Credit: New Economics Foundation and Friends of the Earth. *The (un)Happy Planet Index.* 2006.

years respectively with a much lower GDP per capita (Cuba with nearly 1/10th of Switzerland's GDP — only US$3,500 per capita — and US$9,606 GDP per capita for Costa Rica).

Figure 10.4 shows the top ten countries and bottom ten countries of the world, ranked in terms of life satisfaction. As well as showing statistics on GDP per capita, it presents a Happy Life Years Index (a measure that combines life satisfaction with life expectancy)[13], Ecological Footprint (a measure of how many hectares of the planet land each person uses to meet their material needs),[14] the Happy Planet Index (a new measure that shows the ecological

Figure 10.4. Country rankings (top 10 and lowest 10) by life satisfaction

Country	Life Satisfaction (0–10)	GDP per capita (PPP US$)* 2003	Life Expectancy (years)	Happy Life Years (HLY) Index	Happy Planet Index	Ecological Footprint (gha/ person)	Human Development Index
Top 10 Countries							
1. Denmark	8.2	31,465	77.2	63.3	41.4	6.4	0.941
2. Switzerland	8.2	30,552	80.5	66.0	48.3	5.3	0.949
3. Austria	7.8	30,094	79.0	61.6	48.8	4.6	0.936
4. Iceland	7.8	31,243	80.7	62.9	48.4	4.9	0.956
5. Bahamas	7.7	17,159	69.7	53.7	44.9	4.1	0.832
6. Finland	7.7	27,619	78.5	60.4	37.4	7.0	0.941
7. Sweden	7.7	26,750	80.2	61.8	38.2	7.0	0.498
8. Bhutan	7.6	1,969	62.9	47.8	61.1	1.3	0.536
9. Brunei Darussalam	7.6	19,210	76.4	58.1	41.2	5.6	0.866
10. Canada	7.6	30,677	80.0	60.8	39.8	6.4	0.949
Bottom 10 Countries							
169. Georgia	4.1	2,588	70.5	28.9	41.2	0.8	0.732
170. Belarus	4.0	6,052	68.1	27.2	25.8	3.2	0.786
171. Turkmenistan	4.0	5,938	62.4	25.0	24.0	3.1	0.738
172. Armenia	3.7	3,671	71.5	26.5	36.1	1.0	0.759
173. Sudan	3.6	1,910	56.4	20.3	27.7	1.0	0.751
174. Ukraine	3.6	5,491	66.1	23.8	22.2	3.3	0.766
175. Moldova	3.5	1,510	67.7	23.7	31.1	1.2	0.671
176. Congo, Dem. Rep.	3.3	697	43.1	14.2	20.7	0.7	0.385
177. Zimbabwe	3.3	2,443	36.9	12.2	16.6	1.0	0.505
178. Burundi	3.0	648	43.6	13.1	19.0	0.7	0.378

* PPP=Purchasing Power Parity   Credit: New Economics Foundation and Friends of the Earth. The (un)Happy Planet Index. 2006.

efficiency with which human well-being is delivered)[15] and the UN Human Development Index (a proxy measure of human well-being). Denmark and Switzerland rank one and two (Canada ranks 10th overall) in terms of life satisfaction as well as enjoying high GDP per capita and long lives. But these nations have a relatively higher ecological footprint (i.e. they consume more of earth's resources) than Bhutan with a much lower GDP per capita, relatively high life satisfaction though slightly lower life expectancy. If one considers the "return on life satisfaction" for every dollar of GDP we might choose to live as the Bhutanese do: Bhutanese with a mere US$1,696 (GDP) per capita have a life satisfaction index of 7.6 out of 10.0, an average life expectancy of 62.9 years and a very small ecological footprint of only 3.2 acres per person (compared with the US ecological footprint of 18.3 acres per capita and Canada's 16 acres per capita). Perhaps this is why Bhutan has proposed using a Gross National Happiness index to measure its progress.

These statistics may suggest that capitalism and western democracies, along with their economic policies and technological advances, deserve high marks for creating material prosperity and the conditions for the good life. However, affluent nations face a new challenge. While celebrating the fruits of this economic success we need to turn our attention to genuine well-being, remedying loneliness and improving our relationships with each other and the earth. Affluent nations have much to learn from nations which consume less yet have achieved similar rates of happiness and life expectancy.

Does consuming more of nature buy more happiness?

The New Economics Foundation developed an innovative measure of the ecological efficiency with which human well-being is delivered. Their study examined the relationship between GDP per capita, life satisfaction and the ecological footprint. Figure 10.5 shows that countries with the highest ecological footprints (the United Arab Emirates, the US, Kuwait and Quatar) enjoy actually lower Happy Life Years than countries with small footprints (e.g. Switzerland and Iceland). Even more striking is the fact that countries like Costa Rica, Dominican Republic, Cuba, Bhutan and the tiny South Pacific nation of Vanuatu[16] enjoy remarkably high levels of Happy Life Years on a considerably smaller footprint. The study illustrated that "it is possible to live long, happy lives with a much smaller environmental impact."[17] In other words, well-being does not rely on high levels of consumption, nor does consumption guarantee high well-being. It is indeed possible for those of us from more affluent nations and communities to achieve a high quality of life with a smaller ecological footprint, based on a more moderate and frugal life-style.

Does more income buy more happiness?

Economist Andrew Oswald has been studying how much more money buys incrementally more happiness. From his research he found that an employee earning $10,000 (for example) becomes happier when offered another $10,000, but a person earning $100,000 would need an additional $100,000 to experience the same rise in happiness. According to Oswald's studies, it would take US$1.5 million to move a person from a "fed up" condition to a "very happy" condition.[18]

Oswald has explored whether a nation's economic performance results in extra happiness. He examined economic growth and indicators of happiness and well-being in Western countries, including information on reported happiness, reported life satisfaction, reported job satisfaction and the number of suicides. His study found that in industrialized countries, well-being appears to rise as real national income grows, but that the rise is so small as to be

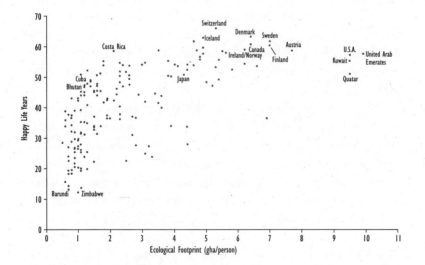

FIGURE 10.5. Happy Life Years relative to the Ecological Footprint of 178 nations, 2003

Credit: New Economics Foundation and Friends of the Earth. *The (un)Happy Planet Index.* 2006.

almost undetectable. According to Oswald unemployment seemed to be the key source of unhappiness in the affluent industrialized countries. Unemployed people are very unhappy. Oswald also found that reported happiness is high among those who are married, on high income, women, whites, the well-educated, the self-employed, the retired and those looking after the home. Richer countries also tend to have higher rates of suicide. Oswald's conclusion is important: "in a country that is already rich, policies aimed at raising economic growth may be of comparatively little value."[19]

Robert Lane, a professor emeritus at Yale University and author of *The Loss of Happiness in Market Democracies,* found that in affluent countries the correlation between income and happiness is close to zero and sometimes negative. The United States ranked near the bottom of this list of materialist nations. Lane found that money has its most positive effect on the poor, but once a person has achieved a minimum standard of living level of income has almost nothing to do with happiness. Lane notes that in fact close relationships, rather than money, are the keys to happiness.[20]

Research conducted by David Myers, Professor of Psychology at Hope College in the US, shows that the number of US citizens who rate their lives as "very-happy" has fallen from 35% of respondents in 1957 to 30% in 2002, even though average income more than doubled (in inflation adjusted dollars) over this same period from $8700 per person in 1957 to over $20,000 in 2002.[21] Using similar self-rated happiness survey data from the US General Social Survey for the period 1972–2005, I have illustrated similar trends showing that extra income does not translate into more "very-happy" citizens in the US (see Figure 10.6).

Indeed the opposite may be true. Myers points out that despite US citizens being materially better off, the divorce rate has doubled, the teen suicide rate has nearly tripled, the violent crime rate has nearly quadrupled (even after the recent decline since the early 1990s) and rates of depression have mushroomed. The genuine bottom line is that more economic growth and materialism have not led to increasing levels of subjective well-being.

In Canada, my analysis of self-reported health and self-esteem shows that there is not necessarily a corresponding link to GDP or income per person. Figure 10.7 shows that Newfoundlanders self-report the highest levels of personal health (66% report of the population reported excellent or very good levels of health) and one of the highest percentage of citizens reporting a "low-stress" life than other Canadians despite having the lowest per capita

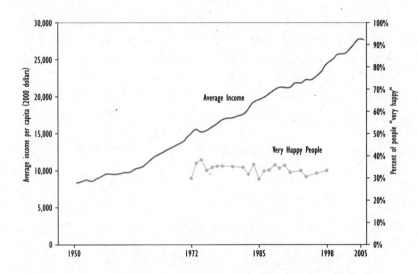

FIGURE 10.6. Average Income and Happiness in the United States, 1950–2005

Credit: US General Social Survey, 1972–1998. U.S. Department of Commerce, Bureau of Economic Analysis

Figure 10.7. Self-rated health, self-esteem, GDP per capita and average income of Canadian provinces, 2001.

	Excellent or Very Good, Self-reported Health, % reporting, 2001	Lowest Self-reported Life Stress, % reporting 1995	GDP per capita, 2001	Average income per capita, 1996
Newfoundland	66	15.2	$26,070	$19,710
PEI	64	13.2	$24,715	$20,527
Ontario	63	10.7	$37,059	$27,309
Alberta	62	9.8	$49,045	$26,138
Yukon	62	12.7	$37,826	$29,079
Quebec	61	18.1	$30,837	$23,198
Manitoba	60	9.5	$30,508	$22,667
Nova Scotia	59	12.2	$26,432	$21,552
B.C.	59	12.0	$31,836	$26,295
Saskatchewan	57	9.3	$32,545	$22,541
New Brunswick	56	15.0	$26,695	$20,755
NWT	54	14.5	$71,394	$31,517
Nunavut	53	16.9	$32,340	$24,193

Credit: Statistics Canada, National Population Health Survey. 1994–95.

income in Canada ($19,710 per capita in 1996). On the other hand, citizens of the Northwest Territories have the lowest level of excellent to very good self-rated health (53% reporting) but the highest average income levels ($71,394). Data also shows that the unhappiest Canadians live in cities where income is highest, and the happiest Canadians live in the Atlantic provinces with lower incomes and GDP. Not only do Atlantic Canadians report lower stress and good health, they also record higher levels of trust, more contact with friends and greater job satisfaction.[22] Indeed this social capital overrides low income and unemployment.

Can we ever have enough money?

So why, in spite of evidence that more money does not buy greater happiness, do we persist in pursuing more financial and material wealth? The answer seems to be our human nature. Dr. Richard Easterlin, who studies the relationship between our material aspirations, income and life satisfaction, offers important insights. Easterlin has found the connection that income growth does not cause well-being to rise because with more income comes a shift in our material aspirations; the more we make the more we want or the more we aspire for more material wealth. We fail to anticipate the rise in material aspirations that will come with growth in income. We are seemingly never materially satisfied with constantly changing material expectations, except when we reach the age of wisdom. In his study, Easterlin found that happiness (subjective well-being) does improve with income but only until retirement age is reached. Indeed, average happiness does not change despite a leveling off and even decline in income after retirement.[23]

Why the sudden interest in the economics of happiness?

The interest may reflect changing demographics as baby boomers enter retirement years and are reflecting on the real meaning of life. This generation may be realizing that once our basic material needs are met, our focus can shift from achieving the means of the good life to the ultimate ends of the good life which include self-actualization. Perhaps society as a whole is growing in wisdom. I also believe there is a growing consciousness that the pursuit of life, liberty and happiness is the ultimate end desired of any human life lived. To measure this shift will require a combination of both objective measures and subjective measures of well-being. It thus makes sense that many care less about the old objective indicators of economic progress and well-being like the GDP, and more about how satisfied we are with life, happiness and our relationships with our children, our community and nature. We care about the joys and pains of those we love. We care about giving and receiving.

Even if there is a growing consciousness amongst individuals that more income and more spending does not buy happiness, there is still tremendous inertia at the macro scale as the Titanic of the economic status quo continues to steam along the course "more growth is always better." We still have much work to shift our consciousness away from materialism. In a University of California/American Council on Education (ACE) survey of a quarter million students entering US colleges 74% said that it was "very important or essential" that they become "very well-off financially" which is up dramatically from the 40% who rated material success as critical back in the 1970s and 1980s. According to Myers, this trend is also prevalent in the general US populace: in 1975 only 38% of Americans defined "the good life" in terms of "a lot of money" while in 1996 this had risen to 63% of those polled. Myers concludes that "materialism was up, spirituality down."[24]

It is my hope that each of us will, based on our own experience, come to realize that true wealth lies in the celebrating life and achieving happiness rather in merely accumulating material wealth. This is not something that can be imposed on society like an economic or social policy or law. Each one of us must be free to pursue what Jefferson's Declaration of Independence set forth: life, liberty and the pursuit of happiness. I imagine a day when the evening news will report on our state of happiness. I hope that Canada, like Bhutan, will one day adopt a Gross National Happiness accounting system which includes national and local indices of well-being, as my colleagues and I are now developing. I agree with Andrew Oswald that "[happiness economics] is going to change the world."[25]

Epilogue

Learn to appreciate what you ARE and already have, and you will find yourself BEING more and having more, of what you appreciate. It's called an Attitude of Gratitude and makes everyday a Celebration of Life.   — OREST ANDRE[1]

GENUINE WEALTH and an economics of happiness are concepts whose time has come. They speak to the deep longing for meaning from citizens all over the world. We know that there is more to life than economic growth, stock price increases, productivity gains, inflation rates, currency exchange rates, more money and more material possessions.

This book is meant to serve those who dream and hope for a better tomorrow. It is a wake-up call to those who are stuck in the illusion of scarcity to rediscover that genuine abundance is all around. Most importantly, it is a call to remember the wisdom of our elders and the past and celebrate our genuine wealth, using all of the practical teachings and tools that are available to us today.

Sharing our genuine wealth — each with our own unique talents, skills, capacities and dreams — means sharing our stories, sharing our living legacy from the youngest to the oldest. It means redefining and measuring progress through the lenses of our hearts. It will mean writing new agreements like the New Economics Foundation's *Well-being Manifesto* that set out how communities might be governed and most importantly measure progress in terms of well-being and happiness. It will mean making new agreements with significant people: with our life partners, our children, our parents, our grandparents and our neighbors. It will mean developing new sustainable and flourishing enterprises like Upstream 21 which believe unequivocally that the responsibilities of business extend to the community and the environment. It will mean redefining money and our relationship with it, as well as eliminating usury and renewing the integrity of banking. At the community level it will mean discovering the joy of genuine cooperation through sharing, giving and receiving of our abundant personal genuine wealth so that communities are stronger, more resilient and happier. And at the personal level it will means discovering our innate beauty, inner capacities, our dreams and inner wealth.

> Authentic development can never be attained solely through economic means. In fact what has become known as the idolatry of the market — a consequence of the so-called civilization of consumption — tends to reduce persons to things and to subordinate being to having. This seriously detracts from the dignity of the human person and makes promotion of human solidarity difficult at best. Instead, recognition of the spiritual nature of the human person and a renewed appreciation of the moral character of social and economic development must be acknowledged as prerequisites for the transformation of society into a true civilization of love.
> — POPE JOHN PAUL II [2]

Genuine Wealth is a practical concept which the 6.5 billion people who live, breathe and have their being on earth can use to appreciate and share the abundance of genuine wealth that lies within everyone. This concept of Genuine Wealth is being supported by a variety of advocates of sustainability and new economics. The opening chapter of the David Suzuki Foundation's *Sustainability Within a Generation* suggests that Canada adopt the concept and supplement the narrow goal of economic growth with the more objective and expansive objective of Genuine Wealth. Raffi's eloquent "Covenant for Honouring Children" calls on all of us to honour the well-being of our young, and the child within us, in all that we do. Perhaps it is time for a similar "elder honoring" declaration to remind us of the importance of elders' wisdom.

The Genuine Wealth model gives us permission to have a new conversation about economics, money, sustainability and quality of life with a practical framework. It also provides tools for appreciating, measuring, managing and investing life energy in building communities and economies of well-being and happiness. I believe we have an opportunity and a responsibility to our children and their children to bring the concept of Genuine Wealth into reality in our daily lives and in national economic policies.

It makes common sense that we define and measure progress in terms of what we value most about life rather than narrow monetary measures of growth such as the GDP. Many of us have been searching for a new story, a new mythology and something that we can believe in. In a world longing for meaning, Genuine Wealth provides a beacon of hope. Rediscovering true meanings in the language of economics has given me personal hope that we can turn our world from a world of unbridled growth to a world of genuine stewardship.

Building societies based on the concepts of Genuine Wealth presented in this book will be challenging. It will require respectful dialogue amongst ourselves, our children, our elders, our neighbors and our politicians to determine good paths forward which are oriented towards well-being. Redefining the nature of money, reclaiming its power over our lives and reinventing it to serve our genuine and common needs is most important for humanity. There will be opposition, but is imperative that we remember the teachings of past generations and religions which condemned usury as incompatible with a life of abundance and love.

Genuine wealth is built with every action and choice we make, no matter how small or large. Genuine wealth is achieved when our decisions and actions are grounded in core values that are rooted in love and respect for each other, respect for nature and creation, and a genuine desire to work together towards improving the well-being of both current and future generations.

It is time for building new societies, based on an economics of genuine wealth and happiness. It is time to transform our society into the civilization of true love Pope John Paul II envisioned. It's time to appreciate the nature of genuine happiness as the Dalai Lama so eloquently states. It will take all of us working in genuine cooperation and in harmony with nature. Indeed, nature can be our blueprint for the most perfect designs. We need to address our own fears and societal mythologies with honesty and integrity so that we can cross the important threshold of hope. We are the ones we have been waiting for. Let's get going on this journey to Genuine Wealth!

Glossary

Canadian Index of Well-being: An initiative to develop a new comprehensive measure of well-being that reflects economic, social and environmental conditions that matter most to Canadians.

Capital: Wealth, in whatever form, used or capable of being used to produce more wealth. Also an accumulated stock of such wealth (money or property) or its value which is owned or used in business by a person, corporation, etc.

Chrematistics: An ancient Greek term which literally means the art of money-making or the science of wealth (e.g. riches).

CIW: Canadian Index of Well-being.

Common Wealth: This phrase (or "the common weal") incorporates the old meaning of wealth which is well-being. Thus the term literally means "common well-being."

Competition: Originally from the Latin *competere* meaning to strive together for some common interest or purpose.

Corporate Social Responsibility: Commitment by an organization to meet stakeholder expectations on economic, environmental and social performance that goes beyond their statutory obligation to comply with legislation.

CSR: Corporate Social Responsibility.

Economics: The study of the science of household stewardship and well-being.

Economy: Originally from the Greek *oikonomia* literally meaning household management. In modern times understood to mean a set of human and social activities and institutions related to the production, distribution, exchange and consumption of goods and services.

Fiat Money: The word *fiat* in Latin means "may it be" as in the term *fiat lux,* words spoken in the Christian Bible at the creation of the world. Therefore fiat money literally means money that is created out of nothing or decreed, usually by governments to be something of value to be used as legal tender for the purpose of exchange of goods and services.

Five Capitals: The Genuine Wealth model consists of five forms of integrated capital accounts: human (people's health, skills, and abilities), social (trust and relationships), natural (environment), built (infrastructure) and financial or economic (money) capital.

Fractional Reserve Banking: The common banking practice of issuing more money, in the form of loans to customers, than a bank holds in its reserves. Banks typically retain only a fraction of their deposits to satisfy demands for withdrawals, lending the remainder and indeed leveraging many times over the sum of all deposits. By lending money out at interest, they can pay interest to depositors and provide prof-its for the bank's owners.

GAAP: Generally Accepted Accounting Principles.

GDP: Gross Domestic Product.

Generally Accepted Accounting Principles: Standard guidelines for financial ac-counting which include standards, conventions and rules accountants follow in recording and summarizing transactions and in the preparation of financial state-ments.

Genuine: Authentic, real, natural, true or pure.

Genuine Progress Indicator: Measure of sustainable economic well-being developed by ecological economists. GPI measures whether or not a country's growth, in-creased production of goods and expanding services have actually resulted in the improvement of the well-being of the people.

Genuine Wealth: The conditions of well-being that are true to our core values of life. Also a model for measuring the conditions of well-being of a community or organ-ization in accordance to its values.

Genuine Wealth Assessment: A tool for measuring the overall well-being of an organ-ization or community using happiness and quality of life surveys combined with an inventory of the perceptions and statistical conditions of the five capitals (human, social, natural, built and financial) which comprise an enterprise, organization or community.

Genuine Wealth Balance Sheet: An accounting framework which reveals the physi-cal, qualitative and monetary (full costs or benefits) conditions of the five capitals (human, social, natural, built and financial capital) of an enterprise, organization, community or nation. The GW balance sheet provides a comprehensive well-being profile that shows community or organizational assets (strengths), liabilities (weak-nesses) and equity (distribution and fairness).

Global Reporting Initiative: An international accounting initiative which has de-veloped Sustainability Reporting Guidelines so that reporting on economic, en-vironmental and social performance by different organizations is as routine and comparable as financial reporting.

GNH: Gross National Happiness.

GNP: Gross National Product.

GPI: Genuine Progress Indicator.

GRI: Global Reporting Initiative.

Gross Domestic Product: The market value of all final goods and services produced within a country in a given period of time.

Gross National Happiness: An official measure of well-being of the Tibetan Buddhist nation of Bhutan used as an alternative to GNP or GDP. The GNH policy of Bhutan recognizes that the Buddhist spiritual principle of happiness should take precedence over material possessions, consumption and economic growth.

Gross National Product: The total value of final goods and services produced in a year by all of the country's nationals (including profits from capital held abroad). For example, the profits from a Mercedes-Benz factory in the USA would count towards German GNP.

GWA: Genuine Wealth Assessment.

Happiness: The ultimate human desire for spiritual well-being characterized by feelings of safety, satisfaction, contentment, health, joy, and love. In Greek *eudaimonia* is the word for happiness consisting *eu* (good or well-being) and *daimon* (spirit).

IGWI: Inuit Genuine Well-being Indicators.

Index of Sustainable Economic Welfare: An economic indicator intended to replace GDP. Rather than simply totalling all expenditures, consumer expenditure in the ISEW is balanced by economically unsustainable factors like income distribution and costs associated with pollution. ISEW is similar to GPI.

Inflation: In mainstream economics a rise in the general level of prices, as measured against some baseline of purchasing power. However, if all money is created in the form of a debt, then inflation could be defined as an increase in money supply when banks issue loans with interest and government prints money.

Integrity: The quality or state of being complete, unbroken, whole, unimpaired, in perfect condition, morally principled, honest and sincere; closely aligned with the original meaning of the word wealth.

Inuit Genuine Well-being Indicators: A set of quality of life indicators of Inuit society aligned with six Inuit guiding principles and values (Inuit Qaujimanituqangit), Inuit skills and social competencies. These indicators can be used to measure community, individual, economic and environmental well-being.

***Inuit Qaujimanituqangit* or IQ**: Six guiding principles that represent fundamental values and life principles of Inuit society in Nunavut, Canada. These principles include environmental stewardship, being useful in service to others, dialogue and communication, learning by observation, experience and practice, teamwork and collaborative relationships and creative problem solving.

ISEW: Index for Sustainable Economic Welfare.

LETS: Local Exchange Transaction System.

Life Assets: Synonymous with life capital. These assets include quality of life attributes that contribute to well-being and happiness such as health (physical and mental), spiritual well-being, healthy relationships, love and respect, the conditions of physical living environment and the well-being of nature.

Life Capital: The human (people), social (relationships), and natural (the environment) capital that contributes to quality of life or well-being.

Life Need: That without which life capabilities are reduced or destroyed (e.g., the need for nourishing food). When people's life needs are satisfied then they have the conditions for a good life.

Local Exchange Transaction System: A local, non-profit exchange network in which goods and services can be traded without the need for printed currency. LETS networks use interest-free local credit so direct swaps do not need to be made. For example, a member can earn credit by doing childcare for one person and spend it later on carpentry with another person in the same network.

Money: Traditionally a medium of exchange usually in the form of bank notes (paper currency) or coins that society agrees to use in trade. However money has no inherent value, and today most money (95% or more) is created out of thin air in the form of a debt when private banks issue loans.

Mortgage: From the French literally meaning a death (mort) pledge (gage). Commonly, a legal device or method of using real or personal property as security for the payment of debt.

National Round Table on the Environment and Economy: An independent body, reporting to the Prime Minister of Canada, which generates and promotes innovative ways to advance Canada's environmental and economic interests, seeking to balance the sometimes competing interests of economic prosperity and environmental conservation.

NRTEE: National Round Table on the Environment and Economy.

Oikonomia: The Greek word for economy which literally means household management.

Poverty: A condition in which a person or community is deprived of or lacks the means (income, education or skills) to the essentials for well-being and life. These essentials include basic needs (food, safe drinking water, and shelter) but also social resources (information, education, health care, social status, political power) or the opportunity to develop meaningful relations with other people in society.

Shabbat: The weekly day of rest from work in Judaism. Derived from the Hebrew *shavat* (which literally means "to cease") or *shev* (which means "sit").

Sustainability: Providing the best well-being outcomes for the human and natural environments both now and into the indefinite future.

Tao: Way. In ancient China the Tao referred to the Way of Nature or of Heaven. According to sages such as Lao Tsu and Confucius the secret of success and fulfilment in life was to renounce one's own way and instead follow the Great Way of "non-action," harmonizing one's personal will with the natural harmony and justice of nature.

Time Currency: A form of money used in most communities of Bali where each household freely commits to giving a few hours of their day to community projects and works. Community projects are organized through a Banjar (3000 operate throughout Bali) which are decentralized, democratic, cooperative (one person-one vote) institutions that operate at the local level. Banjars meet once a month and are open forums for all citizens to discuss, determine and plan for community projects that will sustain or improve quality of life.

Usury: Charging any interest on the use of money, from the Latin usuria meaning "demanding in return for a loan a greater amount than was borrowed." Originally meant charging a fee for the use of money.

Value: The word value originates from the Latin *valere* which means to be strong, be worth or to be well. Standard dictionaries define value as comparative worth in terms of goods or money.

Values: Principles, beliefs and qualities that are really important to our sense of well-being and upon which we base our decisions.

Virtue: The word originates from the Latin *virtus* which refers to the moral excellence of a person as well as a character trait that is valued as being good.

WD: Western Economic Diversification.

Wealth: The word wealth combines two Old English words *weal* (well-being) and *th* (the conditions). Hence the true meaning of wealth is "the conditions of well-being," synonymous with happiness.

Well-being: The state of being well, happy or prosperous. Originally from the Old English word *weal*, meaning well-being.

Western Economic Diversification: A department of the Government of Canada which works to improve the long-term economic competitiveness of the West and the quality of life of its citizens.

Xiaokang: An ancient Chinese Confucian term which describes a society that is moderately well-off, where households have their material needs met and where these needs are equitably available and distributed to all.

Endnotes

Chapter 1

1. Marilyn Waring. *Counting for Nothing: What Men Value and What Women are Worth.* Allen & Unwin, 1988. For the current edition, see the Bibliography.
2. See Chapter 3.
3. Harvard professor Robert Putnam introduced the concept of social capital in his book *Bowling Alone: America's Declining Social Capital.* He defines social capital as the degree to which a community or society collaborates and cooperates through such mechanisms as networks, shared trust, norms and values to achieve mutual benefits. Reading his work, I knew that a new era in holistic capital accounting was possible.
4. Paul Hawkens, Amory Lovins and L. Hunter Lovins. *Natural Capitalism: Creating the Next Industrial Revolution.* Little Brown, 1999.
5. "Measuring Up — Index." [online]. [cited October 20, 2006]. Alberta Government, June 26, 2006. finance.gov.ab.ca/publications/measuring/measup06/index.html.
6. Michael Rowbotham. *The Grip of Death: A Study of Modern Money, Debt Slavery and Destructive Economics.* Jon Carpenter, 1998.
7. See Chapter 9.
8. *The Atlantic Monthly,* October 1995.
9. The Honorable Paul Martin, Minister of Finance. *The Budget Speech* 2000. Department of Finance, Canada, February 28, 2000, p. 14.
10. See Chapter 2.

Chapter 2

1. T.S. Eliot. "Choruses from the rock." In *Selected Poems.* Faber and Faber, 1954.
2. *Webster's New World Dictionary,* Second College Edition, 1986, s.v. "wealth."
3. "2. Spiritual well-being; ... 3a. Prosperity, consisting in abundance of possessions; 'worldly goods,' valuable possessions, esp. in great abundance: riches, affluence.... 4. *Economics:* A collective term for those things the abundant possession of which (by person or a community) constitutes riches, or 'wealth' in the popular sense.... 5. Plenty, abundance, profusion (of what is specified). Also, the condition of abounding in something valuable." From the *Oxford English Dictionary* [online]. [cited December 29, 2006]. dictionary.oed.com/cgi/entry/50281989?single=1&query_type=word&queryword=wealth&first=1&max_to_show=10.

4. Biz/ed Glossary and Diagram Bank. [online]. [cited December 29, 2006]. bized.co .uk/cgi-bin/glossarydb/browse.pl?glostopic=1&glosid=515.

5. *Forbes* Magazine. "The World's Richest People." [online]. [cited December 29, 2006]. forbes.com/lists/2006/10/Worth_1.html.

6. US Central Intelligence Agency. "CIA — The World Factbook — Lithuania." [online]. [cited December 29, 2006]. GDP expressed in PPP (purchasing power parity). cia.gov/cia/publications/factbook/index.html.

7. Oxford English Dictionary, 2d ed., 1989, s.v. "wealth."

8. Entry 2141. Strong's Greek Dictionary. [online]. [cited January 28, 2007]. sacred namebible.com/kjvstrongs/STRGRK21.htm.

9. Gen. 34:28–29 KJV.

10. F.W. Young. *The Interpreter's Dictionary of the Bible,* ed. George Buttrick, vol. 4. Abingdon Press, p. 818.

11. Proverbs 8:11 KJV.

12. David Hagni. "Wealth According to Jesus."[online]. [cited December 29, 2006]. Paper presented to Regent University, Spring 2000. logosword.co.uk/articles/ JesusAndWealth.htm.

13. Meir Tamari. *With All Your Possessions: Jewish Ethic and Economic Life.* Free Press, p.36.

14. Ibid., p. 37.

15. Matthew 16:26 KJV.

16. In Matthew 6:24 the word *mammon* (KJV) or money (financial wealth) is used to refer to something ungodly that entangles or ensnares. Mammon is a transliteration of the common Aramaic word *mmon* for riches and is close to a Mishnaic Hebrew word *mmôn*. See "Mammon." [online]. [cited January 30,2007]. jewishencyclopedia.com and Douglas E. Oakman. "The radical Jesus: you cannot serve God and Mammon." [online]. [cited January 30, 2007]. thefreelibrary.com/The+ radical+Jesus:+you+cannot+serve+God+and+Mammon-a012216251 8.

17. David Hagni. "Wealth According to Jesus." [online]. [cited December 29, 2006]. Paper presented to Regent University, Spring 2000. logosword.co.uk/articles/ JesusAndWealth.htm.

18. Adam Smith. "Introduction and Plan of the Work. " In *An Inquiry into the Nature and Causes of the Wealth of Nations.* [online]. [cited January 1, 2007]. econlib.org/ LIBRARY/Smith/smWN.html.

19. Ruskin Museum. "Unto this Last." [online]. [cited August 12, 2004]. ruskin museum.com/ruskin.htm.

20. Joe Dominguez and Vicki Robin. *Your Money or Your Life.* Penguin, 1992, pp. 118–119.

21. *Webster's New World Dictionary,* Second College Edition, 1986, s.v. "value."

22. Ibid.

23. Eric Patridge. *Origins: A Short Etymological Dictionary of Modern English.* Greenwich House, 1983, p. 760.

24. *Webster's New World Dictionary,* Second College Edition, 1986, s.v. "values."

25. *Oxford English Dictionary,* 2d ed., 1989, s.v. "genuine."

26. *Oxford English Dictionary,* 2d ed., 1989, s.v. "sustain."

27. John R. Ehrenfeld. "Sustainability by Choice." Keynote address to the Sustainable Futures 2002 workshop in Banff, Alberta, February 14–17, 2002.

28. *Oxford English Dictionary,* 2d ed., 1989, s.v. "economy." In addition, the word ecology shares the same Greek root *oikos* (household) plus *logia* (knowledge).

29. Denis Fahey quoting and translating J. Vialatoux in Fahey's *The Mystical Body of Christ and the Reorganization of Society.* Christian Book Club of America, 1995, p. 63.

30. Kim Phillips-Fein. "The Good Life." [online]. [cited October 10, 2006]. inthe setimes.com/issue/26/12/culture1.shtml.

31. *Webster's New World Dictionary,* Second College Edition, 1986, s.v. "economy."

32. *Webster's New World Dictionary,* Second College Edition, 1986, s.v. "economics."

33. John Ruskin. "Unto the Last." [online]. [cited October 29, 2006]. ruskinmuseum .com/ruskin.htm.

34. John Maynard Keynes Quotes. [online]. [cited September 12, 2006]. brainyquote .com/quotes/quotes/j/johnmaynar152041.html.

35. Webster's Dictionary, 1913, s.v. "chrematistics."

36. Herman Daly and John Cobb Jr. *For the Common Good,* 2d ed. Beacon Press, 1994, p. 138.

37. Ibid.

38. Herman Daly and John Cobb Jr. *For the Common Good,* 2d ed. Beacon Press, 1994, p. 139.

39. *Oxford English Dictionary,* 2d ed., 1989, s.v. "competition."

40. Ibid.

41. *Webster's New World Dictionary,* Second College Edition, 1986, s.v. "capital."

42. Personal email communication with Prof. John McMurtry, December 7, 2002.

Chapter 3

1. Robert F. Kennedy. "Remarks at the University of Kansas, March 18, 1968." [online]. [cited January 2, 2007]. jfklibrary.org/Historical+Resources/Archives/Reference+Desk/Speeches/RFK/RFKSpeech68Mar18UKansas.htm.

2. New Economics Foundation. "A Well-being Manifesto for a Flourishing Society." [online]. [cited October 30, 2006]. neweconomics.org/gen/news_wellbeingmanifesto.aspx.

3. Ibid.

4. Based on my own notes taken during Lynne Twist's presentation at the San Francisco Green Festival, November 5, 2005.

5. The GPI follows pioneering work of Cliff Cobb in developing the Index for Sustainable Economic Welfare (ISEW) originally conceived and developed by John B. Cobb, Jr., Clifford Cobb and Herman Daly in *For the Common Good.*

6. Mark Anielski. *Fertile Obfuscation: Making Money Whilst Eroding Living Capital.* Paper presented at the 34th Annual Conference of the Canadian Economics Association, University of British Columbia, Vancouver, B.C. June 2–4, 2000, p. 7.

7. This material is taken from Clifford Cobb, Ted Halstead, and Jonathan Rowe. "If the GDP is Up, Why is America Down?" *Atlantic Monthly*, October 1995, pp. 59–78.

8. John Kenneth Galbraith. Frank M. Engle Lecture in Economic Security, American College, Bryn Mawr, May, 1999. Reviewed in *IMF Survey*, August 2, 1999.

9. The Ecological Footprint is a measure of the ecological sustainability of our lifestyles which contrasts how our consumption of materials and energy relates to the biocapacity of the planet to meet our material and energy needs as well as assimilate our wastes. I have calculated the ecological deficit of the US as the difference between the US Ecological Footprint (expressed in global hectares per capita) and the available biocapacity in the US (also expressed in global hectares).

10. J. R. Grever, R. Kaufman, D. Skole, and C. Vorosmarty. *Beyond Oil: The Threat of Food and Fuel in the Coming Decades.* Ballinger, 1986; Mark Anielski. *Fertile Obfuscation: Making Money Whilst Eroding Living Capital.* Paper presented at the 34th Annual Conference of the Canadian Economics Association, University of British Columbia, Vancouver, B.C. June 2–4, 2000, p. 7.

11. Tim Appenzeller. "The End of Cheap Oil." *National Geographic*, June 2004.

12. Opinion of Dr. David Pimentel of Cornell University reported in "The Oil We Eat." [online]. [cited February 2, 2007]. *Harpers Magazine*, February 2004. harpers .org/TheOilWeEat.html.

13. Hew Crane and Ed Kinderman. "Energy's Inevitable Game Change." SRI Consulting, Business Intelligence Program, Scan No. 2143. 2004.

14. See the ASPO website at peakoil.net.

15. These figures are based on statistics from the US Annual Energy Review 2005 for total fossil fuel consumption (including coal, natural gas and petroleum) by the residential, commercial, industrial, transportation and electric power sectors in comparison with GDP figures for the period 1950 to 2005.

16. David G. Myers. "The Secrets of Happiness." *YES! A Journal of Positive Futures*, Summer 2004, p. 14.

17. World Values Survey (worldvaluessurvey.org) as cited by Michael Bond, "The Pursuit of Happiness," *New Scientist*, October 3, 2003.

18. "WHO Issues New Healthy Life Expectancy Rankings: Japan Number One in New 'Healthy Life' System." [online]. [cited August 25, 2006]. World Health Organization. who.int/inf-pr-2000/en/pr2000-life.html.

19. The Index of Social Health (ISH) is a broad-based gauge of the social well-being. The ISH monitors social conditions using 16 social indicators (such as infant mortality, child abuse, child poverty, teenage suicide, health insurance coverage, income inequality and alcohol-related traffic fatalities) that are combined into a single number for each year, going back to 1970. The US Index shows that while the social health of the nation was strong in the early 1970s, it has stagnated since that time. See Marc Miringoff and Marque-Luisa Miringoff. *The Social Health of the Nation: How America is Really Doing.* Oxford University Press, 1999.

20. David G. Myers. "The Secrets of Happiness." *YES! A Journal of Positive Futures*,

Summer 2004, p. 14. Myers figures are drawn from happiness researchers Ronald Ingelhart and David Lykken.

21. Based on statistics on NYSE and Nasdaq market capitalization values of domestic NYSE and Nasdaq companies.

22. U.S. Department of Commerce: Bureau of Economic Analysis (Real Disposable Personal Income).

23. U.S. Department of Commerce: Bureau of Economic Analysis (Real Personal Consumption Expenditures).

24. Paul Krugman, "The Rich, the Right and the Facts." [online]. [cited August 25, 2006]. pkarchive.org/economy/therich.html.

25. Kennickell and Woodburn, unpublished US Federal Reserve Board paper.

26. "Take back your time." [online]. [cited August 25, 2006]. timeday.org.

27. "Americans work longest hours among industrialized countries." [online]. [cited August 25, 2006]. hartford-hwp.com/archives/26/077.html; International Labour Organization website ilo.org/public/english/bureau/inf/magazine/48/kilm.htm.

28. US Census Bureau, *American Community Survey 2004.* [online]. [cited October 29, 2006]. census.gov/Press-Release/www/releases/archives/american_community_survey_acs/004489.html.

29. US Federal Reserve, *Federal Reserve 2005 Statistics.* Table D.3, Z-1 Federal Reserve, "D.3 Debt Outstanding by Sector." [online]. [cited October 29, 2006]. federal reserve.gov/releases/z1/current/z1r-2.pdf.

30. The scores were derived by converting original raw data for each indicator to an index using a scale from 0 to 100, with 100 set as the best condition of the indicator during the time period for the study—that is, 1961 to 1999. Deviations from that year were measured as movement toward zero. The higher the indicator score, the closer its point is to the outside edge of the circle. For example, in the years between 1961 and 1999, GDP per capita was highest in 1999; thus the score for economic growth in that year was 100, and this point is at the outside edge of the circle. In contrast, suicide rates were high in 1999 compared with 1964, which had the lowest rate and was thus assigned the "best" or "target" score of 100. Therefore, relative to the best year in the study, the 1999 score for this indicator was lower and its point on the circle is closer to the center.

31. Mark Anielski, Mary Griffiths, David Pollock, Amy Taylor, Jeffrey Wilson and Sara Wilson. *Alberta Sustainability Trends 2000: Genuine Progress Indicators Report 1961 to 1999.* [online]. [cited January 4, 2007]. Pembina Institute for Appropriate Development, April 2001. pembina.org/pdf/publications/gpi-ab2000-trends.pd.

32. Pembina Institute."Progress: For Better? Or worse??" [online]. [cited August 23, 2006]. fiscallygreen.ca/gpi/index.php.

Chapter 4

1. Meir Tamari. *With All My Possessions: Jewish Ethics and Economic Life.* Free Press, 1987, p. 208.

2. Rabbi Arthur Waskow. 'Time to Be, Time to Love." *YES! A Journal for Positive Futures,* Fall 2003.

3. Emperor Qianlong was a patron of Taoism, Tibetan and Mongolian Lamaism.

4. St. Thomas Aquinas. *The Summa Theologica.* [online]. [cited January 9, 2007]. ccel .org/a/aquinas/summa/SS/SS055.html.

5. Conversation and e-mail correspondence between the author and Dan Rubenstein.

6. Publishers Weekly review of William Greider's *The Soul of Capitalism.* [online]. [cited January 8, 2007]. amazon.com/Soul-Capitalism-Opening-Paths-Economy/ dp/0684862190/sr=1-1/qid=1168280082/ref=sr_1_1/105-8643493-0194045? ie=UTF8&s=books.

7. William Greider. "The Soul of Capitalism." [online].[cited January 9, 2007]. The Nation, September 29, 2003. thenation.com/doc/20030929/greider.

8. William Greider. *The Soul of Capitalism: Opening Paths to a Moral Economy.* Simon & Schuster, 2003, p. 20.

9. Ibid., pp.325–340.

10. Ibid., p. 326.

11. Amintore Fanfani. *Catholicism, Protestantism and Capitalism.* IHS, 2003, p. 50.

12. Fanfani's teaching is confirmed in Pope John Paul II's encyclical *Centesimus annus* completed May 1, 1991 celebrating the 100th anniversary of his predecessor Pope Leo XIII's encyclical *Rerum novarum.* In 1891 Pope Leo compared the Roman Catholic Church's social doctrines and teachings with the growing forces of capitalism and the spirit of revolution in communism. *Rerum novarum* emphasized the importance of human labor, human private property rights, calling for societies to deal systematically with the conditions of workers.

13. Amintore Fanfani. *Catholicism, Protestantism and Capitalism.* IHS, 2003, pp.53–66.

14. Ibid., pp. 57–58.

15. Ibid., p. 117.

16. Ibid., pp. 117–18.

Chapter 5

1. Comments posted July 28, 2006 by Laurens van den Muyzenberg on Amazon .com. [online]. [cited February 9, 2007]. amazon.com/o/ASIN/0385720270/ref=s 9_asin_title_1/002-8159431-0259249.

2. Publisher's comments posted on Barnes and Noble website. [online] [cited February 5, 2007]. search.barnesandnoble.com/booksearch/isbninquiry.asp?ean=97803 85720274&z=y.

3. E.F. Schumacher. *Small Is Beautiful: Economics As If People Mattered: 25 Years Later.* Hartley & Marks, 1999, p. 251.

4. Ibid, p. 37.

5. A. H. Maslow. "The Theory of Human Motivation." Psychological Review 50 (1943): 370–396. [online].[cited February 5, 2007]. psychclassics.yorku.ca/ Maslow/motivation.htm.

6. Manfred Max-Neef. "Human Scale Development: An Option for the Future." [online]. [cited September 6, 2006]. Rain Forest Information website. rainforestinfo.org.au/background/maxneef.htm.

7. Ibid.

8. Ibid.

9. Joe Dominguez and Vicki Robin. *Your Money or Your Life: Transforming Your Relationship with Money and Achieving Financial Independence.* Penguin, 1999, p.25.

10. New Economics Foundation. *A Well-being Manifesto for a Flourishing Society.* [online]. [cited January 23, 2007]. 2004. p. 2. neweconomics.org/gen/uploads/21xv5yytotlxxu322pmyada205102004103948.pdf.

11. Ibid., p.5.

12. See Chapter 7.

13. See Chapter 8 for more information on The Natural Step.

14. John P. Kretzmann and John L. McKnight. Introduction to "Building Communities from the Inside Out: A Path Toward Finding and Mobilizing a Community's Assets." [online]. [cited October 30, 2006]. October 31, 2005. northwestern.edu/ipr/publications/community/introd-building.html.

Chapter 6

1. Mark Anielski and David Pollock. *The State of Inuit Well-being In Nunavut 2001.* Report prepared for the Nunavut Social Development Council, March 1, 2003, p. 10.

2. Ibid., p.14.

3. Ellen Galinsky quoted by Aime Dunstan (Cox News Service) in "If you asked the kids...: What children really want from their parents." *The Edmonton Journal,* March 18, 2006, p. B-08.

4. See the website of the Simple Living Network (simpleliving.net/main/custom.asp?recid=13) for details.

Chapter 7

1. New Economics Foundation. *A Well-being Manifesto for a Flourishing Society.* 2004, pp. 2–3.

2. FCM definition of a sustainable community. [online] [cited January 20, 2007]. braggcreek.ca/ecotourism/change.htm.

3. Donella Meadows. *Indicators and Information Systems for Sustainable Development.* Sustainability Institute, 1998, p.12.

4. Mark Anielski. *Alberta's International Region's 2005 Genuine Well-being Report.* Prepared for the City of Leduc, Leduc-Nisku Economic Development Authority, Federation of Canadian Municipalities and the Edmonton Community Foundation. May 2006.

Mark Anielski. *City of Leduc 2005 Genuine Well-being Report.* Prepared for the City of Leduc, Leduc-Nisku Economic Development Authority, Federation of Canadian Municipalities and the Edmonton Community Foundation. May 2006.

5. Nunavut Tunngavik Inc. 2002-2003 *Report on the State of Inuit Culture and Society.* [online]. [cited October 10, 2006]. tunngavik.ca/english/pub.html.

6. Mark Anielski and David Pollock. *The State of Inuit Well-being In Nunavut 2001.* Report prepared for the Nunavut Social Development Council, March 1, 2003, p. 11.

7. Santa Monica Sustainability City Progress Report. [online]. [cited January 21, 2007]. hsmgov.net/epd/scpr/index.htm.

9. The population of Bhutan per the Government of Bhutan census in June 2005 was 672,425 (bhutancensus.gov.bt). However, the population estimate in the CIA Factbook is 2,232,291 although it notes that other estimates are as low as 810,000. The United Nations estimate is 2,163,000 (2005). Neither the CIA nor the United Nations documents their methods of population estimate, while the government of Bhutan provides detailed population figures down to the gewog level.

10. 2005 International Monetary Fund statistics for GDP per capita in US PPP, [online],[cited October 16, 2006], Wikipedia website, October 28, 2006. en.wiki pedia.org/wiki/List_of_countries_by_GDP_%28PPP%29_per_capita

11. "Bhutan beats the US in Gross National Happiness", [online], [cited October 15, 2006], Centre for Science and Environment website, cseindia.org/programme/pov -env/bhutan.htm

12. "Gross National Happiness: The True Measure of Success?" Global Village News, Issue 89, August, 2004 [online], [cited October 16, 2006], Global Village News website, gvnr.com/89/1.htm

13. Sander Tideman, "Gross National Happiness: Towards Buddhist Economics", the New Economics Foundation website, neweconomics.org/gen/z_sys_Publication Detail.aspx?pid=47

14. Ibid

15. Ibid

16. *Bhutan 2020: A Vision for Peace, Prosperity, and Happiness.* Planning Commission, Royal Government of Bhutan. Accessed April 11, 2007. www.unpan.org

17. Interview with the Prime Minister of Bhutan, For Q & A in Times of India by Rajni Bakshi found in Gross National Happiness Report on Conference on Gross National Happiness, February 18-20, 2004, Bhutan.

18. David Suzuki Foundation, Sustainability Within a Generation, David Suzuki Foundation website, davidsuzuki.org/WOL/Sustainability/

19. *Bhutan 2020,* op. cit.

20. Atkinson Founation, "The Canadian Index of Well-being" [online], [cited October 20, 2006], Atkinson Foundation website, atkinsonfoundation.ca/ciw

Chapter 8

1. Mike Lewis."Mapping the Social Economy in B.C. and Alberta: Towards a Strategic Approach." April 2006, p. 4.

2. Joel Bakan. *The Corporation: The Pathological Pursuit of Profit and Power.* Viking Canada, 2004. The film can be downloaded from thecorporation.com.

3. Joel Bakan. *The Corporation: The Pathological Pursuit of Profit and Power.* [online]. [cited January 23, 2007]. Movie script, p. 14. thecorporation.com/media/Transcript_finalpt1%20copy.pdf.

4. "One day early in this journey, it dawned on me that the way I'd been running Interface is the way of the plunderer. Plundering something that's not mine, something that belongs to every creature on earth, and I said to myself 'My goodness, the day must come when this is illegal, when plundering is not allowed.' I mean, it must come. So, I said to myself 'My goodness, some day people like me will end up in jail.'" Ray Anderson in Ibid., p. 18.

5. Russell Mokhiber and Robert Weissman. "Corporation as Psychopath." [online]. [cited October 20, 2006]. Published February 18, 2004. commondreams.org/views04/0218-01.htm.

6. Personal communication with Bryan Redd, October 31, 2006.

7. *Webster's New World Dictionary,* Second College Edition. 1976, s.v. "integrity."

8. David Williams. "Look within for growth." *Oregon Business,* November 2005, p. 9.

9. Vancity's statement of its mission, values and commitments can be downloaded from vancity.com/SharedContent/documents/sovac.pdf.

10. Paul Hawken. *The Ecology of Commerce: A Declaration of Sustainability.* HarperCollins Canada, 1994.

11. Ray C.Anderson. "GETTING THERE Ray's Story." [online]. [cited October 23, 2006]. interfaceinc.com/getting_there/Ray.html.

12. Interface Inc. "Sustainable Enterprise." [online]. [cited October 23, 2006]. interfaceinc.com/eur/company/sustainability/frontpage.asp.

13. Ray C. Anderson. *Mid-course Correction: Toward a Sustainable Enterprise: The Interface Model.* Peregrinzilla Press, 1999.

14. Brian Nattrass and Mary Altomare. *The Natural Step for Business: Wealth, Ecology and the Evolutionary Corporation.* New Society Publishers, 1999.

15. Karl-Henrik Robèrt. "That Was When I Became A Slave." [online]. [cited October 26, 2006]. Excerpts from an interview by Robert Gilman and Nikolaus Wyss. *In Context,* #28, Spring 1991. context.org/ICLIB/IC28/Robert.htm.

16. "The Natural Step's Principles of Sustainability". [online]. [cited January 19, 2007]. naturalstep.org/com/What%5Fis%5Fsustainability/.

17. Brian Nattrass and Mary Altomare. *The Natural Step for Business: Wealth Ecology and the Evolutionary Corporation.* New Society Publishers, 1999, p. 112.

18. Personal communication with Leslie Christian, October 25, 2006.

19. "Creating the Vision and Charting the Course for the Future Corporation. Welcome." [online]. [cited January 19, 2007]. corporation2020.org.

20. Corporation 20/20. *New Principles of Corporate Design.* [online]. [Cited October 26, 2006]. corporation2020.org/Papers_files/papers_for_workshop4/Annotated_Principles.pdf.

21. Mountain Equipment Co-op. "Marking Our Route: MEC Accountability Report 2005." [online]. [cited January 19, 2007]. Section 1, page 2. mec.ca/Main/content _text.jsp?FOLDER%3C%3Efolder_id=2534374302883013&bmUID=116227 3633051.

22. Ibid., Section 1, p. 7.

23. Ibid.

24. Ibid.

25. Mondragón Corporación Cooperativa. "Who We Are — Economic Data." [online]. [cited January 22, 2007]. mcc.es/ing/magnitudes/cifras.html. For an excellent description of MCC see Greg MacLeod's book *From Mondragon to America: Experiments in Community Economic Development,* University College of Cape Breton Press, 1997.

26. Greg MacLeod. *From Mondragón to America: Experiments in Community Economic Development.* University College of Cape Breton Press, 1997, pp. 14–15.

27. White Dog Café Foundation. whitedogcafefoundation.org.

28. Business Alliance for Local Living Economies. "Our History." [online]. [cited January 22, 2007]. livingeconomies.org/aboutus/whoweare/history.

29. balleseattle.org.

30. ballebc.com.

31. BALLE BC. "Mission, Vision, Objectives." [online]. [cited January 22, 2007]. ballebc.com.

32. BALLE BC. "Welcome to BALLE BC." [online]. [cited January 22, 2007]. ballebc .com.

33. Janine M. Benyus. *Biomimicry: Innovation Inspired by Nature.* Harper, 2002.

34. Raffi Cavoukian. "What is Child Honouring: Organizing Principle, Catalytic Power." [online]. [cited October 25, 2006]. raffinews.com/child_honouring/ what_is_child_honouring.

35. Raffi Cavoukian. "A Covenant for Honouring Children." [online]. [cited January 22, 2007]. raffinews.com/child_honouring/covenant_principles. Raffi©1997, 2004 Troubador Music Inc.

Chapter 9

1. Michael Rowbotham. *The Grip of Death: A Study of Modern Money, Debt Slavery and Destructive Economics.* Jon Carpenter, 1998, p. 316.

2. Joe Dominguez and Vicki Robin. *Your Money or Your Life: Transforming Your Relationship with Money and Achieving Financial Independence.* Penguin, 1999, pp. 219–258.

3. Thomas Jefferson in the debate over the Re-Charter of the Bank Bill (1809). [online]. [cited February 6, 2007]. moneyreformparty.org.uk/quotations.htm.

4. Quoted on The Money Masters website. [online]. [cited October 24, 2006]. the moneymasters.com/presiden.htm.

5. Quoted in Patrick Carmack and Bill Still. Video documentary "The Money

Masters: How International Bankers Gained Control of America." 1998.

6. Patrick Carmack and Bill Still. Video script from the documentary "The Money Masters: How International Bankers Gained Control of America," 1998, pp. 78–79.

7. Mark Anielski. *Fertile Obfuscation: Making Money Whilst Eroding Living Capital.* Paper presented at the 34th Annual Conference of the Canadian Economics Association, University of British Columbia, Vancouver, B.C., June 2–4, 2000.

8. Based on Lynne Twist's address at the Green Festival in San Francisco in November, 2005.

9. Bernard Lietaer. *The Future of Money: Creating New Wealth, Work and a Wiser World.* Century, 2001, p. 52–53.

10. Gospel of Matthew 5:22 KJV. See "Aramaic of Jesus."[online].[cited February 6, 2007]. reference.com/browse/wiki/Aramaic_of_Jesus.

11. John Kenneth Galbraith. *Money: Whence It Came, Where It Went.* Houghton Mifflin, 1975, p. 5.

12. Deut. 23:19 KJV.

13. Bernard Lietaer. *The Future of Money: Creating New Wealth, Work and a Wiser World.* Century, 2001, p.41.

14. Frederick Soddy. *Wealth, Virtual Wealth and Debt: A Solution to the Economic Paradox.* Allen and Unwin, 1926, p. 137–141.

15. Ibid., p. 72.

16. Herman Daly. "The Economic Thought of Frederick Soddy." *History of Political Economy* 12:4 (1980), p. 474.

17. Ibid., p. 475.

18. Ibid., p. 476.

19. Benjamin Tal. "Are We Sitting on a Debt Time Bomb?" *The Edmonton Journal.* January 21, 2005. p. F1.

20. John Kenneth Galbraith from *Money: Whence It Came, Where It Went.* Houghton Mifflin, 1975. [online]. [cited February 7, 2007]. quotes.liberty-tree.ca/quote/john_kenneth_galbraith_quote_e08d.

21. Bernard Lietaer. *The Future of Money: Creating New Wealth, Work and a Wiser World.* Century, 2001, p. 33.

22. Reginald McKenna. *Postwar Banking Policy.* Heinemann, 1928.Quoted in Michael Rowbotham. *The Grip of Death: A Study of Modern Money, Debt Slavery and Destructive Economics.* Jon Carpenter, 1998, p. 29.

23. Minutes of the Proceedings and Evidence Respecting the Bank of Canada, Standing Committee on Banking and Commerce, Ottawa. [online].[cited February 6, 2007]. michaeljournal.org/appenE.htm.

24. David. C. Korten. *The Post-Corporate World: Life after Capitalism.* Berrett-Koehler, 1999, p. 24.

25. US Central Intelligence Agency. "Gross world product." In World Factbook. [online]. [cited February 7, 2007].cia.gov/cia/publications/factbook/rankorder/2001rank.html.

26. See T. W. Baxter. "Early Accounting, The Tally and the Checkerboard." *The Accounting Historians Journal.* 16 (1989), pp. 43–83. "Tally sticks were an ancient method of accounting used by the Treasury. Notches were cut into wooden sticks according to a code. The sticks were then split down the middle and the Treasury kept one half and the debtor the other. When the debt was paid the two halves were matched to see if they 'tallied.' Tally sticks were abolished in 1783, but their use continued until 1826. The fire at the Palace of Westminster in 1834 was caused by the burning of old tally sticks. The fire soon got out of control as there were huge numbers of these sticks." [online].[cited February 6, 2007]. explore.parliament.uk/ Parliament.aspx?id=10166&glossary=true.

27. Michael Rowbotham. *The Grip of Death: A Study of Modern Money, Debt Slavery and Destructive Economics.* Jon Carpenter, 1998, p. 16.

28. *Toronto Star.* "Money is $O Last Century." September 18, 2005, pp. D1 and D9.

29. Ibid.

30. Margarit Kennedy. *A Changing Money System.* Permaculture Publications, 1991, p. 2–3.

31. Personal email communication with Margrit Kennedy, October 8, 2003.

32. Quoted on The Money Masters website. [online].[cited February 6, 2007]. themon eymasters.com/presiden.htm.

33. Anthony Sutton quoted in chapter 1 of G. Edward Griffin's *The Creature from Jekyll Island.* [online]. [cited February 6, 2007]. radio.goldseek.com/edwardgriffingron vall.php.

34. Ronald Paul. "Paper Money and Tyranny." [online]. [cited January 22, 2007]. pop ulistamerica.com/paper_money_and_tyranny.

35. Federal Reserve Bank of Chicago. *Modern Money Mechanics: A Workbook on Bank Reserves and Deposit Expansion.* 1992, p. 3. Also available at landru.i-link-2.net/mon ques/mmm2.html.

36. Frederick Soddy quoted in chapter 5 of Thomas H. Greco. "New Money for Healthy Communities." [online].[cited February 6, 2007]. ratical.org/many_ worlds/cc/NMfHC/chp5.html.

37. Pat Carmack. "How does the Fed 'create' money out of nothing?" [online]. [cited November 1, 2006]. themoneymasters.com/faq.htm#q5.

38. Personal communication with Pat Carmack, November 1, 2006.

39. Carroll Quigley. *Tragedy and Hope: A History of the World in Our Time.* GSG & Associates, 1975. [online].[cited February 6, 2007]. www.themoneymasters.com/.

40. Henry Ford. [online], [cited February 6, 2007] brainyquote.com/quotes/quotes /h/henryford136294.

41. Aristotle quotation. [online]. [cited February 7, 2007]. www.knowprose.com/ node/11805.

42. Quoted on The Money Masters website. [online]. [cited October 30, 2006]. the moneymasters.com.

43. Deuteronomy 23:19 NIV.

44. Deuteronomy 23:20 NIV.

45. Thomas Aquinas. *Summa Theologica*. [online].[cited February 6, 2007]. intra-text.com/IXT/ENG0023/_P9R.HTM. See also Dennis Fahey. *The Mystical Body of Christ and the Reorganization of Society*. Christian Book Club of America, 1995, p. 76.

46. Al Baqarah 2:275. [online]. [cited February 20, 1007]. www.reference.com/browse/wiki/Usury.

47. Excerpt from Al Baqarah 2:276-280. [online]. [cited February 20, 1007]. reference.com/browse/wiki/Usury.

48. Ali Zohery. "Textual Analysis of the Last Sermon of Prophet Muhammad." [online]. [cited October 30, 2006]. prophetmuhammadleadership.org/textual_analysis_of_the_last_ser.htm.

49. Mark Anielski. *The JAK Members Bank Sweden: an Assessment of Sweden's No-Interest Bank*. Prepared for Vancity Capital Corp., 2004, p. 5.

50. My analysis examined why I believe JAK Members Bank might become an international model for "sustainability banking" serving the interests of citizens, businesses and communities committed to sustainability and improved quality of life. I examined the step-change opportunities which existing North American savings and credit unions could use to adopt (in whole or in part) the JAK model. The study contrasted the full benefits and costs of operating JAK versus Vancity and assessed the tangible and intangible benefits of no-interest banking. The full results of the can be found on my website anielski.com.

51. According to the Economic Policy Institute, living wage levels are equal to what a full-year, full-time worker would need to earn to support a family of four at the poverty line (US$17,690 a year, or US$8.20 an hour, in 2000).

52. See ecobank.com.

53. See grameen-info.org.

54. See "Making Sweden an OIL-FREE Society." [online]. [cited January 23, 2007]. 21 June 2006. sweden.gov.se/sb/d/2031/a/67096.

55. Quoted in Patrick Carmack and Bill Still. Video documentary "The Money Masters: How International Bankers Gained Control of America." 1998.

56. The Money Masters. "Monetary Reform Act."[online]. [cited February 6, 2007]. themoneymasters.com/monetary.htm.

57. Milton Friedman. *A Program for Monetary Stability*. Fordham University Press, 1960, pp. 66–76.

58. "Reviews and Comments of *The Money Masters*." [online]. [cited January 23, 2007]. themoneymasters.com/viewcim.html.

59. Frederick Soddy. *The Role of Money*. Harcourt Brace, 1935, p. 24.

60. Herman Daly and John Cobb Jr. *For the Common Good,* 2nd ed. Beacon, 1994, p. 428.

61. John Maynard Keynes. *Essays in Persuasion*. Norton, 1963, p. 371–372.

Chapter 10

1. George J. Irbe's Favorite Quotes from Aristotle on Selected Topics. [online].[cited February 6, 2007]. radicalacademy.com/philosophicalquotations36.htm.

2. Erin Anderssen. "Come on, get happy." *Globe and Mail*, October 9, 2004, p. F1.

3. "Homo economicus — The model." [online], [cited February 6, 2007]. fascism .com/wiki/?title=Homo_economicus.

4. US Declaration of Independence. [online]. [cited August 23, 2006]. archives.gov/ national-archives-experience/charters/declaration_transcript.html.

5. Hugh McDonald. "Saint Thomas on the Ethics of Business Practice." [online]. [cited February 6, 2007] vaxxine.com/hyoomik/aquinas/negotiatio.html; John Ikerd. "The Economics of Happiness." [online][cited February 6, 2007] ssu.missouri.edu/ faculty/JIkerd/papers/SFTHappiness.htm.

6. *Eudainomia* in Greek is broken down into *eu* (meaning well, good or happy) and *daimon* meaning an attendant spirit or an inferior deity (dictionary.reference.com /browse/demon). "Literally 'having a good guardian spirit', the Greek term 'eudai-monia' has a much more objective meaning. To be eudaimon is to be successful, to have what is most desirable, to flourish. There is some disagreement about what sort of life is most flourishing. Some say it is a life of pleasure, others of honor, some a wealthy life, others a virtuous one." [online]. [cited Fberuary 8, 2007]. philosophos .com/knowledge_base/archives_13/philosophy_questions_1378.html

7. E. Diener and C. Scollon. "Subjective well-being is desirable, but not the summum bonum." Paper presented at the University of Minnesota Interdisciplinary Workshop on Well-Being, 2003.

8. John Helliwell. "Well-being and Social Capital: Does Suicide Pose a Puzzle?" Unpublished paper, August 17, 2004.

9. Helliwell notes that suicide rates do differ greatly by gender (men successfully commit suicide more often than women) while life satisfaction is similar for men and women.

10. Daniel Hoornweg, Fernanda Ruiz Nuñez, Mila Freire, Natalie Palugyai, Maria Villaveces, and Eduardo Wills Herrera. "Annex 7: Indicators of Subjective Well-being in Cities" in *City Indicators: Now to Nanjing*. World Bank Working Research Working Paper 4114, January 2007, pp. 61–64.

11. Tom Spears. "The rich aren't that happy after all, researchers suggest." [online]. [cited October 29, 2006]. *The Ottawa Citizen,* June 30, 2006. canada.com/vancouver sun/news/story.html?id=d30b622b-f238-4167-adbd-07f484475023&k=4954.

12. Benedict Carey. "What Makes People Happy?" [online].[cited February 6, 2007]. New York Times, December 2, 2004. nytimes.com/2004/12/02/health/02cnd-mo od.html?ex=1259816400&en=54a7945951ff647f&ei=5088&partner=rssnyt

13. The New Economics Foundation defines the happy life years (HLY) as the "degree to which people live long and happily in a country at a certain time." The concept is derived from R. Veenhoven. "Happy life expectancy: a comprehensive measure of quality-of-life in nations." *Social Indicators Research* 39 (1996), pp. 1–58.

14. The Ecological Footprint (EF) measures the biologically productive area necessary to support current consumption patterns given prevailing technical and economic processes. It is a means of measuring how much nature we use to sustain our current lifestyles.

15. The Happy Planet Index (HPI) measures well-being, considering life satisfaction, the Ecological Footprint and life expectancy of human populations.

16. Vanuatu scored the highest Happy Planet Index in NEF's study.

17. New Economics Foundation. *The un(Happy) Planet Index.* 2006, p. 3.

18. Erin Anderssen. "Come on, get happy." *Globe and Mail.* October 9, 2004, p. F1.

19. Ibid.

20. Robert Lane. "The Loss of Happiness in Market Democracies." [online].[cited February 6, 2007]. *Miami Herald,* May 28, 2000. commondreams.org/views/05280 0-105.htm.

21. David Myers. "The Secret of Happiness." [online].[cited February 6, 2007]. YES! Magazine, Summer 2004. yesmagazine.org/article.asp?id=866.

22. Erin Anderssen. "Come on, get happy." *Globe and Mail.* October 9, 2004, p. F1.

23. Richard Easterlin. "Income and Happiness: Towards a Unified Theory." *The Economic Journal,* 111 (July 2001), pp. 465–484.

24. David Myers. "The Secret of Happiness." [online].[cited February 6, 2007]. *YES! Magazine,* Summer 2004. yesmagazine.org/article.asp?id=866.

25. Erin Anderssen. "Come on, get happy." *Globe and Mail.* October 9, 2004, p. F1.

Epilogue

1. Personal communication with Orest Andre, Edmonton, October 30, 2006.

2. Pope John Paul II. April 28, 2003 address to Pavel Jajtner, the Czech Republic's ambassador to the Holy See. Reported in "Pope Warns of Idolatry of the Market." *The Wanderer,* May 22, 2003, p. 2.

Bibliography

The following books, paper and articles were used as source material for this book and have been formative in shaping my thoughts and ideas. I have included a more complete list of my papers. They may be of use to readers and practitioners interested in further exploring well-being, sustainability measurement and reporting using the Genuine Wealth model at the individual, community, business and organizational, and societal scale.

Anderson, Ray. *Mid-Course Correction: Toward a Sustainable Enterprise: The Interface Model.* Peregrinzilla Press, February 1999.

Anielski, Mark. *The 1998 U.S. Genuine Progress Indicator Methodology Handbook.* Redefining Progress, 1999.

Anielski, Mark. The Alberta GPI Blueprint: The Genuine Progress Indicator (GPI) Sustainable Well-Being Accounting System. Pembina Institute, 2001.

Anielski, Mark. Alberta's International Region's 2005 Genuine Well-being Report. Prepared for the City of Leduc, Leduc-Nisku Economic Development Authority, Federation of Canadian Municipalities and the Edmonton Community Foundation, May 2006.

Anielski, Mark. City of Leduc 2005 Genuine Well-being Report. Prepared for the City of Leduc, Leduc-Nisku Economic Development Authority, Federation of Canadian Municipalities and the Edmonton Community Foundation, May 2006.

Anielski, Mark. Fertile Obfuscation: Making Money Whilst Eroding Living Capital. Paper presented at the 34th annual Canadian Economics Association conference, Vancouver, B.C., June 2–4, 2000.

Anielski, Mark. The Genuine Progress Indicators (GPI) Accounting Project: Charting a Sustainable Future for all Canadians. Pembina Institute for Appropriate Development. Paper prepared for the National Round Table on the Economy and the Environment, January 2001.

Anielski, Mark. "GPI: Alberta's Sustainability Trends, 2000" in Bringing Business on Board: Sustainable Development and the B-School Curriculum ed. Peter N. Nemetz. University of British Columbia Press, 2002.

Anielski, Mark. Integrated sustainability and well-being indicator accounting systems for sustainability performance measurement and policy evaluation in China. Presentation to the Chinese National Academy of Sciences and the China Council for International Cooperation on Environment and Development, Cheng De, China, August 26, 2005.

Anielski, Mark. Is Alberta Running Out of Nature's Capital — Physical and Monetary Accounts for Alberta's Oil, Gas and Timber. Paper presented at the Institute for Public Economics, University of Alberta, Edmonton, March 5, 1997.

Anielski, Mark. JAK Members Bank Sweden: An Assessment of Sweden's No-Interest Bank. Paper prepared for Vancity Capital Corp., January 2004.

Anielski, Mark. Measuring the Genuine Wealth of Communities. Anielski Management Inc., 2003.

Anielski, Mark. Measuring the Sustainability of Nations: The Genuine Progress Indicator System of Sustainable Well-being Accounts. Paper presented to the Fourth Biennial Conference of the Canadian Society for Ecological Economics: Ecological Sustainability of the Global Market Place, Montreal, Quebec, August 2001.

Anielski, Mark. Misplaced Concreteness: Measuring Genuine Progress and the Nature of Money. In Proceedings of the Third Biennial Conference of the Canadian Society for Ecological Economics Nature, Wealth and the Human Economy in the Next Millenium, Regina, Saskatchewan, August 1999.

Anielski, Mark. "Natural Capitalism." In Assault on the Rockies, ed. Ian Urquhart. Rowen Books, 1998.

Anielski, Mark. Santa Monica's Sustainability Indicators Reporting System. Report prepared by Anielski Management Inc. for the City of Santa Monica, April 22, 2004.

Anielski, M. A Sustainability Accounting System for Canada: An Assessment of the State of Sustainable Development Accounting and Indicator Reporting at the National, Provincial, Municipal-Community and Corporate Level. Research paper prepared for the National Round Table on the Environment and the Economy, June 15, 2002.

Anielski, Mark. Towards a Measurement of Ecological Integrity. Paper prepared for the National Round Table on the Environment and the Economy, November 15, 2001.

Anielski, Mark and David Pollock. The State of Inuit Well-being in Nunavut, 2001. Report prepared for the Nunavut Social Development Council and the Nunavut Tunngavik Inc., March 1, 2003,

Anielski, Mark and Jonathan Rowe. The Genuine Progress Indicator — 1998 Update. Redefining Progress, 1999.

Anielski, M. and C. Soskolne. "Genuine Progress Indicator (GPI) Accounting: Relating Ecological Integrity to Human Health and Well-Being." In Just Ecological Integrity: The Ethics of Maintaining Planetary Life, eds. Peter Miller and Laura Westra. Rowman and Littlefield, 2001.

Anielski, Mark and Jeffrey Wilson. The Ecological Footprints of Canadian Municipalities and Regions. Prepared for the Federation of Canadian Municipalities. Anielski Management Inc., September 2004.

Anielski, Mark and Mark Winfield. A Conceptual Framework for Monitoring Municipal and Community Sustainability in Canada. Research paper prepared for Environment Canada, June 17, 2002.

Anielski, Mark, Mary Griffiths, David Pollock, Amy Taylor, Jeffrey Wilson, Sara Wilson. *Alberta Sustainability Trends 2000: Genuine Progress Indicators Report 1961 to 1999.* Pembina Institute, 2001.

Anielski, Mark, Heather, Johannesen, and Shelagh Huston. *First Nations Socio-Economic Assessment: Jumbo Glacier Resort Project: A Genuine Wealth Analysis.* Prepared by Anielski Management Inc. for the B.C. Environmental Assessment Office, December 16, 2003.

Balkan, Joel. *The Corporation: The Pathological Pursuit of Profit and Power.* Viking Canada, 2004.

Benyus, Janine M. *Biomicry: Innovation Inspired by Nature.* Harper Perennial, 2002.

Boyd, David R. *Sustainability Within a Generation: A Vision for Canada.* Vancouver: David Suzuki Foundation, 2004.

Carmack, Pat and Bill Still. Video documentary "The Money Masters: How International-al Bankers Gained Control of America." 1998. themoneymasters.com.

Cavoukian, Raffi and Sharna Olfman eds. *Child Honouring: How to Turn This World Around.* Praeger, 2006.

Daly, Herman and John Cobb Jr. *For the Common Good, 2d ed.* Beacon, 1994.

Dominguez, Joe and Vicki Robin. *Your Money or Your Life: Transforming Your Relationship with Money and Achieving Financial Independence, new ed.* Penguin, 1999.

Douthwaite, Richard. *The Growth Illusion.* New Society, 1999.

Elkington, John. *Cannibals with Forks: The Triple Bottom Line of 21st Century Business.* New Society, 1998.

Fanfani, Amintore. *Capitalism, Protestantism, and Catholicism.* IHS Press, 2003 (original-ly published in 1934).

Fisher, Irving. 100% Money designed to Keep Checking Banks 100% Liquid; to Pre-vent Inflation and Deflation; Largely to Cure or Prevent Depressions; and to Wipe Out Much of the National Debt. City Printing, 1945.

Friedman, Milton. *A Program for Monetary Stability.* Fordham University Press, 1960.

Galbraith, John Kenneth. *The Good Society: The Humane Agenda.* Mariner, 1997.

Galbraith, John Kenneth. *Money: Whence It Came, Where It Went.* Houghton Mifflin, 1975.

Gladwell, Malcolm. *The Tipping Point: How Little Things Can Make a Big Difference.* Back Bay, 2002.

Greider, William. *The Soul of Capitalism: Opening Paths to a Moral Economy.* Simon & Schuster, 2003.

Greider, William. *Secrets of the Temple: How the Federal Reserve Runs the Country.* Simon & Schuster, 1989.

Grever, J. R., R. Kaufman, D. Skole and C. Vorosmarty. *Beyond Oil: The Threat of Food and Fuel in the Coming Decades.* Ballinger, 1986.

Hawken, Paul. *The Ecology of Commerce: A Declaration of Sustainability.* Harper Collins, 1994

Hawken, Paul, Amory Lovins and L. Hunter Lovins. *Natural Capitalism: Creating the Next Industrial Revolution.* Little, Brown, 1999.

Jacobs, Jane. *The Nature of Economies.* Vintage, 2001.

James, Sarah and Torbjorn Lahti. *The Natural Step for Communities: How Cities and Towns can Change to Sustainable Practices.* New Society, 2004.

Kennedy, Margarit. *A Changing Money System.* Permaculture Publications, 1991.

Keynes, John Maynard. *Essays in Persuasion.* Norton, 1963.

Korten, David. *The Great Turning: From Empire to Earth Community.* Berrett-Koehler, 2006.

Korten, David. *Post-Corporate World: Life After Capitalism.* Berrett-Koehler, 2000.

Korten, David. *When Corporations Rule the World, 2d ed.* Berrett-Koehler, 2001.

Küznets, Simon. "Towards a Theory of Economic Growth" in *Economic Growth and Structure.* Norton, 1965.

Lane, Robert. *The Loss of Happiness in Market Democracies.*

Lietaer, Bernard. *The Future of Money: Creating New Wealth, Work and a Wiser World.* Century, 2001.

MacLeod. Greg. *From Mondragón to America: Experiments in Community Economic Development.* University College of Cape Breton, 1997.

Maslow, A. H. "The Theory of Human Motivation." Originally published in *Psychological Review* 50 (1943): 370–396.

Max-Neef, Manfred. "Human Scale Development: An Option for the Future." Rain Forest Information website. rainforestinfo.org.au/background/maxneef.htm.

McKnight, John. *The Careless Society: Community and its Counterfeits.* Basic Books, 1996.

McMurtry, John. *Value Wars: The Global Market Versus the Life Economy.* Pluto Press, 2002.

McQuaig, Linda. *All You Can Eat: Greed, Lust and the New Capitalism.* Penguin, 2001.

Meadows, Donella. *Indicators and Information Systems for Sustainable Development.* Sustainability Institute, 1998.

Milani, Brian. *Designing the Green Economy: The Postindustrial Alternative to Corporate Globalization.* Rowan and Littlefield, 2000.

Miller, Peter and Laura Westra, eds. *Just Ecological Integrity: The Ethics of Maintaining Planetary Life.* Rowman and Littlefield. 2001.

Miringoff, Marc and Marque-Luisa Miringoff. *The Social Health of the Nation: How America is Really Doing.* Oxford, 1999.

Myers, David G. "The Secrets of Happiness." YES! A Journal of Positive Futures, Summer 2004.

Nattrass, Brian and Mary Altomare. *The Natural Step for Business: Wealth Ecology and the Evolutionary Corporation.* New Society, 1999.

New Economics Foundation. *The (un)Happy Planet Index.* 2006.

New Economics Foundation. *A Well-being Manifesto for a Flourishing Society.* London, 2004.

Nunavut Tunngavik Inc. 2002–2003 Report on the State of Inuit Culture and Society. [online]. [cited October 10, 2006]. tunngavik.ca/english/pub.html.

Polanyi, Karl. *The Great Transformation: The Political and Economic Origins of Our Time, 2d ed.* Beacon, 2001 (originally published in 1944).

Pope John Paul II. *Crossing the Threshold of Hope.* Knopf, 1995.

Putnam, Robert. *Bowling Alone: The Collapse and Revival of American Community.* Simon & Schuster, 2001.

Rowbotham, Michael. *The Grip of Death: A Study of Modern Money, Debt Slavery and Destructive Economics.* Jon Carpenter, 1998.

Schumacher, E. F. *Small Is Beautiful: Economics As If People Mattered: 25 Years Later.* Hartley & Marks, 1999.

Sacco, Pier Luigi Paolo Vanin and Stefano Zamagni. The Economics of Human Relationships. Unpublished paper, November 2003. Available at philia.ca/files/pdf/economics.pdf.

Sen, Amartya. *Development as Freedom.* Knopf, 2000.

Smith, Adam. An Inquiry into the Nature and Causes of the Wealth of Nations. 1st ed. 1776.

Soddy, Frederick. *The Role of Money.* Harcourt Brace, 1935.

Soddy, Frederick. *Wealth, virtual wealth, and debt: The solution of the economic paradox.* London: Allen & Unwin, 1926.

Tamari, Meir. *With All Your Possessions: Jewish Ethic and Economic Life.* Free Press, 1987.

Twist, Lynne. *The Soul of Money: Transforming Your Relationship with Money and Life.* Norton, 2003.

Wackernagel, Mathis and William Rees. *Our Ecological Footprint: Reducing Human Impact on the Earth.* New Society, 1995.

Waring, Marilyn. *Counting for Nothing: What Men Value and What Women are Worth, 2nd ed.* University of Toronto Press, 1999.

Waskow, Rabbi Arthur. 'Time to Be, Time to Love." YES! A Journal for Positive Futures, Fall 2003.

Willard, Bob. *The Sustainability Advantage: Seven Business Case Benefits of a Triple Bottom Line.* New Society, 2002.

Wright, Ronald. *A Short History of Progress.* Carroll & Graf, 2005.

Index

About the Author

MARK ANIELSKI is a well-being economist, entrepreneur, professor and president of Anielski Management Inc. specializing in well-being measurement. In 2004, *Adbusters* magazine recognized Mark as a "rising star" amongst international progressive economists. He has pioneered natural capital accounting in Canada and alternative measures of economic progress, including the US Genuine Progress Indicator (GPI) and the Alberta GPI Sustainable Well-being measurement system. For 14 years he served as senior economic policy advisor to the Alberta Government. He is currently advising the Chinese government on greening GDP accounting. Mark is Adjunct Professor of corporate social responsibility at the School of Business, University of Alberta and also teaches ecological economics at the Bainbridge Graduate Institute near Seattle. Mark is past-President of the Canadian Society for Ecological Economics and a Senior Fellow with the Oakland-based economic think-tank Redefining Progress. He lives in Edmonton, Alberta, Canada with his young family. More information about Mark and his Genuine Wealth work can be found at www.genuinewealth.net.

Mark can be reached by email at: anielski@genuinewealth.net

If you have enjoyed *The Economics of Happiness*,
you might also enjoy other

BOOKS TO BUILD A NEW SOCIETY

Our books provide positive solutions for people who want to
make a difference. We specialize in:

Environment and Justice • Conscientious Commerce
Sustainable Living • Ecological Design and Planning
Natural Building & Appropriate Technology
Educational and Parenting Resources • Nonviolence
Progressive Leadership • Resistance and Community

New Society Publishers

ENVIRONMENTAL BENEFITS STATEMENT

New Society Publishers has chosen to produce this book on Enviro 100, recycled paper made with **100% post consumer waste**, processed chlorine free, and old growth free.

For every 5,000 books printed, New Society saves the following resources:[1]

29	Trees
2,604	Pounds of Solid Waste
2,865	Gallons of Water
3,737	Kilowatt Hours of Electricity
4,734	Pounds of Greenhouse Gases
20	Pounds of HAPs, VOCs, and AOX Combined
7	Cubic Yards of Landfill Space

---

[1]Environmental benefits are calculated based on research done by the Environmental Defense Fund and other members of the Paper Task Force who study the environmental impacts of the paper industry.

For a full list of NSP's titles, please call 1-800-567-6772 *or check out our website at:*

www.newsociety.com

NEW SOCIETY PUBLISHERS